D1559516

To Stretch a Plank

A Survey of Psychokinesis

To Stretch
a Plank

A Survey of
Psychokinesis

Diana Robinson

Nelson-Hall nh Chicago

To

John, Joanne, and Stephen

with love, and thanks for all they

have endured during the writing of

To Stretch a Plank

and

to the memory of

J. Gaither Pratt

Library of Congress Cataloging in Publication Data

Robinson, Diana.
  To stretch a plank.

  Bibliography: p.
  Includes index.
  1. Psychokinesis. I. Title.
  BF1371.R6   133.8′8   80-12335
ISBN 0-88229-404-0

Manufactured in the United States of America

10   9   8   7   6   5   4   3   2   1

Contents

Preface

The idea that man, without moving a muscle, may affect his material environment is hard to accept. The phrase "mind over matter" is generally spoken with a laugh, and very few people really believe that their minds may indeed have an effect on their physical surroundings. Yet this expression, mind over matter, offers the simplest explanation of what psychokinesis, PK, is generally considered to be. In spite of its apparent impossibility, PK is receiving increasingly serious study from scientists in many fields.

Once the little-noticed baby sister of the psychical research family, PK in recent years has begun to claim its share of the spotlight as such headline grabbers as Uri Geller, Ted Serios, and Matthew Manning have attracted public attention. The forte of all three is psychokinesis.

The term covers a wide variety of phenomena. As we shall see in the following chapters, PK ranges from the simple (if anything is simple in the field of psychical research) fall of dice in a certain direction to the spectacular bending of spoons, from helpful psychic healing to terrifying poltergeist disturbances.

Mediums in trance may produce PK. So may mystics, saints, schoolboys, and drunken elevator operators. Or, say some, perhaps nobody produces any genuine PK effects at all.

The subject is, of course, still controversial. Many people believe that any significant effects shown in modern experiments with PK must be the result of fraud or sloppy experimental method. I have found it surprising, however, how many of those who condemn parapsychology out of hand admit, when pinned down, that they have read nothing of modern research and must hark back to the criticism of early 1930s work by J. B. and Louisa E. Rhine to bolster their opinion. For them the matter is a closed book, and their attitude creates a vicious circle: they don't believe in PK, so they won't waste their time studying it, so they won't learn about the results of modern, rigorously controlled experiments, many of which support PK. Since they are not aware of these experiments, they continue to believe that there is no real evidence for PK.

It is true that questions and doubts exist, and certainly not everything that is claimed to be PK really does involve the paranormal. Some people are too credulous to think objectively. Some experimenters have "helped" their results along in the desired direction. Some enthusiasts regard any investigation as a denial of the existence of psychic phenomena, or psi, and any slight coincidence as evidence of psychic events. All these facts must make us very careful in what we accept as being true psychokinesis. On the other hand, some occurrences do seem very hard to explain in terms of our present knowledge except as forms of PK.

This is what *To Stretch a Plank* is about. In it I try to examine psychokinesis from all points of view: what is believed about it, what used to be believed in the past; what has been discovered under scientifically controlled conditions, and how PK seems to manifest in less controlled circumstances.

A great deal has been written about psychic phenomena in general, and most of this material includes something about PK. However, few books deal specifically with the subject. Of those that do, fewer still are aimed, as my publishers express it, "at the intelligent layman." The one survey that is, and that probably always will be a classic reference work is *Mind Over Matter* by Dr. Louisa E. Rhine. However, it was published in 1970, and the explosion of interest, research techniques, and new approaches since that time makes some kind of update necessary.

In writing *To Stretch a Plank* I have attempted to survey the facts, fallacies, and theories of psychokinesis while picking my way along a path that lies somewhere to the left of the ponderously scientific and to the right of the "ooh, aah!" attitude taken by the overly credulous.

Obviously, like all writers, I owe a tremendous debt to the "doers" whose hard work and research have provided much of the material for this book, and whose names and relevant works are listed in the bibliography. In addition, I have received direct help, for which I am very grateful, from many people. Most notable among these are Jim Kennedy, Jim Davis, and Dr. K. R. Rao of the Foundation for Research on the Nature of Man and Dr. Rex Stanford of the Center for Parapsychological Research, who gave advice on portions of the manuscript, and Charles Honorton of Maimonides Medical Center and Bill Roll, Jerry Solfvin and Joan Krieger of the Psychical Research Foundation, who gave time to advise and encourage. However, if this book should contain any misinterpretations of their work, or of the work of others, that is my responsibility.

I regretfully note that since the completion of the manuscript of *To Stretch a Plank,* the deaths of Gardner Murphy, J. Gaither Pratt, and J. B. Rhine have been reported.

Part 1

In and Around the Laboratory

Chapter 1

Introducing Psychokinesis

What are the relations of mind to matter? Are mental processes always and everywhere intimately and utterly dependent upon material or physical organizations? Do the volitions, the strivings, the desires, the joys and sorrows, the judgments and beliefs of men make any difference to the historical course of the events of our world, as the mass of men at all times have believed?

William McDougall (162)

A young man concentrates on a computerlike machine with flickering dials. The machine, best described as an electronic coin-flipper, should end up with roughly equal "scores" for heads and tails. Yet it shows a score of 60 percent heads when the man is concentrating on heads, and 42 percent heads when he is concentrating on tails.

In Toronto a group of people sit together, laughing and singing, waiting for the "appearance" of an entirely imaginary person whose life story they have concocted out of thin air. After a while loud raps from the table before them seem to indicate that he has arrived.

In New York a young Israeli showman gently and thoughtfully strokes one end of a key, the other end of which is lightly held by a man of considerable experience in both sleight of hand and psychical phenomena. Though the latter can feel no pressure on the key, which does not leave his hands, the key bends.

What have these varied and unlikely events in common, apart from their apparent impossibility? Each has two possible explanations. It may be the result of very clever trickery, or, possibly, it may have been caused by some form of psychokinesis, or PK.

PK, also popularly but inaccurately known as "mind over matter," is the moving or affecting of an object without the use of any

3

physical intermediary. Something happens. You do not *physically* make it happen—no muscle power is involved—yet apparently you make it happen in some other, mysteriously mental, nonphysical way.

Perhaps a die falls in a certain direction, or with the desired face uppermost, just a little more often than might be expected. Or a pendulum may change the speed of its swing; a random generating machine produces a certain number more often than it "should." Perhaps, just possibly, a metal object may bend; a watch, silent for months, may start to run. As we will see, PK seems to take many different forms.

All such phenomena are, of course, quite plainly impossible by all our presently understood laws of physics, but, nonetheless, things sometimes happen, even under tightly controlled conditions, that can only be explained if PK is a fact.

The alternative explanation is that a large number of extremely intelligent, methodical, well-trained scientists are either deluded or involved in a web of fraud that spans the globe. Given political events over the past few years such fraud might be a plausible explanation were it not for the fact that there is no apparent motive for such deception. Success or fame cannot be the spur. Mere involvement in the field of parapsychology is often sufficient to get researchers condemned by many colleagues from other disciplines, and the more impossibly successful their experiments become, the louder and more vicious are the attacks on them. The most obvious motive for fraud—money—can also be ruled out. The last people to make any money out of parapsychological inquiry are the researchers. In fact, more than one, after producing extremely important and significant experimental results, has quit the field simply because he could not afford to stay in it.

It must be admitted that the same is not always the case with those who perform the apparently psychokinetic tasks ("applied specialists in parapsychology" for those who enjoy pseudoscientific jargon). Occasionally, whether possessing genuinely psychokinetic abilities or not, they become both famous and wealthy. When a man appears able to do the impossible, a lot of people are willing to pay good money to see it done, and a smart businessman can parlay such eagerness into a hefty bank account.

No doubt even in prehistory the shamans or witch doctors who could produce the most incredible phenomena accumulated the largest herds of animals—a measure of wealth. Whether they used what we would call PK or were simply adept at fooling all of the people all of the time, a close parallel still exists between them and some modern PK "superstars."

The throwing of bones in divining is little different from the throwing of dice today, and if the guidance given to the community via those bones should just happen to result in more advantage to the shaman, or to those who seek his help, no one could implicate him—hadn't they seen him throw the bones themselves? They could attest to the fact that he hadn't influenced their fall. Or could they?

Despite the awe with which shamans were regarded, one suspects (mankind being what it is) that even in prehistory there was an occasional skeptic. He would notice that certain shamans consistently produced advice that would aid their own friends or family more than other members of the community. Was part of it done by sleight of hand and trickery? Was the shaman himself responsible rather than the spirits? These questions must have been asked, and the first man who quietly (and fearfully) set about a systematic study of his shaman's techniques and the effects he produced was, in a way, the first psychical researcher. No doubt many more of his ilk came after him, even though to question or study the workings of the supernatural has long been a perilous course.

We know that in the seventeenth century Francis Bacon published a plea for investigation of both ESP and PK and indicated that he had done some research with the former. However, it was not until the mid-nineteenth century, when spiritualism in all its varieties blossomed, that psychical research began to take an organized form. The first parapsychological organization, the Society for Psychical Research, was formed in London in 1882 to study the sensational seances that were being reported there, and similar groups soon sprang up in continental Europe and the United States.

Since then we have come a long way. Physiological measurements and random-number generating machines are part of most parapsychologists' stock-in-trade. Physicists, psychologists, mathematicians, and stage magicians contribute their knowledge to the attempt to discover just how, or whether, someone may influence the fall of dice or affect the outcome of what should be an entirely random event. Frankly, we have not come quite as far in our knowledge as in our technical ability. Exactly *what* energy is used, if it is used, is still a matter for debate among scientists. Some nonscientists deride their arguments, believing that PK reflects some form of "nonmaterial energy" that can never be comprehended by the methods of the physical sciences. Still others, as we have mentioned, maintain that psychokinesis is a myth, that its claimed effects are actually the results of a combination of coincidence, credulity, and skilled magicianship.

Whatever the eventual answers will be, a large body of literature is now devoted to the various forms of psychical phenomena, including PK. Some is sane and objective, some is wildly overcredulous, and some bends just as far from objectivity in the direction of skepticism.

The field has also developed its own terminology, some of which requires brief explanation.

The term *psychokinesis* has already been discussed. Another term used by some people to mean almost the same thing is *psychotronics*. As originally coined in 1967, *psychotronics* was supposed to mean "the study of energies released in the processes of human thought or volitions" (120), which seems reasonably analogous to PK. However, in recent years the term has acquired some less scientific connotations so, though *psychotronics* is popular in some European countries, the term *psychokinesis* or *PK* will be used in this book.

Psychic phenomena (psi) refers to events that cannot be explained by present knowledge about psychology or physics. It is generally divided into three areas, *survival research, ESP,* and *PK*.

Survival research, the search for proof of some form of survival after bodily death, had its heyday in the early years of psi, when the great mediums claimed that their "messages from beyond" brought proof of life after death. In the last few years, the subject has experienced quite a revival, minus mediums, due mainly to a large bequest made for that purpose.

Later *extrasensory perception, ESP,* held center stage. ESP is "knowing" something without the use of any of the five senses. It is usually broken down further into *telepathy, clairvoyance,* and *precognition. Telepathy* is knowing what is in the thoughts or mind of someone else. *Clairvoyance* is awareness of a scene or object even when it is not known to anyone else, so that telepathy is ruled out. *Precognition* is the seeing of the future—an added complication that most theorists would prefer to do without were it not that, as with telepathy and clairvoyance, considerable experimental data indicate that it very probably does occur. The people who seem skilled at the various forms of psi are known as "sensitives," "mediums," "psychics," "gifted subjects," "applied specialists in parapsychology," or "frauds," depending on one's point of view.

Many scientists switched to the study of ESP after becoming discouraged in their work with mediums. They realized that a great percentage of evidential material received through a medium could be explained by telepathy or clairvoyance. In other words, if a medium tells you she sees your long-dead grandfather and describes him perfectly, she could be getting the information from some surviving "part" of him, but she *could* instead be getting the information from your mind (by telepathy) or from a photograph or other record that exists somewhere in the world (by clairvoyance).

So, though some mediumship may be genuine, research in the field can at the moment offer no *final* proof of the type demanded by the more careful scientists. In addition, the field is subject to considerable fraud. Both the well-meaning amateur, who seeks only to comfort the bereaved and further their belief in the hereafter, and the slickly organized professional medium, who trades information about her clients with other mediums and supplements her performance with expensive stage-magic gimmicks, have brought the subject into disrepute and caused irreparable damage to those of their kind who may in fact be genuine.

It was because of this "contamination" that, when PK began to be studied under properly controlled laboratory conditions (Chapter 2), the new term *psychokinesis* was introduced in place of the older *telekinesis,* which had been used in earlier psychical research and spiritualist circles. As Drs. Louisa E. and J. B. Rhine, pioneers of parapsychology, commented,

> . . . to those who are familiar with this word [*telekinesis*] it connotes "Oectoplasm," mediums, dark room seances, and other associations which it has accumulated and which we do not deal with in these

experiments. We believe we are legitimately avoiding unnecessary difficulties by not adopting the name telekinesis. (247)

Sterling work had already been done on PK, the third aspect of psi, but it was extrasensory perception that was gaining the attention of the news media and, therefore, the public. It is not terribly hard to accept the possibility that an individual can somehow "read" someone else's mind. Most people feel that they have had the experience at some time or other. ESP, therefore, was somewhat believable even to those who could not or would not get involved in the complex statistics and scientific reports on the subject. But that a person could affect the environment by some sort of "mind power"—that Muhammed might indeed have been able to move the mountain, or at least a small part of it, or that King Canute might have held back the waves if he had had sufficient faith in his power to do so—that was far too much for most people to accept. And it was definitely contrary to the known laws of physics. So, despite the work of parapsychologists such as J. B. Rhine, Ed Cox, Helmut Schmidt, and many others who had conducted carefully controlled and statistically significant PK experiments for many years, the public paid little attention to scientific PK research until the emergence of Uri Geller, the controversial Israeli who reduces most people to a state of shock and whom we will meet again in Chapter 5.

Whether Geller impresses people because of his PK abilities, his magicianship, or simply his egotism is another matter, but when it seemed that spoons and keys could bend at his lightest touch, when he spoke of being teleported from one place to another in a moment of time, then people did start to wonder whether, perhaps, it might be worthwhile to take a second look at PK. Psychokinesis research, which had been quietly jogging along behind the scenes all the time, began to be noticed by the public.

Of course, the development of PK within parapsychology cannot be judged without knowledge of the growth of parapsychology itself, both as a scientific field and as a subject of popular interest.

Fifteen years ago an interest in psychic phenomena was pretty much an underground pursuit as far as the general public was concerned. Though a growing number of people were reading popular books on such "seers" as Edgar Cayce and Jeane Dixon, few cared enough about scientific investigation of psi to know that in 1968 the Parapsychological Association was already eleven years old and boasted 84 full members and 103 associate members. The PA is an international organization of scientists involved in the study of psi. To become a full member one should have a graduate degree and have made some significant scientific contribution to the field of parapsychology, so its population of superstitious kooks is kept quite low. Few people outside the PA noticed that in 1969 the organization was accepted as an affiliate of the prestigious American Association for the Advancement of Science (AAAS), a signal to scientists everywhere that the methods of research used by parapsychologists had been approved by some of the nation's top researchers in all fields.

In fact, public knowledge of parapsychology, and particularly of parapsychology in the United States, was very limited. The publication in 1970 of a book called *Psychic Discoveries Behind the Iron Curtain* (184) was quite damaging to the public image of Western parapsychology because it discussed with great enthusiasm various parapsychological and pseudoparapsychological programs in Eastern Europe. The book gave the overall impression that official recognition and immense amounts of money were being received by researchers in other countries, with significant results, while practically nothing was being done in the United States.

Predictably, resentment among researchers in the United States was strong, and some reviews of the book were harsh. Every inaccuracy, unverified assertion, and exaggeration (of which there were indeed quite a few) was picked up, examined, and denounced. However, its publication had interesting side effects. It aroused some public protest over the small amount of official recognition given to psi in this country. It prompted a few young people to think seriously about doing research in parapsychology and to inquire about, sometimes even to demand, college courses in the subject. It also caused some people to react with near panic as they contemplated cold war being waged by some form of thought control.

Parapsychology would, of course, have grown anyway, and unfortunately many of those who read *Psychic Discoveries Behind the*

Iron Curtain and nothing more no doubt remain in some ways misinformed to this day. Nevertheless, since 1970 the number of college courses offered, though often in noncredit adult education programs, has increased enormously, and parapsychology is now reasonably respectable in many circles. Acceptance by the AAAS and general publicity have no doubt helped, but it is probable that, despite its inaccuracies and negative attitude toward Western psychical research, *Psychic Discoveries* was at least a little helpful to American parapsychologists in gaining public interest in their field of endeavor.

Actually, at that time the psychic grass was probably no greener in Russia than in the United States. Milan Ryzl, a parapsychologist who defected from Czechoslovakia in 1967, has said that he considered most of the much-heralded Eastern European research to be undercontrolled and overpublicized (261).

Dr. Robert A. McConnell, research professor of biophysics at the University of Pittsburgh, examined the Russian parapsychology scene in 1975 and suggested that it was only very recently that the government there, after allowing a great deal of somewhat amateurish work on psi for some years, had at last judged the subject worthy of closer study (161). However, whether governmental recognition constitutes any breakthrough for parapsychology in Russia is questionable, since it apparently means that *all* such research will now be carried out under strict government control and, probably, secrecy. Parapsychologists of all nations tend to be a somewhat freethinking lot who do not care to have their wings clipped, and whether future research will progress under such conditions remains to be seen.

Another country popularly believed to be very receptive to psi is the present author's native country, England. British "spiritual healers" must by law be allowed as much access to hospital patients (at each patient's request) as are medical doctors. Such freedom has given rise to a folklore that the entire field in Britain is far ahead of its American counterpart as far as official acceptance is concerned, a view frequently encouraged by "seers" and "healers" who visit the United States giving lectures and demonstrations for high fees based, they say, on the immense demand for their services in their own country. While some of these people are indeed talented and highly regarded, others are entirely unknown to their fellow countrymen. Nor is interest in psi much stronger in England than here, particularly as far as careful research is concerned. Because universities in England are government-funded, it is also much harder to obtain private funding for research in a university setting than it is in America.

In actual fact, parapsychologists in this country have much to be thankful for. The development of electronic equipment has added greatly to the range of experiments that can be conducted and to the speed with which they can be completed. Increased sophistication in experimental and statistical methods has produced a level of competence that can rarely be seriously attacked by objective critics. To be sure, fanatics and publicity-seekers still raise their voices in derision (occasionally with merit when some scientists who are new to parapsychology and therefore naive about its history and pitfalls are involved), but few critics are willing to venture into a modern laboratory to discover for themselves how things are done.

Parapsychologists are increasingly aware of the need for strict controls and self-examination and are no longer willing to accept on faith that a subject, or even an experimenter, could not cheat in an experiment just because he or she is a nice person. It is other parapsychologists themselves who most closely examine and criticize any experiment, ensuring that scientific standards are steadily raised.

In 1977 faculty and/or students in about a dozen academic institutions were conducting serious experiments. New privately funded research institutions are springing up and attracting some of the best researchers because of their ability to provide up-to-date facilities.

One might think that another hopeful sign for psi is the fact that the number of colleges offering courses in parapsychology was well over one hundred at last count. In fact, however, only about twenty are taught by members or associates of the PA. Many others are not for academic credit, and no universal standards exist to ensure that witchcraft, herbalism, and astrology do not get lumped into the same course.

This confusion between psi and the occult is perhaps the greatest hindrance to general academic and scientific acceptance of psi. A fine line separates psychic phenomena, which are the legitimate field of study of the parapsychologist, and occultism. Many people, not clearly understanding that parapsychology is a strictly scientific field (not surprisingly, since the term is often abused), think that its study indicates an acceptance of, or involvement in, the occult. Often people who know that I am involved in psychical research have asked me questions concerning astrology, witchcraft, and black magic, as though taking it for granted that an interest in one denotes an interest in all. Most people who consider themselves too rational to believe in the occult dismiss parapsychology without a second thought because they believe that the two are one and the same. In areas where logical, linear thinking is emphasized, as in most colleges, the experiments of those who feel that psi can be studied scientifically are often an embarrassment.

One might expect that acceptance by the AAAS would have given pause to the skeptics, causing them to reexamine the subject and their prejudices. Many skeptics, however, genuinely believe that they have reevaluated the subject quite objectively. Unfortunately, their reexaminations have often been based on outdated data.

Historically, some of the most publicized laboratory experiments in PK were the very early ones at Duke University. Examination of these first reports showed that the work done there was not in fact as well controlled as it might have been. Immediate criticism from other scientists brought immediate reforms, as discussed in the next chapter, and under the new conditions significant results continued to be produced. However, in some minds the damage was done and has not yet been remedied. Not long ago an acquaintance of mine in his fifties, on hearing that I was interested in psi, commented that he had been interested in the subject when he was a young man, but that he had read the criticisms of the early work and realized that in fact there was nothing to it. End of interest in psi.

Nor is the ambivalent attitude of the academic world the only crimp in the style of those who would like to see parapsychology flourishing. Money is a major factor. What concrete gains can a parapsychologist promise an organization to whom he is applying for a research grant? Greater understanding of human beings, their inner workings, their relationship to the environment? Perhaps, if the experiment can be successfully repeated, but where's the profit? If psi should ever be harnessed, will it lead to new technologies? Greater sales? Quite the reverse. If that great psi breakthrough should ever come about, so that mankind could use psi easily and at will (and frankly I doubt whether that time will come in the foreseeable future) it would enable man to do *without* many gadgets that are now highly profitable to their manufacturers. As a result, sources of funding, though increasing, are still few and far between. In fact, one prominent member of the PA recently estimated that in 1976 no more than $800,000, including salaries, was spent on parapsychology in this country. Others have given even lower estimates.

With so little money available, most parapsychologists are some-thing else first—psychologist, physicist, mathematician, writer—and can spend time on psi only as an avocation. One man who *is* a full-time parapsychologist once commented rather wistfully, as he sat in my home and talked with my children, that he often wished he might have married and had a family.

"But," he added, "then I couldn't have been a parapsychologist. It's far too risky a field if you have other people dependent on you."

The situation is improving, and perhaps one side effect of women's liberation will be that more people—of either sex—can devote themselves to such risky and financially thankless work as psychical research while the other member of the family supports them both, but that time is here for only a very few.

Another human quirk may be slowing down progress in psychical research. Much has been written in recent years about the "will not to succeed," which causes people to give up, or to change direction, just as they are approaching their original goal. This seems to be particularly pronounced in parapsychologists.

In 1971 psychologist Robert Van de Castle suggested to members of the PA that the implications of psi, some of which will be discussed in Chapter 15, are so mind-boggling that, though researchers consciously try to find out all they can about the subject, unconsciously they may put up roadblocks at almost every step of the way (321). They may treat subjects so coolly that they are unable to perform, "accidentally" sabotaging an experiment by forgetting something vital, lose records, choose less than ideal methods or conditions for an experiment, or simply become "too busy" with other things to conclude a nearly finished project. Whatever prompts such actions, this tendency does form yet another block to progress in our understanding of psi.

Yet all is not gloom, as the following chapters will show.

Historians may wince because I start my account of PK with the early dice work done at Duke University. As later chapters will show, I am well aware that some forms of PK work, under other names, were done elsewhere before the Duke work began. However, I believe that the skeptic is entitled to know whether it is worth his while to spend time on a book before he has spent *too* much time on it. If PK is not a fact, then why should he read on? Accordingly, the next two chapters are devoted to an account of experiments that, for the most part, attempt to demonstrate the existence of PK. The more controversial aspects of the subject come later, since they can be seen in better perspective after one has decided for oneself whether or not the existence of PK has indeed been established.

Some readers may wonder at the fact that healing and religion are mentioned in a book that claims to have a scientific base. Others may go utterly frantic at my inclusion of the "fringy" subjects discussed in Chapter 12. However, experimental work with healers does seem to indicate that whatever they do, if they do it, may relate to PK. In the same way, many events categorized as miracles in days past might well, if they occurred today, be referred to the parapsychologist rather than to the theologian. An example is the legend from which comes the rather unlikely title of the book.

In *Tales of the Dervishes,* Idries Shah says:

> It is further related that one day Jesus, the son of Mary, was in the workshop of Joseph the Carpenter. When a plank of wood was found to be too short, Jesus pulled it, and it was found to have become in some way lengthened.
> When this story was told to the people, some said:
> "This is a miracle, therefore this child will be a saint."
> Others said: "We do not believe it, do it again for us."
> A third party said: "This cannot be true, therefore exclude it from the books."
> The three parties, with their different feelings, yet got the same answer because none knew the purpose and the real significance lying within the statement: "He stretched a plank." (276)

Whether or not the incident is true is irrelevant. What is interesting is the attitudes of the people who heard it. They seem to sum up very well the attitudes of those of us who, today, hear of a case of psychokinesis.

"This is a miracle."

"We do not believe it; do it again for us."

"This cannot be true; therefore exclude it from the books."

None of the three reactions dealt with the reality of what apparently happened, any more than most of us can deal with the reality of a PK event today. Each reaction leaves us with yet more questions and very few answers. We still do not know the full significance of the words "He stretched a plank."

It is because of this lack of answers, after so many years of research, that I have included Chapter 12, covering a few things that may be considered too far out for scientific acceptance. Of course they are controversial, unscientific, and improbable. So, in the opinion of many people, is PK. On the other hand an open-minded look at the beliefs of other cultures, other idea systems, cannot help but give us a new look at ourselves and our own ideas. Foxglove tea was used for heart complaints long before medicine discovered that the foxglove plant contains digitalis—a most useful drug for the treatment of heart complaints. More than one skeptical Westerner has fallen ill in the wilds of Africa or South America and found himself inexplicably healed by the attentions of a local shaman or witch doctor.

Dr. Gardner Murphy, famed psychologist and parapsychologist at Columbia University for many years, was told by the distinguished scholar W. I. Newbold, professor of philosophy at the University of Pennsylvania, that the main task of psychical research is to "combine sound, modern scientific method with the ancient lore which has been forgotten." (178)

Coming from a man whose fields of study included philosophy, psychology, and archeology, this advice perhaps should not lightly be dismissed. Unfortunately, what he referred to as ancient lore is usually considered today to be superstition or occultism, and is therefore dismissed. If we already had all the answers, perhaps our logical, Western arrogance in treating all "superstition" as unworthy of our attention might be justified, but we don't. We have no more idea of *how* PK works, if it works, than had the people in Shah's Sufi story. It is possible that some aspects of occultism, though not acceptable to us in their present guise, may yet provide us with ideas that might lead to hypotheses testable in the laboratory. Perhaps one day such an approach may shed light on the many unanswered questions about psi that we spend so much effort trying to answer. It is for this reason that I have risked scientific condemnation by including them, not because I believe that in their present form they constitute scientific facts.

For myself, I have no answers. This book will not tell you how PK works, nor even whether it works. It will simply look at what other people have said, done, discovered, and speculated as it relates to PK and, I hope, present a reasonably clear and concise picture of a subject that in itself is neither clear nor concise.

Chapter 2

The Die Is Cast

There was no expressly designed experimental program at the start: it was all naturally an exploratory venture which went on from day to day as time permitted. The records were all kept and customary procedures followed. After some experience with high dice that looked much like something beyond a chance effect, we recognized the need for a procedure controlling the experiment for possible dice imperfections . . . later on . . . the manner of throwing too was changed.
Louisa E. and J. B. Rhine (247)

If every gambler felt totally at the mercy of chance and the house there would be few gamblers; yet there are many. It is against all logic to feel that at times one has an edge, either because lady luck is smiling or because somehow one can "go with" the dice or the roulette ball and *make* them come up winners. Perhaps human beings are not logical, and many a gambler's bank account will so testify. Yet, why is there that persistent feeling that occasionally the dice *do* respond?

Perhaps a certain young gambler was prompted by some such questions, a desire to know more, or perhaps by simple braggadocio. In any event, he is now a legend in parapsychology, because it was he who first approached J. B. Rhine in 1934 and claimed to be able to influence dice.

Rhine and his wife, Louisa, had become famous for their research at the Parapsychology Laboratory at Duke University, where they had attempted to legitimatize and standardize ESP tests under scientific control using properly applied statistical methods. They seemed to be showing fairly clearly that one can become aware of what is in the environment without using the "normal" sensory system. J. B. Rhine's first major publication, *Extrasensory Perception* (225) was in press, and he must have been awaiting with some trepidation the public's reaction to it. Then in walked the gambler with his outlandish claim.

To his credit, Rhine did not duck the issue, but promptly put the man to the test. The two of them hunkered down on the floor and started throwing dice. The results were interesting enough to start Rhine working on a more thorough test, and before long dice throwing was a fad throughout Duke. Parapsychology had started on a trail that would indicate fairly clearly, as time went by, that man can affect his environment without using his "normal" motor system.

During this early period, experimentation was freewheeling, highly exploratory, and lightly controlled. Gradually more people heard of what was being done and put their minds to work on *how,* other than by PK, the sometimes highly significant results could be obtained. In response to their criticism, controls were tightened and record-keeping became more standardized. Before long, a PK "run" was established at twenty-four individual dice throws. When two dice were being thrown at the same time, the run was twelve throws. If six dice were used, four throws made a run, and so on. The chance scores for the various types of targets were calculated to provide a firm base against which experimenters could analyze their results.

Significant results appeared, but Rhine, ever cautious, refused to publish any reports of PK work in the *Journal of Parapsychology (JP),* which was published from the Parapsychology Laboratory and carried reports of ESP experiments. It was too soon, Rhine felt, and the results, though indicative, were perhaps not convincing enough.

So, through the rest of the 1930s and the early 1940s, though experimentation continued, nothing found its way into print. It was not until 1942, with resources strained by World War II and fewer active experimenters working around the lab, that there came a lull. It was decided to go back over the already completed experiments and reanalyze them. So hectic had the early work been that many records had barely been looked at once the experiment was complete and its significance calculated. Researchers had always had new ideas to test and new experiments just begging to be run—much more exciting than a dreary review of the preliminary statistical analyses that were carried out as a matter of course. However, the reanalysis that was done in 1942 turned up a fact that was far from dreary to those at Duke. Nearly (though not quite) all of the test records showed what became known as the *decline effect* (200, 238). Scores dropped as the experiment proceeded. Further, on a given record sheet they dropped both vertically and horizontally. In other words, if one vertical column were assigned to each run the rate of scoring would tend to drop through the run, and also in each succeeding run. If a record sheet was divided into four quarters, the scoring rate in the top left-hand quarter was nearly always higher, often significantly higher, than that in the bottom right-hand quarter. This phenomenon became known as the *quarter distribution* (QD). Another finding was that when pages themselves were divided into sets (so many runs to a set) those sets, if divided into quarters, also showed a QD effect.

At first glance this may not seem to be the most exciting finding in the world. So PK subjects start off better than they finish. Maybe they get tired or bored. So what? What excited the Rhines and their colleagues was the fact that the declines occurred so frequently through the eighteen major series analyzed that they appeared to constitute some kind of lawful trend. They indicated that something other than chance *was* happening in the PK experiments.

Three major criticisms can be made of the kind of dice experiment that was being run in those early days—face tests they were called, because the aim was to make a specific die face, or groups of die faces, finish uppermost.

The first criticism was that the dice might be biased. This bias is possible because most dice are excavated; the numbers are indicated by little holes dug out of them. Since the six-face has six holes dug out of it, it should be fractionally lighter in weight than the one-face, which has only one hole dug out of it. The other numbers provide a continuum between the two. Later sophistication produced controls against such bias, but the earliest tests did not. They were usually run with high faces as the targets, and it was easy for critics to dismiss successful results on the grounds that the dice would naturally fall with the higher faces up more often because those faces were lighter. However, dice bias would not explain why the scores were now found to go steadily down throughout the tests. If biased dice were responsible for the higher number of sixes, then the high number of sixes should have occurred throughout the tests, for nothing physical was changed that could account for the decline. It therefore follows that something other than biased dice, something that could change during the course of the test, must be responsible for the decline. Since all physical conditions were kept the same, that something had to be related to the state of mind of the subject, very strong evidence that the subject was in some way influencing the fall of the dice.

Another criticism frequently levied during the early tests was that the results were obtained by skilled throwing. These charges were soon countered by experiments comparing scores when the dice were thrown from a cup and when they were balanced on a ruler placed on two nails. When the ruler was smartly removed the dice tumbled down the chute (247). This was known as the semimechanical method and was soon replaced by a machine that made handling the dice unnecessary. The apparatus, consisting of a wire mesh cylinder that rotated end to end, stopping each time it reached the vertical position, ensured that skill could have no part in the results obtained (226). Still later a camera was installed to photograph the dice in the cage each time the device stopped. However, even the earliest tests, in which dice were thrown by hand, without using a cup, were vindicated when the analysis in 1942 showed a strong decline in many of them. Had skilled throwing been involved, one would have expected the scores to go up as the subjects got more practice.

The third major criticism against the PK work was that record-keeping might have been less than honest, or just plain sloppy. Wishful thinking or careless counting of the die faces, particularly when many dice were used for each throw, could have resulted in more hits being recorded than actually occurred. Again, the decline effect made this unlikely. Since it had not been noticed at the time the tests were done, the experimenters could hardly have doctored the scores to show it at the time of the experiments. Nor is it likely that the record-keepers would have started each experiment carelessly, recording extra hits, and gradually have become more exact so that the scores appeared to drop steadily. In fact, one would expect just the reverse, that carelessness would set in as the test, and boredom, proceeded.

The decline effect seemed to refute all three major criticisms of the dice experiments. This new evidence for PK was not the only reason for Rhine's decision to start publishing results of PK experiments, however. World War II had decimated his staff and slowed other research in parapsychology. Few people had the time to work on new ESP research, yet the Parapsychology Laboratory was committed to publishing four issues of the *JP* every year (237). Accordingly, in 1943 the first PK reports were published, and for the next several years a major part of the *JP* was devoted to reports of work on PK.

For the first time those outside the parapsychological fraternity became aware of the evidence for PK that had been mounting for nearly ten years. In fact, as they reported on their first experiment, the Rhines revealed the full extent of that work:

> As we rewrite this report in December, 1942, there are available . . . for publication in due order, twenty-four other reports of comparable character and content. Several others wait only for the authors concerned to find time for the analyses and writing . . . A score of experimenters have been involved in the conduct of these investigations to date. (247)

That first report told of the first experiment, run in 1934 and based on the habits of that gambler who had just provided the impetus for the whole PK program. He was used to throwing for high dice—two dice thrown together showing a total of eight or more—so that is how the first experiment was designed. The results were encouraging, but at that point controls were sorely lacking. However, proper records were kept, and they were later found to show a consistent decline.

Readers were introduced to the Main Series run by the Edmond Gibsons (106), who would later report a number of other tests from their home in Grand Rapids, Michigan. Since much of the significance of the Main Series came from Mrs. Gibson throwing for the six-face only, the results were suspect. However, a light/dark series of twelve throws for each die face in three conditions was interesting. The conditions were white light, red light, and darkness. In the dark condition considerable "psi-missing" was shown, with a score of twenty-four less than the seventy-two that would have been expected by chance.

A note on chance is in order here. The chance score is the score that, on average, would be expected to occur if twenty-four dice throws were made for a specific type of target without the intrusion of any nonchance factors such as biased dice, skilled throwing, or, of course, PK. The further the score deviates from chance, the lower is the probability that it could have occurred by chance alone, and the greater the "significance," or the possibility of PK being responsible—assuming that the experimental controls are adequate. In many cases that follow throughout this book, results will be indicated in their simplest form by giving the probability, or P, of their occurring. If $P = .01$ this means there is only one chance in a hundred that such a result would occur by chance or, to put it another way, if one hundred identical tests were run, only one score at that level would be expected if only chance were responsible. $P<.01$ means that the probability is less than one in a hundred, making the results even more significant. $P= .001$ means one chance in a thousand. There is no arbitrary point at which significance is attained. Each scientist decides, before starting an experiment, what P value he will consider significant. However, in general, parapsychologists have been somewhat stricter than scientists from most other fields and have demanded a P of .01 or .02 before calling a result significant. In other disciplines $P = .05$ (one chance in twenty) is considered significant, but in parapsychology it was considered only marginal. In the past it was sometimes taken to indicate a tendency, but not to be evidential in itself as far as proof of the existence of psi was concerned. However, in more recent experiments, which largely deal with differences between conditions in an experiment, where the existence of psi is already accepted, the .05 level of significance has become acceptable among parapsychologists, who feel that they should not be required to carry a far more excessive burden of proof than do their colleagues in other fields.

The lower than chance score ($P = .007$) obtained by the Gibsons when throwing in the dark was particularly interesting because significant PK-missing had not been observed before, though it was not uncommon in ESP tests. Subjects are said to psi-miss when they obtain scores significantly below the chance score, and according to the laws of probability such scoring is just as much evidence for psi as is high scoring. It does, however, make research rather more difficult.

Sensitive to criticisms of high-dice tests in which biased dice might be involved, Rhine had also run some low-dice and sevens tests, using two dice per throw (228). Low-dice tests have a target aim of six or less; sevens have a total of seven as the aim. The chance score for low- and high-dice tests is five hits in a run of twenty-four throws. For sevens the chance score is 2. These tests, intended as a control against the first high-dice experiment, used the same dice. If they *were* biased toward the six-face and PK were not operating, then high dice should continue to predominate, thought the experimenters. On the other hand, if PK were responsible, the lower faces should turn up more often in the low-dice tests.

Neither of these things happened! It was the in-between sevens that scored a deviation (+42) well above chance (P = .005). It seemed, thought the researchers, as though the subjects were able to avoid the high dice, as they had been instructed to do, yet were not quite able to overcome their inner prejudices against low dice, Accordingly, they sat on the fence by throwing far more than the expected number of sevens.

This bias against low dice is very understandable, even in people who have not been working hard to throw high dice, as had some of these subjects. From childhood we are conditioned to aim for high dice. Every game of chutes and ladders, or any other childhood (or adult) game that involves progressing around a board according to the fall of a die is most likely to be won by the person who throws fours, fives, and sixes. In some games one cannot even begin to play until he has thrown a six. Accordingly, an inner prejudice against low dice probably runs quite deep in most of us.

Another form of subject bias can occur when a subject develops a preference for a particular die face (208) and keeps throwing that regardless of the target face. An experimenter can design an experiment that is controlled against biased dice, but to control against biased subjects is far harder.

Since subjects so often had difficulty throwing for low dice, the skeptics' explanation of biased dice was not easily brushed aside. One method of attempting to control against die bias was to have control runs in which the dice would be thrown in the same manner as in the actual experiment, but with no specific target. It was thought by some people that any bias in the dice would show up in the control runs. This did not take into account the subconscious nature of psi. As J. B. Rhine and Betty Humphrey commented after analyzing many PK experiments, "The one thing that stands out most clearly in the PK research, as in the ESP work, is the fact that *the essential mental act is unconscious.* No one knows how he influences the die, or even when he is succeeding and when he is failing" (238).

If an experiment has just given very significant results, but the targets have been sixes throughout, it is very natural for the experimenter to hope that the dice are not biased toward sixes, for if they are this would cancel out all his nice, significant results. Accordingly, as he conducts the control runs he can't help wishing for sixes *not* to appear more often than usual. He may resolutely dismiss such unscientific thoughts from his conscious mind, but, as we shall see in greater detail in Chapters 3 and 13, since psi seems to operate quite unconsciously at times when we have no idea it is operating, it is far more likely to follow the dictates of the unconscious mind than of the conscious. Thus it is possible for the experiment to produce apparently significant results that are actually caused by biased dice, and for the following control runs to present apparently chance results that are actually the result of experimenter PK counteracting the dice bias. For this reason no great weight can be given to experiments whose main control against biased dice is the control run.

The problem of controlling against biased dice was finally solved when it was realized that if a die were biased *toward* one face it had to be equally biased *away from* the opposite face. This applies most strongly to the six/one face combination, though to a lesser extent it also fits the five/two and four/three pairs. The only necessary control, therefore, was to make sure that every test was "round-the-die"—that is, for each die-face in turn, and with an equal number of tries for each face. The totals for all faces could then be pooled, and any bias in the dice would cancel itself out with the negative and positive deviations. If the bias were toward the six, and sixes showed a positive deviation of +31 (31 above chance) then the one should show an approximately equal negative deviation (about 31 below chance). When totaled, these would cancel each other out, bringing the score very close to chance.

The Gibsons were moving toward this method in another experiment (105). Though the spectacular psi-missing under the earlier dark condition made it unlikely that their dice were biased, they wisely chose this time to throw around the die, though not, unfortunately, for exactly the same number of each face throughout the entire experiment. Some runs were not witnessed—also unfortunate. However, in the 6,033 runs that were witnessed, 1,057 hits above chance were obtained. This margin may seem small, since it comes to little more than one extra hit in every 5.7 runs. However, over such a large number of runs (144,792 die throws), one would expect that the score would have come very close to chance had only chance been operating. That it remained consistently higher gives very strong evidence for PK. It is possible that the dice were biased: the one-face score was a little under chance with a mean run score of 3.97, and the scores for the three higher faces were well above those for the low faces. However, the mean run score for the six was 4.33, which more than cancels out the negative deviation of the one-face. In actual fact, the three low faces together had a positive deviation, which, though lower than that for the three high faces, makes it clear that biased dice alone were not responsible for the high scores obtained. When this experiment was originally reported it was stated that the odds against chance for such results were "more than a trillion to one." Hindsight has modified this to "one in millions" (243) but either way, the evidence for PK from this test is strong.

Such tests became increasingly common, with increasingly exact counterbalancing of die faces. Round-the-die work also freed the experimenter from the restrictions of two dice per throw that had been in effect while the gambler's methods were followed. Tentatively at first, with a two-dice condition and a six-dice condition, experimenters began to spread their wings. It was found that the scoring "gave almost exactly the same rate when six dice were thrown at a time as when two were used" (227). In fact, these early tests were not well controlled and their results, although significantly above chance, were dismissed until the later analysis showed a significant decline effect. However, they were the forerunners of tests that would eventually see up to ninety-six dice being used in one throw.

At about the same time (late 1934 to early 1935), another experiment using various numbers of dice was being run at Wayne University (239). This had the additional variation of introducing different *size* dice in each throw, with scores recorded separately. Of the four series using six, twelve, twelve, and twenty-four dice per throw, only the latter attained significantly high scores—high enough to raise the overall deviation of all four series almost to significance, though not quite ($P = .015$). The fourth series itself was significant at the $P = .001$ level. Since the entire experiment was not significant, it might not be of great interest were it not for the fact that the highest scores came when the largest number of dice were being thrown, and that much higher scores were obtained with the larger dice than with the smaller. Both features provided some evidence that a normal energy was not responsible for the scores, since an energy would have less effect as it was divided among more dice, and, presumably, would also be less effective on larger, heavier dice than on small dice.

Readers of the *Journal of Parapsychology* in the mid-1940s found that experimenters had been working in many parts of the country, some of them in correspondence with and under advice from Rhine, some of them quite independently. Dr. Carroll Blue Nash, then of American University, had devised an experiment in 1940 without any awareness of Rhine's work (180A). Using 113 subjects, far more than had ever been used for PK at Duke at that time, Nash found that scores were higher when dice were thrown six at a time than when thrown one at a time.

In those exciting days, anything was fair game for a PK experiment. Can one person stop another from performing well in a test? One subject who regularly scored well using the dice-throwing machine was challenged by one of the experimenters who believed that she could distract him sufficiently to reduce his score. His undistracted score was 298 in sixty runs, fifty-eight above chance ($P < .00006$), but when she started discouraging and distracting him he dropped to thirteen below chance in eighty runs ($P < .0004$). The difference between the two scoring rates was highly significant (213).

A similar help/hinder test, in which two subjects aimed either for the same target or for different targets, without any overt distraction, also showed better results for the cooperating part of the experiment (132).

Major differences in scores under different conditions are, in many ways, better evidence for the existence of PK than the straight, one-condition experiment that seeks only to show that PK exists. The results of one-condition experiments could be said to be due to some unnoticed experimental error or lack of control. On the other hand, if two parts of an experiment are physically the same, differing only in the psychological attitude of the subject, and yet show results that change along with that psychological attitude, then this is a strong indication that the physical results and the psychological attitude are connected. If psychological attitudes can manifest in physical results, this is PK—there can be no other explanation.

In 1946 the American Society for Psychical Research (ASPR) ran the first of its PK experiments with fifty-four subjects throwing round the die, using four dice per throw, for 1,296 runs (67). The total score was 171 above chance. This, and a "striking" decline in scoring from the first to the fourth run were considered significant enough to warrant a further ASPR experiment. The second experiment, however, achieved near chance results. It was reported in the *Journal of the American Society for Psychical Research,* with the comment: "The purpose of the present report is to put on record *all* the formal PK research that has been carried out at the Society since publication of the first report" (68).

This statement highlighted a publication policy of the *Journal of Parapsychology,* which was to publish only results that were significant. To a certain extent this policy may have given teeth to critics who pointed out that if a specific type of experiment was performed a hundred times, the laws of probability would predict one result with a *P* of .01 purely by chance. If experiments were not reported unless their results were significant, then perhaps hundreds of non-significant tests were not being reported, and therefore the reported results appeared significant but were actually due to chance.

That this criticism was invalid becomes apparent if one takes a look at the number of experiments reported (particularly in the next chapter) and the statistics involved. An astronomical number of nonsignificant experiments would have to have been run if all these results were due only to chance. A look at the small number of researchers in the field and the time and facilities available to them makes it clear that there were not enough people around to have run nearly that many experiments.

In any event, in 1958 the *JP* adopted a new policy and now publishes abstracts (summarized reports) of experiments with chance results. Any researcher wishing to know more about such an experiment can then obtain a copy of the full report through the *JP*. This policy allows information on chance-score experiments to be published without using up valuable space on the full report and has satisfied most—though perhaps not all—critics of the former policy.

In 1951 a major step forward in PK work was reported, a step that was to free experimenters from the confines of die faces and lay the groundwork for a great variety of types of PK research.

Since 1946, W. Edward Cox, a businessman much interested in the Duke work, had been experimenting with what he called placement experiments. The aim was not to have dice fall with a certain face uppermost, but to have them fall *in a certain direction.* The first placement experiment reported by Cox was extremely complicated, involving 252 squares that were the targets within which the dice were willed to land, plus a system of primary and secondary targets so that every dice throw had two purposes. The results were not particularly significant, and the method was soon changed, but the concept of placement had been introduced (55).

The same issue of the *JP* carried two other reports of placement work. One of these used marbles, coins, and cubes (241) and the other various sizes and different densities of dice—plastic, wood, and lead. The former showed no clear differences in scoring, and in summarizing the results of the latter J. G. Pratt remarked that the significant differences in results "did not show any consistent relationship between scoring rate and the physical characteristics of the dice. These findings suggest that psychological factors were responsible for the differences" (209).

Apparently the psychological explanation was not accepted by Haakon Forwald, a Swedish engineer whose placement experiments were also reported with Cox's (230). Forwald had corresponded with Rhine and had been told of the placement work in progress at Duke. He based his first experiments on Rhine's advice and proceeded with a marathon series of tests, reported from time to time in the *JP* and later summarized in a separate monograph (94).

Though his first experiment, like most placement work, simply involved willing the released dice to fall on the target half of the apparatus rather than the nontarget half, Forwald later progressed to using various types of cubes and to covering them with materials of differing atomic weights. This he combined with calculations of the sideways movements of the cubes into the target area (did they travel far into it or just cross the dividing line?) and the amount of energy that would have been necessary to move them that far. He concluded that a physical relationship, related to gravitational effects, existed between the distance traveled by the cubes and the material of which they were made or with which they were covered. The thickness of the covering was also taken into account in his calculations.

The quantity of work done by Forwald is monumental, and his theories may yet prove relevant to our understanding of PK. However, their impact is unfortunately lessened because he served as his own subject, observer, and experimenter. As an engineer, he probably had a natural tendency toward a physical explanation for PK, and the extent to which his own beliefs and preferences may have influenced his results cannot be calculated (see also Chapter 4, which discusses this preferential effect).

Other die experiments from those early days are discussed in Chapters 4 and 6. They provided the basis for present-day PK research, and in their variety still provide a rich fund of material for the researcher seeking experimental ideas or theoretical concepts. Placement made available a huge new range of research methods, and, though in 1951 the day of the die was far from over, those first placement reports heralded a new era in parapsychology.

Chapter 3

The Wonders of Modern Science

Several minutes and millions of trials later, I suddenly realized that we had just collected more trials in those few minutes than had been reported during the entire sixty year period between 1880 and 1939.

Charles Honorton (127)

Foremost among the experimenters who gave free rein to their imaginations in designing experiments without using die faces was Ed Cox, the Rube Goldberg of parapsychology. Cox has made PK machines out of bits of an old car radiator, discarded trash, aquarium equipment, paper straws, and anything and everything that has come to hand (to the despair of some of his colleagues, who try to have all equipment compatible with their beloved computer).

As targets he has used dice, coins, balls, BB slugs, water spray, mercury globules, soap film, air bubbles, and electric relays. His enthusiasm and ingenuity kept him swimming against the tide when the mainstream of parapsychology was directed almost entirely toward ESP. Indeed, in 1975 Charles Honorton, then president of the Parapsychological Association, observed that "had it not been for the work of W. E. Cox [who] nurtured PK research for nearly two decades" interest in PK might well have faded away in the late 1940s (127).

Freed from die face constrictions, Cox compared spheres and cubes as targets, experimented with different surfaces for the targets to roll over, and developed an assortment of multitiered placement machines including, as he has remarked, "a fancy one with so many balls it nearly fell by its own weight" (64).

In a dice/spheres placement experiment (56) he found that the spheres (marbles) scored somewhat above chance while the dice scored below. Such a finding could produce speculation on the physical attributes of the objects, lower friction, lack of corners, and the like. However, as Pratt once suggested, it could as well be because subjects just plain preferred working with marbles, perhaps because dice were becoming old hat around Duke at the time. As we shall see in the next chapter, a preference for one part of an experiment can lead to a higher score for that part.

At least Cox had found that spheres worked well in PK experiments. Later he began to develop his tiered apparatus. The theory was that perhaps PK, once it started to influence a ball, would stay with that particular ball until it reached its ultimate destination. Accordingly, each tier of the apparatus was divided into halves, target and nontarget. Usually one section was used as the target for half of a run or session and the other section during the other half, to overcome any tendency to bias in the floor or equipment. Balls that fell into the target area of the first tier fell on down to the second tier, which was again divided. If PK stayed with certain balls, then the non-PK balls should have been filtered out at an ever-increasing rate, leaving mainly PK-influenced balls to fall through the lower tiers. The percentage of hits in the lower tiers should then have been much higher than in the higher tiers. In the first three-tier experiment only the bottom tier showed significant results, and comparison with the other tiers proved unclear. Cox then built a five-tier model, only to find that here, too, the bottom tier alone showed significant scoring (57). Since the upper tiers did not show any pattern of scoring at all, it seems possible that subjects were interested only in the bottom tier because that was where the balls ended, and they could see immediately how many were in the target area. For the other levels they had to await the experimenter's calculations, which would have been less interesting. This was partly confirmed when Cox shielded the bottom tier from view and the scores immediately dropped (246).

A major contribution of Cox's was to adapt the cumulative scoring method, sometimes used in ESP and later called the majority vote technique, to PK. In this form a series of units (trials, throws, dice, droplets of water, or whatever) are totalled. If more have gone into the target area than into the nontarget area, the result is counted as one hit. An example is the water droplet experiment reported in 1962 (58). Water was sprayed onto a surface in which were a number of slits. Half the slits led to one glass tube and half to another. If more water went through the slits into the tube designated the target for that test than into the nontarget tube, a hit was scored. Thus one hit was scored not by each droplet, but by an accumulation of droplets. Two series were run, and each reached considerable significance ($P=.00003$ and $P=.002$, respectively).

Later Cox returned to steel balls as units in cumulative experiments, in which, again, the balls fell into various combinations of chutes divided into target and nontarget sides. Further development of cumulative work of this kind was reported by Cox to the PA in 1965 (59) and 1966 (60), and confirmatory work was done by a colleague, Robert Morris (172). It was found that scores calculated by the cumulative method (rather than by counting each ball as a separate trial) showed much clearer evidence of PK than had previous placement machine scores. In these experiments, Cox's work scored at the $P=.001$ and $P=.004$ level respectively, while Morris reported results with a P of .01.

(It is noticeable that, as in Morris's case here, confirmatory work by an experimenter using a machine or method not of his own invention tends to produce scores at a lower level of significance than work done by an experimenter using a machine or method that is his own "baby".)

From steel balls Cox switched to clock-time machines, using time clocks activated by an assortment of units. Water spray was the first, and later sodium and chlorine ions were used—at least Cox *thought* they were used. However, to determine what part of the equipment was really affected by PK he short-circuited the saline solution in which the PK process had been intended to work, only to find that scoring levels remained as significant as before (246).

Later Cox returned to cubes with a clock-timed cube-placement device that used a light beam shining from one end of a cylinder to an electric eye at the other end. Whenever the beam was interrupted a circuit was connected and the clock hand moved (61). In addition to the light beam, the cylinder contained sixteen rubber cubes which, tumbling about as the cylinder revolved, interrupted the light beam and so connected the circuit, causing the clock hand to move. For half the sixteen trials per run, the subjects were told to make the clock hand move clockwise as far as possible, then when the hand had stopped and the motor had been reversed, to hope for as little counterclockwise movement as possible. For the other eight trials, the greater movement was to be counterclockwise and the lesser one clockwise. The measure of success or failure was whether the hand finished to the left or right of zero, and how far from zero it was. In other words, after a long clockwise movement and short counterclockwise return, the hand would not have returned to zero, and the farther to the right of zero it was, the greater success the subject had achieved in creating a difference between the two successive movements—if that was the direction in which he was aiming.

Another series of Cox machines consisted of pendulums whose swings were timed mechanically (62). A slow swing would keep a counter going for a longer time than would a quick one, though subjects' attention was directed more to the counter than to the pendulum. Again each trial consisted of one high aim and one low aim in differing orders, so that at different times subjects had either to speed up or to slow down the pendulum.

At times Cox must have felt that his was a PK voice crying in the parapsychological wilderness. To be sure, he received help and cooperation from staff members at the Parapsychology Laboratory, both when it was at Duke and later when, upon Rhine's retirement from Duke, the lab became a part of the privately funded Foundation for Research on the Nature of Man (FRNM). Yet, with the exception of Haakon Forwald in Sweden, very few other people were working on PK research. However, the cavalry was galloping to the rescue, two regiments of it, each bringing a new viewpoint with new ideas for experimental design. They were, to coin a few terms, the "living systems PK-ers" and the "microdynamic PK-ers."

The living systems group wondered whether PK could be used to affect growth, speed up enzyme reactions, or change the direction of a primitive animal's movement (though the question remains whether this last would be PK or telepathy). Some of this work relates very closely to research on PK as a form of healing, and similar experiments will be found in Chapter 7. The living systems group of experiments is quite separate from those designed to discover whether animals themselves can use PK to affect their environment, which we will discuss later.

In 1951, while reporting on a dice experiment, Paul and Christiane Vasse of Amiens, France, mentioned in an aside that Mme. Vasse had apparently succeeded in increasing the rates of both germination and growth of seedlings (324). In England, Nigel Richmond reported success in influencing paramecia to move into a specific quadrant of a circle as seen through a microscope lens (248), but he acted as his own subject and record-keeper, making his task extremely complicated. A later attempt at replication of Richmond's work by John Randall, also acting as his own subject, did not show evidence of psi (218). A similar attempt by Randall using students as subjects and woodlice as targets produced insignificant overall results (219). (Several individual subjects did attain significant scores, but one strong psi-misser canceled their scores, and breaking the scores down individually is not an acceptable scientific procedure.)

An experiment using fungus was reported by Jean Barry of Bordeaux in 1969 (8). Using a fungus that is often responsible for disease, Barry thought it suitable to have each subject try to retard growth in five culture dishes, with five other dishes serving as controls subject to identical conditions except for the attention of the subjects. Subjects sat for fifteen minutes four to five feet from the dishes, doing whatever they felt would help their PK operate. When the fungus had finished growing, a scorer, blind to the experimental or control status of the dishes, drew an outline of each fungus colony as it had been at the moment of maximum growth. The outlines were cut out, weighed, and compared. If the experimental group weighed less than the controls it was considered a hit. Of thirty-nine trials, thirty-three were hits, with only three misses. In the remaining three the weight of the control and experimental groups were the same. The probability of such a score occurring by chance is only one in a thousand.

More recent tests by William Braud of the Mind Science Foundation in San Antonio, Texas, have successfully used the orientation of electric fish (swimming horizontally or vertically in relation to electrodes on two sides of the tank) and the speed with which a gerbil turned an activity wheel as targets in this type of PK work (26A).

It would seem possible that some psi experiments involving lower life forms may be complicated by human feelings toward such creepy crawlies and a reluctance to "get one's mind too close" to them. One wonders whether such feelings might explain Randall's lack of success, and whether a measure of his students' attitudes towards woodlice might have correlated with their varied scores. From this point of view, a nice, clean, objective electronic machine should be less subject to individual variances. In addition, machinery can be ignored when not in use, adapted in many ways, and adjusted according to the speed found most comfortable to individual subjects. It can also be designed to keep its own records, free from experimenter error. The randomness of targets generated by machines can be assured, and they can be connected with an assortment of feedback devices that immediately tell the subject how successful or unsuccessful he is being.

Enter the "microdynamic PK'ers" and the random number generator (RNG), developed into the parapsychologist's best friend by physicist Helmut Schmidt, once a senior research scientist for Boeing, later director of research at FRNM, and most recently a researcher at the Mind Science Foundation.

Schmidt reported harnessing the randomness with which radioactive nuclei decay as a way of ensuring randomness in a PK machine. Actually, he was not the first to do this. Beloff and Evans of Edinburgh reported on such a technique in 1961, but their results were not significant (12). Nor were those of Wadhams and Farrelly of Cambridge, England (244). However, a French experiment in which children tried to speed up or slow down the blips counted by a Geiger counter seemed very successful, although it was considered by the experimenters, Chauvin and Genthon, to be only exploratory (245). Another experiment without significant overall results was reported by Professor Brenio Onetto of Santiago, Chile (182). Of the eighty-three subjects tested, one, Onetto's own son, scored at a rate of $P=.002$. Although the law of probability predicts that in a large group of subjects a few will score well by chance, such a score does seem promising. However, Onetto decided not to continue testing the boy, now an adult.

Despite these not very encouraging developments, Schmidt worked at his own machine design, particularly trying to simplify methods of feedback. Before long he was the father of generations of "Schmidt machines" that were to serve parapsychology as faithfully as had Cox's mechanical devices before them.

To illustrate the revolution brought about by these microdynamic PK machines, Charles Honorton has told of his introduction to a machine he describes as a "third or fourth generation version" of a Schmidt machine. "Eager to play," he and a colleague, Ed May (a physicist and consultant at Stanford Research Institute), ran a random check on the machine. (This means letting the machine run nonexperimentally to be sure that when not influenced by PK it will produce results very close to chance. The procedure has to be followed before and after every test, and even more frequently during long sessions, to be sure nothing has gone amiss with the delicate insides of the machine. Although necessary, a random check is not entirely proof against machine malfunction, since the experimenter may use unconscious PK to cancel out machine bias, as discussed in regard to control runs in dice throwing in Chapter 2.)

"Several minutes and millions of trials later," says Honorton of their random check, "I suddenly realized that we had just collected more trials in those few minutes than had been reported during the entire sixty year period between 1880 and 1939" (127). He was referring to all psi trials, both ESP and PK, during those sixty years.

In a typical Schmidt machine, the aim is to obtain either a +1 or a −1. A switch oscillates rapidly between the plus and minus positions and is stopped when a radioactive decay particle is detected. The subject, trying to get more pluses than minuses, for example, is actually trying to get a nucleus to decay at a time when the particle emitted will stop the switch while it is in the plus position—a little tricky in view of the fact that the switch oscillates a million times per second (272).

Such machines, with just two positions and a fifty-fifty chance of success, are known as binary random generators, or, more familiarly, electronic coinflippers, since the plus and minus positions can just as well be described as heads and tails, thus making more sense to the subject and helping him feel more at home. The same operating principle can be used for similar machines that have more than two positions, usually four, five, or ten. Other Schmidt-type machines may operate on specially generated internal electronic noise instead of radioactive compounds. Either way the selection of target is entirely random.

However the machine works, the subject need not worry about it and may not even know anything about the workings of the apparatus. His task is simply to affect whatever form of feedback he is being given. Feedback may take the form of a circle of lights in which one lamp is lit at a time. A plus may move the light clockwise, a minus counterclockwise, and the subject attempts to keep it moving in one direction or the other as instructed by the experimenter. He may be told to watch a pen moving over a chart and try to keep it to one side of the central line; again, he is actually trying to generate more of one signal than the other. He may wear earphones and try to keep a certain tone going or to speed up clicks fed to one or both ears. All are effective techniques for letting the subject know how well he is doing, though some may distract him from his task. New forms of feedback are reported at every parapsychological convention, and the aim is always to make the situation as stimulating as possible for the subject while interfering with his state of mind as little as possible. When the apparatus operates at high speeds, the feedback may let him know how he has done over the last one-fifth of a second or over the last ten or twelve trials, or use some similar form of averaging.

Psi-missing is shown as clearly on these machines as is psi-hitting. In fact, if an experimenter finds a group of subjects who tend to psi-miss in exploratory tests he may predict below-average scores and so still get a successful main experiment. In just such a case, Schmidt used fifteen subjects who he knew tended to psi-miss (265). He told them to associate the test with feelings of failure and frustration, ran 32,768 trials, and obtained an overall deviation of -302 ($P<.001$).

Experience with PK is not necessary for success with RNG machines. In Utrecht in 1976, Scott Hill of the University of Copenhagen reported that a teenage girl with no record of previous psi experiences had in two days, over 13,600 trials, scored 172 above chance expectation (124).

To see whether the speed of a machine makes a difference to the subject, Schmidt has run tests at varying speeds. In one the selected speeds were 30 and 300 trials per second (270). Obviously at such speeds the subject may not be able to affect each trial individually, but he can put his mind in what he conceives to be a "PK condition" and attempt to keep it there, making adjustments to his mental technique as he receives feedback. Although subjects were allowed to choose whether they would take the test at the fast or slow speed, so that all would feel good about the way they were being tested, the faster tests were consistently less successful than the slow ones.

Another of Schmidt's machines uses the previously described principle of trying to make a counter run for as long or as short a time as possible. Again using a fast electronic process, a counter advances or stops, with sixty-three chances of advancing and one chance of stopping, making the random "decision" to stop or advance twelve times every second. Schmidt pointed out that by chance it would stop after an average of sixty-four trials, or about 5.3 seconds, but in the pilot experiment, with subjects trying to lengthen the run, 250 runs averaged seventy-five trials before a stop, and two confirmatory tests of 530 and 105 runs averaged seventy-seven and ninety-two trials respectively, giving extremely significant results (267).

Microdynamic machines, some like the simple ones originally developed by Schmidt and others later developed by him and by other electronic tinkerers into fourth-, fifth- and sixth-generation psi machines based on the same principles, are now used throughout the world, and several reports on such research are read at each annual PA convention. In fact, of the eighteen papers* read at the 1977 convention in Washington, D.C., ten involved PK, and of these eight were based on the use of microdynamic machines.

In 1975 Honorton summarized the sixteen PK studies using Schmidt-type machines that had been reported between 1970 and 1975. Thirteen of these, over eighty percent, gave significant

---

*This is far less than the usual number of experimental papers read at a PA convention, due to a change of format for 1977.

results, and when all the results were pooled they showed a significance of $P < 10^{-10}$. In other words, there was less than one chance in ten billion that such results could have been achieved by chance (127)!

Some of the more recent machines can measure, or be connected to machines that measure, tension, indicated by galvanic skin response (GSR) and muscle tension (EMG); brain waves, shown by EEGs; and various other physiological functions, and chart them alongside the PK results graph, making it easy to see whether any distinctive physiological traits regularly accompany PK. So far no reliable correlations have been obtained.

One of the laboratories using such equipment is the Psychophysical Research Laboratory (PRL) at Princeton Forrestal Center, New Jersey. (This organization was until recently better known as the Division of Parapsychology and Physics at Maimonides Medical Center, Brooklyn.) Here Charles Honorton works with a gadget affectionately called Psifi. In the lab, Psifi is connected with an impressive array of these physiological indicators in a complicated system that allows feedback and other information to be directed in almost any combination between two experimental rooms and the room in which Psifi and the experimenter are located. However, Psifi itself is small enough to be packed into a (heavy) suitcase and taken out into the field when necessary.

Still another advance, "Psiborg," is being developed at the PRL. Psiborg already handles up to seven physiological measurements while presenting PK targets, and is eventually expected to use artificial intelligence techniques to correlate the physical state(s) with deviations in the PK scores, modifying its own program as it goes along. In other words, if at the start of an experiment, the subject shows a high alpha amplitude at the same time as high PK scores, Psiborg will adjust its program so that it separates out trials made during high alpha amplitude from trials made during lower alpha. If, as the experiment continues, the high alpha fades but some other physiological measurement seems to correlate with high scores, Psiborg will adjust its program to isolate trials made while that higher or lower reading is present.

Psiborg can create cartoon-type pictures as feedback. Eventually it will be possible to change these according to the interests of the subject, but the basic format is that of a car race. Two cars, one red and one blue, race up the screen. Each is moved by the "heads" randomly generated by the coin-flipper aspect of Psiborg, but the subject tries to make "his" car move faster than the other, which would mean that the set of random events generated for his car contains more target heads than the set moving the other car—which should be at chance. Chance scoring by the subject would cause his car to move at the same speed as the chance car; psi-missing would cause the car to move more slowly, so losing the race.

An even greater complexity that Honorton hopes might be incorporated into electronic equipment is the possibility of sending binary coded information via PK. For example, if sending information about a picture, the first bit of information might be "has color/has not color." The sender would try for, say, heads to indicate color, tails for not color, for a certain length of time. If the picture did have color, the next task might be to identify which colors, one at a time, perhaps with each small segment of the picture being dealt with in map grid fashion in turn. Square A1 "has red/has not red," "has blue/has not blue," and so on. The receiver would watch the output of Psiborg, knowing how much time was to be spent on each item in turn. If he saw more heads being generated he would know that the picture did have color, so the next information coming up would be the identification of the colors. Knowing that A1 was the first square to be worked on, and knowing the order in which the color questions would be presented, he should expect that continued heads would indicate that square A1 would have red in it, or tails would mean no red in that area, and so on, until the complete picture had been put together mosaic style. This, of course, assumes fairly reliable PK ability on the part of the sender (or senders—more than one person could take part simultaneously in this form of sending), but it is an interesting and not impossible concept.

Not everybody approves of either the extremely high-speed trials attainable or some of the multipurpose designs now becoming popular. At FRNM the researchers prefer to have their experimental versatility provided by software programs running on a standard PDP-11 computer system, with experimental procedures being implemented in the form of programs rather than having actual adjustments made to the hardware.

Jim Davis, an experienced computer expert and research associate at FRNM, has pointed out that the faster a machine runs, the harder it is to be sure that its output is consistently random (70). If it is not random, then the statistical analyses used in parapsychology become useless. Another problem is that the greater the variety of tasks such a device is required to do, the more difficult it is to test and the greater the chance of a malfunction, which, particularly at high speeds where a run may take only a few seconds and trial-by-trial targets may not be recorded, might not even be detected. (Indeed, the idea and length of a run has become a matter of convenience, subject to arbitrary decision, since the high-speed experiments began.) Such criticisms may not apply to all high-speed machines. Honorton claims that the targets for Psifi, for example, are alternated in such a way that even with a systematic bias the machine could not produce a significant deviation (129).

Be that as it may, both approaches to experimental equipment serve the purposes of their adherents, and it is certainly healthier for parapsychology as a whole that there is room for both to exist and for disagreement rather than total conformity.

Another PK gadget, named a tychoscope by its inventor, Pierre Janin of Epernon, France, is "a cylindrical device with the approximate size of a drinking glass" (133). The tychoscope is self-propelled and changes both its direction and the length of each movement between directional changes quite randomly. Janin suggests that such a device may be an ideal PK target. One can attempt to control its movements by PK, and it can be made to draw a record of its movements (called a tychogram) for later detailed analysis. No formal studies using tychoscopes have been reported at the time of writing, but initial reaction to Janin's description of the gadget has been enthusiastic, with Rex Stanford, director of the Center for Parapsychological Research in Austin, Texas, calling it "one of the most ingenious and potentially useful of the feedback modes for possible PK effects" (287).

With the development of so much sophisticated hardware, human foibles were effectively removed from the generation of targets, the keeping of records, and measurement of many variables. The next step was to try to remove human inconsistencies from the PK process altogether, by using animals as subjects. Unlike the "living systems" experiments mentioned earlier, in which living things were the targets, animals would now be the subjects attempting to demonstrate that they could use PK to affect the random generators.

When a random generator is set to produce plus or minus, heads or tails, it can also produce "on" or "off" in just about any condition using an on/off switch. Lights, heat, electric shock, delivery of food or water, all can be controlled by the random generator or, if PK can affect the generator, then by PK. An environment can be set up in which an animal is just slightly uncomfortable if the generator runs at chance, and the experimenter hopes (unscientifically, but perhaps also humanely) that it will use PK to improve its situation.

Once again the forerunner in this work was Helmut Schmidt, whose subject in a preliminary test was his family cat. Since cats like warmth, Schmidt put his cat in a cold environment, set up his equipment so that when plus was generated the room was warmed, and observed "encouraging" results. In other words, the plus came up more often than not, and the cat got warmer.

Next, less kindly, he turned his attention to cockroaches, two at a time (266). When plus was generated, they received an electric shock; when minus came up, no shock. The cockroaches were more frequently shocked than expected by chance, with $P<.01$ in the first experiment of 6,400 trials; $P<.0001$ in the second, with 25,600 trials; and $P<.001$ in the last, with 1,280 trials. The last experiment was run at night while Schmidt was at home, away from the laboratory, for he feared that the results might stem from an inherent human dislike of cockroaches, and that *he* might be the source of the PK that was causing the additional electric shocks. Since distance limits have not yet been established for PK, this precaution may not have provided the additional control that Schmidt sought. Perhaps, even while sleeping, his subconscious reached out to harass the pestiferous insects! Assuming his experimental controls *were* adequate, however, alternative explanations are that he had landed on a group of extreme psi-missers, or that cockroaches like electric shocks.

The ethics of using such tactics as electric shocks on living things are of great concern to parapsychologists, and most are trying to find ways of giving positive rather than negative feedback when using animals for experiments.

Siamese fighting fish (bettas) have been subjects in one such series of experiments. Male bettas are naturally aggressive. The sight of another of their own kind causes an immediate display of aggressiveness, spreading of the fins, and the like. William Braud of the Mind Science Foundation used this fact in running a microdynamic test in which PK hits were rewarded by presentation of a mirror, to which the fish reacted as though he were seeing another fish. Since bettas apparently enjoy putting on such displays, the mirror acts as a positive reinforcement. Nonaggressive fish that did not care whether they saw another fish were used as a control group. The aggressive fish soon got used to the mirror, so it was decided to use first-day scores only, and for these the combined scores of the next three experiments showed a probability of .02. The scores of the nonaggressive fish were close to chance (24). Similar results were obtained when, acknowledging that the experimenter effect could not be ruled out, Braud and James Kirk replicated the experiments using "person-fish teams" (28).

Conscious human intervention in experimental results is not called the experimenter effect. It is called fraud. During the early 1970s parapsychologists became hopeful that they were nearing the long-sought repeatable experiment that could be set up and demonstrated to any and every skeptic who came along. Small rodents (mice, hamsters, and gerbils) were the subjects. They ate little, did not have temper tantrums or scheduling problems like human subjects, and could be tested at any time. In short, they seemed the ideal subjects. The ideal experimenter seemed to be Dr. W. J. Levy, a brilliant young worker at FRNM who rose to be director of research. Following on some earlier French experiments, Levy had been running a number of tests in which small rodents sought to avoid a mild electric shock by being in the half of the cage where they would not be shocked when the current was turned on (by an RNG, of course). These experiments actually tested precognition, although it is possible that PK might have been involved. Levy had also done several PK experiments similar to those of Schmidt, using baby chicks and chick embryos whose "task" was to make their environment warmer. Results were so consistently good that hopes for a repeatable experiment soared.

In May 1974, some of Levy's colleagues noticed that during experiments he was spending an unusual amount of time near the recording apparatus—a paper punch machine attached to the test equipment. The tape for the period of his presence showed a very high rate of scoring. Incredulous, they set up a duplicate recording apparatus in another room, and in June one of them arranged to watch him covertly. The duplicate recorder confirmed what the watcher observed—that Levy was doctoring the records (234). Faced with the evidence, Levy admitted tampering with the records in question but denied having done so in the many experiments he had done over the previous five years. In the following months, however, evidence accumulated that his deception might have been more extensive than he admitted, and J. B. Rhine suggested that no work conducted by Levy should be cited as evidential in the future (235).

As a result, a large amount of work on animal psi has had to be dismissed. Even the work of other researchers with whom Levy had worked was discounted if he had had access to the recording equipment. The shock to parapsychology was great, but the fact that the problem had been discovered by other parapsychologists, and been promptly and openly dealt with instead of being swept under the rug, did much to counteract the damage that could have been done to the entire field. (FRNM now has attached to its computer an additional printout device, which can be checked against individual experimental records for most experiments beyond the preliminary stages. The same mistake will not easily be made again.)

On the face of it, replication of Levy's very promising methods should have been easy, but it was not. Scattered reports of success were mixed with a majority of failures. It is as though the Levy work and methods are now covered by a cloud in other people's minds, so that their own feelings are too negative to allow successful results. The experimenter effect can be negative as well as positive. In general, parapsychologists have decided to move forward, developing their own new experiments, rather than spend time looking over their shoulders at might-have-beens.

One area of parapsychological research that does not come under the PK heading, but may yet relate to it, is on out-of-body experiences (OBEs). Readers of Raymond Moody's bestseller *Life After Life* (171) will be familiar with a phenomenon that has been reported by thousands of people through the years and about which many books and studies were written prior to Moody's work (170, 278, 303, 304). This phenomenon is the sensation, usually when sick, injured, or near death, that one's consciousness is floating out of the body. It is of interest to the survival part of psychical research, because if a part of a human being can really leave the body during life, then perhaps that same thing (designated *theta* by W. G. Roll of the Psychical Research Foundation) can continue to exist after the body has died. An additional connection with parapsychology is the fact that when a person claims to have left the body and describes a scene or object in some other location, he could instead be using clairvoyance to get the information.

The connection with PK is tenuous. For the most part, OBE proponents say that in their out-of-body state they cannot affect the physical world. They speak of being unable to open doors, for example, though they often feel that they have passed through unopened doors. If they *could* affect physical things while away from the body, we might start to wonder whether that same something was moving out of the body and causing PK in general.

In recent OBE work, experiments have included devices to measure heat energy changes, electromagnetic field strength, and both visible and invisible light in the area of the target. (The target itself is usually visual, something the subject cannot see from his physical position but is supposed to get to so that he can describe it later as proof that he did get "out" of the body.) Usually the expensive gadgets fail to detect anything unusual when OBE subjects claim to be in their vicinity, but anecdotal reports have referred to occasional changes in electrical fields at the time that a subject reported being near those fields.

Charles Honorton has mentioned a regular PK experiment with Psifi during which the subject reported an unexpected and spontaneous out-of-body experience. At the same time, Psifi produced "a strongly biased output" whose likelihood of occurring by chance was only one in fifty thousand (128). However, Honorton and other researchers emphasize that the occasional "interesting" effects obtained in this way are too sporadic to be regarded as anything more than coincidences.

Another feature of PK that we have already touched on, and will return to, is its unconsciousness. We know that subjects can do as well at "blind PK," in which they do not consciously know their targets, as when they are aware of them. In 1972, Bert Camstra of Amsterdam reported an experiment in which he seemed able to condition people toward achieving better PK if they did *not* concentrate, while such conditioning was less successful if they did concentrate. He was most successful when subjects did not even know they were to perform PK, but believed they were taking part in a telepathy test (40). Later work would see this discovery taken even further.

The indefatigable Helmut Schmidt also ran an experiment to discover whether people who had no idea they were using PK could in fact affect the counter (mentioned earlier) that averages one stop in every 64 trials. Schmidt had the equipment generate a very faint signal at the end of each run, while his subjects (one at a time) listened (271). Great alertness was required, and he expected that their eager anticipation of each signal would shorten the runs in order to make the signals come more quickly. Subjects were not told that the test involved psi. Though two sets of control runs showed averages of 63.8 and 63.5 steps per run, the experimental run in the pilot tests averaged 54.2, significantly less than chance ($P<.001$). The confirmatory test average run was 55.3 steps ($P<.001$).

The second half of this experiment leads to another aspect of current PK research—the apparent ability of PK to reach backward in time just as precognition seems to reach forward. This time Schmidt had his equipment make tapes of randomly spaced signals in the same way, while he was away from it. To further avoid affecting the tapes himself, he had the equipment produce two groups of runs, and it was not until shortly before the experiments were conducted that he determined (by complex calculator figuring) which was the target and which was the control group.

Several days after the tapes were prepared he played them to subjects under circumstances similar to those in the first half of the test, except that, since the tapes were preprepared, it should not have been possible to affect them by PK. Yet the average length of the experimental runs was 56.4 ($P<.001$) as against 62.9 for the average control run.

Schmidt's next step was to see whether a tape that was played several times to a subject would be affected more than a tape that was played only once. In this experiment, which used the binary electronic coinflipper (274), subjects knew that they were attempting PK but did not know that some of the signals were actually being prepared while they talked to Schmidt before the experiment. During the experiment, a complex system was used to intermix these prerecorded signals with others generated during the experiment, but the prerecorded signals were presented to the subject four times, as against once each for the others. The subject's task was to make as many heads or tails come up as he could. By chance, the average scoring rate should have been 50 percent. For the targets presented once it was 50.82 percent—a marginally significant result ($P<.05$) in view of the large number of trials (20,480). The average scoring rate for the targets that were presented four times was 52.95 percent ($P=.0005$). The difference between the two was significant at $P=.025$.

This makes it appear that a target can be affected even though the subject does not know until later that he is meant to affect it. However, attempts by other researchers to replicate this work have not shown significant results (36). Schmidt points out that an experimenter effect cannot be ruled out, for he did know that the targets were being generated and taped while he talked with the subjects at the start of the experiment.

All this microdynamic work is, of course, quantitative. It deals with how much and how often, but not necessarily with how well. If a subject can affect the minute circuits of a Schmidt machine, what does that mean? It may help prove that PK exists. Perhaps a well-designed experiment may give insight into the whys and hows of PK, but that is all. It does not necessarily show that the subject can in any way use PK in day-to-day life—except insofar as his life may be affected by such equipment. As researcher David Rogers has commented, "In much of psychical research...precise work is often done at the price of relevance while relevant work is often too imprecise" (250).

For this reason this chapter is best seen balanced against Chapter 5, in which we will look at the "PK superstars" and reports of far greater achievements, many of which, however, occurred under far less well controlled conditions. The present chapter could be said to represent the more precise, quantitative techniques of parapsychology, while Chapter 5 offers relevance (though some may question the relevance of a bent spoon). Even more relevance, as well as some quantitative work, will be seen in Chapter 7.

I do not mean to imply that the work with superstars is *totally* different from day-to-day parapsychological lab work. In fact, innovations developed in work with the superstars are gradually being introduced into regular lab work with less spectacular, but perhaps more tractable, subjects. However, there is usually less control, and if the microdynamic work had not been done it would be fairly easy to dismiss the superstars as skilled magicians. Since such work has been done, and since it gives strong evidence that PK, which "cannot exist," may exist, we must give the feats of the superstars careful attention.

First, however, let's turn to some experimental problems that arise in parapsychological research.

Chapter 4

Murphy's Law—
The First Rule of
Parapsychology

(a) Nothing is as easy as it appears to be; (b) everything takes longer than you expect; (c) if anything can go wrong it will!

Perhaps the foregoing chapters have made it appear that parapsychology is a relatively simple field of endeavor. In fact, however, it is incredibly complicated, so much so that it seems the complications deserve a chapter of their own. Had they been included with the straightforward accounts of research, the reader by now would be completely bogged down in suggested alternative explanations.

The complications go back a long way. In the 1890s F. W. H. Myers, writing of raps apparently produced by mediums, was asking:

Are we to suppose that actual sound-waves are produced in the air? If so, of course the smallest "rap" is an interference with the ponderable world every whit as definite as the "levitation" of a medium on to the table. Or are they mere hallucinations—with some origin, perhaps, outside the minds of the sitters, but operating upon these minds in some direct fashion, and not upon the air of the room? (179)

At first glance, we may assume that such a simple question is easily dealt with by the use of a modern tape recorder during a seance. If the raps are recorded on tape, then clearly actual sound waves *are* produced in the air. But then we have to wonder whether it might be just as simple (or complicated) for a medium to affect the magnetic tape directly, and so produce the effect of noise on the tape, as to affect the air molecules that transmit sound. Conclusion? Probably none, except that Murphy's Law *(a)* holds.

Many more concrete problems face today's researcher, who works in an atmosphere far removed from that of Myers's seance rooms. One major problem mentioned in Chapter 2 is that of psi-missing, sometimes referred to as negative psi.

It is easy to see that when a die is thrown you have one chance in six of getting the desired face upward just by chance if the die is perfectly balanced. Equally, it is clear that if someone consistently scores well above the one in six chance score he may be using PK. What, though, are we to think of the person who consistently scores well *below* chance? Anyone not used to statistics may assume that the lower the score the less likelihood that PK is being used, but this is not the case. The statistician knows that a score well below chance is just as unlikely as a score well above chance and just as much an indication that *something* is probably causing these unlikely events.

It is as though, at some level of consciousness, a part of the subject is inhibited from scoring well. His PK works, but it works to *prevent* the target faces from coming up even as often as they should by chance. This is a case of PK operating without the conscious control of the subject. Psi-missing may be explained by such factors as personality, state of mind, fear of psi, or other undiscovered variables, but the result is always a low score. Even a normally high-scoring subject may psi-miss when slightly uncomfortable, physically or mentally.

Recently I telephoned a subject who had scored very low in a group ESP test and, in conversation, asked if she had been too hot during the test, since the room had been quite warm.

"Oh, no," she replied. "I felt fine...except that just before we started someone made a remark about my smoking. That was rather hurtful."

Any experimenter should be careful to avoid such a guilt-evocative situation, but unfortunately I was not. I only wished I knew which subject made the remark, for, having made it, he or she too might well have been in a psi-missing mood and it would have been interesting to check that score.

While researchers look for clues that may help them identify psi-missing people and situations, so far they have few conclusions. As Louisa Rhine remarked in 1965, "It is a tendency which may vary in degree from person to person and from situation to situation" (242).

In the analysis of results, psi-missing causes complications that can be overcome, but that do require rather more complex methods than we could otherwise get away with using. In computing the mean, or average, score of a group, for example, we may find five strong psi-hitters and five psi-missers, with scores equally far from chance but in opposite directions. As an unlikely example, if the average run score is four, half the subjects might score eight each (every researcher should be so lucky) while the other half score zero. The odds against this happening are very high and, if the experiment were properly designed and controlled, this result would in itself be strong evidence for psi. Yet if these scores were simply added together and averaged, the mean score would be four—right on chance and nothing to get excited about.

Fortunately, use of the correct statistical methods can easily overcome this problem as they can overcome many others.

During the early years of lab research the development of good statistical methods became one of the most important underpinnings of parapsychology, and it remains so today. Statistical techniques help researchers ascertain whether differences in scoring rates are big enough to be worth further study, or whether they simply reflect the fact that no two groups of figures can be expected to be identical. They give parapsychologists a way of comparing one experiment with another and of stating in their reports just how likely or unlikely any single result, or any difference between groups of results, is. Without some knowledge of statistics, it is now almost impossible to understand most of the papers published on parapsychological experiments, and no experiment, no matter how well designed, can be properly assessed without a knowledge of statistics.

In the case of psi-missing, a variety of techniques are used to measure how much the score varies from chance, regardless of whether the variance is up or down, and such techniques can prevent psi-missers and psi-hitters from canceling out each others' scores.

Psi-missing seems to appear quite prominently in conjunction with what is often called the preferential effect—itself an infuriating complicater of experiments. The preferential effect was noticed when researchers realized that some subjects always did much better with one kind of target, or in one set of conditions, than another, according to which they preferred.

Many times an experimenter has thought he had discovered a particular condition that helped get better psi scores, only to discover that, though it helped some subjects, the same condition was a hindrance to high scoring in others. It was not the condition itself that helped; it was the effect of the condition on the mind of the subject. If he liked it, he would score better. If not, his score would drop when the new condition was introduced. The problem has harassed researchers since the days of early dice—and probably before. One example is the preference for high dice discussed earlier, but the preferential effect does not confine itself to die faces. It interferes with almost every experiment in which subjects know that they are working under two different conditions.

Does the experimenter want to find out whether the size of the dice affects the rate of scoring? Such a finding might shed light on just *what,* if any, type of physical force is involved in PK, but if the subject knows that he is sometimes working with one size and sometimes with another he may quickly establish a preference for one of them. From then on he is very likely to score higher on his preferred size than on the other. He may even proceed to psi-miss on the nonpreferred target. Result? An experimenter who cannot tell whether his results, however significant they may be, reflect the fact that one size of die is more responsive to PK, or simply that the subject preferred that size, felt more comfortable with it, and so was able to score better with it.

The same problem occurs when trying to discover, as did Cox and others, whether different shapes may facilitate PK, or, as in Forwald's work, whether different substances may bring about different results. The problem is particularly acute in Forwald's case because he was his own subject. Subject Forwald therefore always knew what hypothesis was involved in each experiment and what result Experimenter Forwald was seeking. (Although every conscientious experimenter tries not to hope too hard that the results will prove his theory correct, experimenters are, after all, human, and the thought that several years of work may be disproven, literally at the toss of a die, cannot help but provoke a little subjective bias.)

The subject's state of mind is very important in parapsychology. As we have seen, a tense or unhappy subject is unlikely to achieve high scores. One approach that is very likely to create tension and unhappiness is for the experimenter to approach a new subject as though he is a potential fraud, determined to fool the experimenter, with magic tricks up his sleeve and a confederate behind every door. It is important that the subject feel liked, trusted, and comfortable; yet, if an experiment is to be properly controlled to satisfy the rigid demands of science and skeptics, the experimenter *must* think of the subject as having potential magic tricks up his sleeve and a confederate behind every door.

The commonly accepted solution is for the experiments to start with a casual, relaxed method that is not necessarily well controlled. The results, while noted, are not used in support of a hypothesis. As the subject becomes more confident, more accustomed to the lab, the experimenters, and the work involved, the experimenters gradually introduce new conditions, stronger controls. Slowly the experiment is tightened until it is being performed under the kind of strict controls that help assure that the results will relate to the hypothesis and not to some uncontrolled variable, fraudulent or accidental.

This procedure sounds fine, but once again the preferential effect interferes. If a subject has become comfortable under one set of conditions, he is often uncomfortable when those conditions are changed—not necessarily because they are unpleasant or reflect distrust, but simply because they are different. Once again the skeptics crow triumphantly that as soon as properly controlled conditions were introduced the results returned to chance. This, they say, is proof that any significant results obtained before proper controls were in force were due to sloppy method or conscious or unconscious fraud. They may, of course, be right. However, if the experimenters and subjects have developed a truly good relationship, and if they persist, they will often find that as the new becomes the familiar, scores will rise again.

Then there are times when it seems that PK operates slightly "off target"—the displacement effect. Displacement was first noticed in work with ESP when it seemed that some subjects would consistently hit the target ahead of, or behind, the one they were aiming for. Less attention has been paid to displacement in PK, but from time to time it has seemed to appear in dice work (181). In PK, displacement can manifest as a tendency for the target face to be on the bottom (farthest away from the target position) *less* often than would be expected by chance. Or, when the target face is changed after a trial, results may show more of the previous or next target face than expected. Another phenomenon described as a form of displacement was the appearance of a large number of sevens in Rhine's experiment in which the aim was low dice (Chapter 2).

When the face that was the previous target keeps appearing the explanation may also be the "linger effect."

If PK has affected an object, or a location, there is some evidence that the effect continues *after* the subject's attention has moved elsewhere. This has been studied mainly in relation to healing (Chapter 7) but has been noticed in other experiments, too (332). The linger effect may complicate placement experiments in which the target side is switched randomly from side to side of the equipment at frequent intervals, because PK may still be operating on the side that *was* the target side but is now the nontarget side.

The question raised by the linger effect is whether it exists because the PK subject's mind is still unconsciously involved with the previous target or because PK has had a *physical* effect on the object or area that continues to work for a while before dying down. Consider an analogy with an object warmed by direct heat from a space heater. For a while after it is turned off the heater continues to emit heat, and it is hard to tell to what extent the object remains warm because of this continued heat from the heater, and to what extent it remains warm because it is storing the heat previously received. So far, no one has found a way of determining an answer.

A constant complication for those seeking to isolate PK or ESP is the way the two functions—or whatever they are— seem to merge. Where does ESP end and PK begin? The two are often referred to as the opposite sides of the coin of psi. That seems to separate them clearly—until one remembers that somewhere in the middle of a coin is a place where the two sides meet or merge. Is there a neat, tidy cutoff point? Here is the inside of the heads side; here is the inside of the tails? Or, if they merge gradually, at what point does the "influence" of heads cease to spread into tails? Similarly, it is difficult to separate PK and every aspect of ESP. Let us look at some examples relating to each form of ESP, one at a time, for in many studies of PK they are a complication indeed.

In 1897 Dr. P. Joire of the University of Lille, France, reported a series of experiments in which he moved his limbs and willed blindfolded subjects to imitate him. Even when Joire stood behind the subjects, he reported a high degree of success (136). For each movement, Joire would visualize the successive contractions of the various muscles involved, fasten his eyes on the subject, and then, with "a considerable effort of will," attempt "as vividly as possible, first to imagine such a series of muscular contractions and then to induce the subject to carry them out."

Even if the results were not due to sensory cues, a question remains. Were Joire's movements discerned by the subject using ESP? Was the experimenter actually influencing the subject's muscles, causing him to respond? Or was the experimenter affecting the brain or motor nerves and so causing the movements? If the experimenter influenced muscles, brain, or nerves, a form of PK was being used.

In 1962 in Russia, parapsychologist L. L. Vasiliev reported on work that he had done inducing hypnotic sleep in certain subjects while he was a considerable distance away from them. Vasiliev, professor of physiology in the University of Leningrad at the time, achieved a remarkable record of success. In one series of seventeen trials, the sender and the subject were in different rooms, separated by two passageways and with all doors closed. The subject fell asleep an average of 4.05 minutes after the sender started to "will" her to do so and woke an average of 3.67 minutes after he willed her to wake, though she had no idea of when the silent commands would come or how long each experiment would last.

Under the same conditions another subject took part in thirty-five such trials, with average delays of only 3.87 and 3.60 minutes before responding to the orders to sleep and wake. Again a considerable question arises as to whether this effect was induced telepathically, as Vasiliev believed, or by a form of PK working directly on the brain (323).

Another experiment, often quoted by parapsychology historians, was reported at the First International Congress of Psychical Research in Copenhagen in 1922. Three researchers at the Psychological Laboratory at Groningen, Holland, sought to influence a subject named Van Dam so that he would point to one of forty-eight squares on a board in front of him. As with a map, the squares were identified by numbers along the side and letters across the bottom, and before each trial the target square was chosen by lot and known only to the one experimenter who was to attempt to influence the subject. For half the experiments, the researchers were in a darkened room, looking down through a double glass window in the floor at the blindfolded subject sitting in a cubicle in the room below them. For the other half they were in the same room as the subject, but shielded by the walls of the cubicle. While four successes would be expected by chance in the 187 trials conducted, Van Dam pointed to the correct square sixty times.

Though this was an unsophisticated experiment when compared with those conducted today, and though details of the procedures were not adequately reported, it is of interest because, when asked about this experiment by Gardner Murphy, the chief experimenter, Brugmans said, "We could *push* the hand this way and that" (175).

Like Vasiliev, Brugmans considered the results to be achieved by telepathy, but this was before PK had been subjected to serious laboratory investigation. In light of the fair amount of evidence for the existence of PK, perhaps the alternative explanation, that PK might have directly affected the subject's muscles or motor nerves, should be borne in mind.

Many researchers have suggested the existence of two forms of telepathy, one in which the percipient or receiver is the active person, and one in which the agent or sender is active (see also the *Shin* theory, Chapter 14). Rex Stanford has suggested that the latter form is actually a kind of PK and should be termed "mental or behavioral influence of an agent" (MOBIA) to avoid confusion with telepathy, in which the percipient is the active participant (284).

That clairvoyance and PK are often so intertwined as to be inseparable has been recognized for many years. In 1953 Karlis

Osis (now of the American Society for Psychical Research) reported an experiment in which three subjects threw dice *without being told which faces were the targets.* Two simply tried to hit the target, whatever it was, and the third tried to miss it. The first two achieved significantly high scores, and the third scored below chance, as he had tried to do, though not significantly so. (Perhaps, again, because of the preferential effect. No one likes to throw to lose.) Osis concluded that, "There must therefore be a close relationship between ESP and PK. Whether they are two different aspects of the same process...cannot be conclusively determined at our present state of knowledge" (183).

More recently Helmut Schmidt and Lee Pantas, both then on the research staff of the Institute of Parapsychology, conducted an experiment in which subjects were sometimes being tested for PK and sometimes for precognition. The test machine had four lights and four buttons. For each trial, the subject pressed a button corresponding to the light that he expected to light next. Earlier, similar tests had been intended to be for precognition alone, but it was realized that once the subject had pressed the button he could presumably be "willing" the chosen light to come on, in which case PK might come into play. To correct for this possibility, Schmidt adapted his machine so that, at the flick of a switch, it would convert from generating targets that the subject had to forecast (for precognition) to recording a hit only when a specific target was generated. Presumably unconscious PK could affect the frequency with which that target was generated. Despite this internal difference, the machine appeared to be running in exactly the same way at all times, so the subjects, and even Schmidt's coexperimenters, did not know that more than one type of test was being conducted.

In a test series using groups of visitors to the institute (mainly students and teachers), the score for PK was a little higher (deviation of +32 in 500 trials) than for precognition (+24), though the difference was not significant.

In another series, using coexperimenter Lee Pantas as a subject, the precognition score was higher than the PK score, but, again, no significant difference appeared. Schmidt pointed out that he could not rule out PK under the precognition condition, nor prevent someone from using precognition to aid in the PK test, stating:

> The precognition-oriented and PK-oriented tests cannot be considered to be "pure" precognition or PK tests, respectively. Just as in the precognition test the subject could use PK to enforce the generation of a chosen target, in the PK tests the subject could use precognition to determine when the conditions for the generation of the target seemed favorable, and then push a button. The difficulty of distinguishing between precognition and PK may be of a rather basic nature and not just a feature of the present experiment. It may even be that such a distinction is, in principle, conceptually and experimentally impossible. (275)

Many parapsychologists now feel that not only is it impossible to talk of telepathy, clairvoyance, and precognition as separate functions (they seem to be different modes of the same thing), but it may be impossible to separate ESP and PK. An illustration of the way this fact may confuse an experiment comes from Charles Tart of the University of California, who not long ago wrote that he had not done much work with PK, but added, "I may be forced to look at it because I suspect that some of our better scoring subjects in my ESP learning experiment may have been unconsciously using PK on the electronic random number generator" (307).

The ESP/PK linkage may cause problems outside the laboratory as well as in it. A friend of mine who seems to do well at precognition was unwise enough to make one or two minor predictions to colleagues at work. When she was proven right, she faced a result she had not foreseen—they decided that she must have *made* the events occur. They were mistaking her precognition for PK, but, knowing little of parapsychology, carried their beliefs further and concluded that she was a witch!

The last chapter described experiments that seem to show that many people use PK when they are not aware of doing so. Obviously this presents the experimenter with more complications, not least of which are his own emotions and desires. Is *he* causing experimental results that he believes are brought about by his subjects? Remember Schmidt and his cockroaches? Do the experimenter's preferences (usually about the hypothesis he is trying to prove, but sometimes also about his subjects) *cause* the results for which he is hoping? Is unconscious experimenter PK responsible for the fact that, with some experimenters, subjects are consistently successful, while with others they regularly score at chance? If this is the case, then the experimenter is a co-subject in every experiment he runs.

Helmut Schmidt may have been quite prepared, in the interests of science, to allow his cat to remain a little on the cool side, but another less scientific and more humane part of him may have felt guilty at creating such a situation, even though it was only temporary. Could it not, then, have been his PK, trying to make amends, rather than PK on the part of the cat, that caused the random number generator to produce more hits and so warm up the cat's living area? Again, we still have evidence for the operation of PK, but it may be human, not feline, in origin.

Is it possible to guard against the experimenter effect? In an attempt to do so, some researchers have run experiments in which the apparatus operated through the night while they were away from the lab, so that they could not be consciously aware of when it was "aiming" for hits and when for misses. In a continuation of his sixty-three-steps-advance, one-step-stop counter experiments (267), Schmidt shortened the probable run from sixty-four steps to thirty-two and arranged that brine shrimps in a trough of water would get a mild electric shock at the end of each run. It was therefore to the shrimps' advantage to make the runs longer than average so that they would get fewer shocks. In his exploratory series, when 1,878 shocks would have been expected, 1,760 were actually given. Then, as his control against any experimenter effect, Schmidt introduced control runs in which no shock was given to alternate with test runs. Everything was done automatically, including the record-keeping, so Schmidt did not know which runs were control and which were experimental. In the control runs the shocks were very close to the chance number, but in the experimental runs, where 3,347 shocks would have been expected, only 3,164 were delivered.

This may sound like a proper control method, but if we accept the possibility that PK may work in conjunction with ESP, the experimenter may know by ESP which mode is required when and adjust his PK accordingly, all at the unconscious level where it appears that psi operates best, without any conscious awareness whatsoever. Of course, such unintentional manipulation of results may not invalidate an experiment entirely; it may still provide proof of PK. However, a particular hypothesis may appear to be supported or unsupported when in fact the variables responsible may be in the experimenter's mind, not in the conditions of the experiment.

Such an experimenter effect may be the explanation for the famous (or infamous) Backster effect, named for Cleve Backster, who obtained results indicating that plants and simple cells have an apparently telepathic awareness of what is happening to other plants and cells and of the emotions and intentions of humans around them. Backster's results need not be denied, but a number of attempted replications by other researchers have failed, and he may, in all innocence, have been the victim of his own PK, working either directly on the instruments or on the metabolism of the plants themselves.

Whether PK might also invalidate actual measurement of psi effects is another complication that will eventually have to be faced. If a person can deflect the needle of a compass or similar device, then can such a device safely be used for measuring anything in the area where PK events are taking place?

Dr. Hans Bender reported on the Rosenheim poltergeist (see Chapter 9) in the late 1960s. This case largely involved electric fittings and surges of power in electrical lines. A voltmeter connected with one of the lines in question showed erratic surges of power, though similar instruments attached to the external electric lines showed no such surges entering the building (14, 199). What really threw everyone for a loop was the fact that when they disconnected the voltmeter *it continued to show the same type of needle movement.* So *was* it originally measuring power surges that could have explained the other events in the building (regardless of whether they were normally or paranormally caused) or was the voltmeter simply responding, like a compass needle, to a form of PK from Annemarie, the suspected poltergeist agent in this case? How can we ever know?

If the experimenter does indeed have a direct effect on the results of his experiments, we can see why skeptics remain skeptics and believers continue to believe. The confirmed unbeliever, however hard he tries to remain open-minded, will automatically have a negative effect on any experiment in which he is involved. No matter what wondrous results were achieved in his absence, if they never occur when he is there "to see that things are done right," it will not be surprising if he concludes that in his absence other experimenters must use slightly different methods, be less alert, or in some way allow their control over the experiment to slip, so permitting a skillful fraud to affect the results.

Even pairing such a skeptic with a usually successful experimenter might not work, if we remember the help/hinder experiments mentioned in Chapter 2. It seems likely that a skeptic, observing an experiment that would upset his entire belief system if it proved significant, would consciously or unconsciously have a hindering effect on the subject who was trying to use PK and/or on the inadvertent PK of any other, less skeptical experimenters or observers who were present.

This fear of upsetting one's world view is a major problem for parapsychologists. As young children we are taught that if you can't see it, touch it, or measure it—whatever *it* is—it probably doesn't exist. Every parent, faced with the problem of teaching a child the difference between "reality" and imagination, fact and fiction, comes down hard—must come down hard—on the side of the see-it/touch-it school of thought. When dealing with a screaming preschooler who has just heard his first "the ghost is gonna get ya" or "I'll put a spell on you" story, one *must* dismiss all nonmaterialist ideas as utter nonsense. With most children this denial is thankfully accepted as the only truth; it has to be accepted, because, if it is not, the world becomes a fearful place where ghosts roam and enemies can hurt you just by thinking about it. So that little pigeonhole of belief is mercifully closed and locked and the key thrown away. The child grows up convinced, as his teachers continue to assure him, that only physical pressure can alter or move physical objects, that nobody can know something unless awareness comes via the five "normal" senses, and that the world is, therefore, safe, predictable, and, as far as presently known laws of nature are concerned, law-abiding.

It is hardly surprising that many people find parapsychology threatening. The acceptance of psi may mean the reopening of that safely locked door, the reemergence of who knows what fears that never had to be dealt with before because they could always be dismissed as superstitious nonsense. For some, it is easier and safer to deny that the door exists than to face those ancient terrors.

Of course, we could hardly admit this as the basis for our skepticism, even to ourselves. Rather, we cling to the flotsam of a physics that has been largely discarded by physicists. We state flatly that a table is a solid object, even though we know that it is made up of atoms consisting largely of empty space. We say "you can't stop the clock" and assume that time moves irreversibly forward at a constant speed, ignoring the fact that the theory of relativity shows that time is not constant, and that subatomic physics suggests that some elementary particles may even go "backward" in time. Life must be commonsensical, and our minds find it hard to accept anything else, so we reject psi, which does not appear to be commonsensical.

On the whole, though, parapsychologists themselves accept the micro-PK events that we have discussed in the previous two chapters. Small PK effects, apparent only when repeated hundreds of thousands of times and then subjected to statistical analysis, are not, after all, too threatening. In cases of macro-PK, however, the situation is quite different. Macro-PK refers to PK in which the effects are large enough to be visible to the naked eye; it is sometimes called "directly observable PK." Poltergeist events involve macro-PK, according to current theories, and so may some seance effects, but the most controversial sources of all, at this time, are the PK "superstars" who have appeared in several different countries in the last few years. From the violence of the reaction to them, both pro and con, it would seem that if their apparent abilities are eventually proven to the satisfaction of most parapsychologists (and this is not yet the case by any means), the result may well be an outbreak of acute parapsychologist anxiety the like of which has not yet been seen.

But then, perhaps this will never happen. It may be that they are not superstars, but superfrauds. Let us look further.

Chapter 5

Superstars
or
Superfrauds?

In order to establish that not all crows are black you have only to find one white crow. In order to establish directly observable PK as a fact you have only to find one instance of it having occurred under totally controlled circumstances. The question is, has there ever been such an instance?

Micro-PK,* the kind of effect that can be measured only by statistical analysis of a large number of trials, is obviously intensely frustrating to the psychical researcher. Declines and psi-missing, experimenter, linger, and preferential effects, all combine to make him wonder at times whether what he is seeking—an understanding of psi—is a will-o'-the-wisp that may lead him stumbling through the marshlands of science for the rest of his life, all to no purpose. Even while the quantitative approach to PK was being developed, the cry was going up: "Where are the great physical mediums now that we have the tools to measure their phenomena?"

Seemingly, the great mediums were gone, vanished in a cloud of ectoplasm before the onrush of scientific method. However, in the late 1960s rumors began to percolate out of Russia. There was a lady—perhaps there were two ladies—who could make things move! Objects almost danced before them, moving from left to right, backward and forward, on demand. In 1968 participants in an international meeting on parapsychology in Moscow were shown a movie in which one Nina Kulagina did indeed appear able to move objects without having any physical contact with them. From then

---

* Meaning psychokinesis discernible only by statistical analysis, *not* necessarily the same as microdynamic PK, which means PK on electronic equipment.

on the desire of almost every parapyschologist who visited anywhere near Russia was to visit and test Kulagina.

Unfortunately, the vagaries of politics being what they are, not all such trips have been fruitful. Tests in a laboratory situation are rarely possible, contact with Kulagina being usually informal and taking place either in her apartment or in the hotel of her visitors. At times she is suddenly unavailable, and every trip to see her is a gamble that may or may not work out. Nevertheless, some important phenomena have been demonstrated during the handful of semisuccessful meetings that Western scientists have had with her. They are labeled semisuccessful only because controls have not been of laboratory quality, so the question of trickery has never been totally ruled out. At the same time, no Western scientist has ever detected trickery, or even the possibility of trickery, on Kulagina's part. Four reasonably conservative and widely disparate scientists from three nations have reported, after an intensive study of their own experiences with Kulagina and of other published reports of work with her, "From all the evidence now at our disposal it seems reasonable to conclude that Kulagina does not behave like a person who is trying to conceal something" (141).

In 1970, during a visit by Kulagina to their hotel room, J. G. Pratt and Champe Ransom, both of the Division of Parapsychology, University of Virginia, watched while a metal cylinder slid along a table and even moved after it had been placed under a glass. They spread aquarium gravel on the table and then saw the cylinder move "toward Kulagina while clearing a path through the gravel." Pratt later rated the first event as the "best evidence of PK," which he termed "good, but not conclusive"(211).

Also during the fall of 1970, Montague Ullman, then of the Maimonides Medical Center in Brooklyn, observed Kulagina moving,

> . . . without any apparent contact, a number of small objects placed on a table which was covered by a tablecloth. The objects included two pen tops placed upright (one of which was plastic), several large paperclips and a box of wooden matches. The objects moved both independently and together toward Mrs. Kulagina in short jerky movements of about an inch at a time. (316)

In 1971, the political climate was not good for working with Kulagina, but in July 1972 Benson Herbert of the Paraphysical Laborarory in England was able to visit her. The weather was hot and thundery, both factors which bother Kulagina, and she said she could not perform. The conversation turned to healing, which Kulagina is reported to do quite frequently. She gripped Herbert's arm and, after a moment or two, he felt "a new sensation, which I described at the time as a kind of 'heat,' but which now, after much reflection, I believe to be more akin to a mild electric shock" (118).

The sensation was unpleasant enough to make Herbert "writhe" and "grimace" and remove his arm after about two minutes. His colleague, Mr. Cassirer, felt nothing under similar circumstances, but, as Herbert points out, Cassirer "has a reputation for remaining unaffected by most electrical experiments that we conduct from time to time at the Paraphysical Laboratory." Kulagina then turned her attentions to the hotel receptionist, who was acting as interpreter. The receptionist behaved much as Herbert had and quickly asked to be released.

A later visit in which Kulagina repeated this performance convinced Herbert that, after all, the effect was "pure heat and not electrical in nature" (119). However, during a more recent visit by H. H. J. Keil of Tasmania and Jarl Fahler of Finland she raised painful red welts on Fahler's arm by placing her hand on it, even though a thermometer placed between her and his arm showed no change from normal body temperature (140).

That September, Pratt and Keil made an unannounced visit to the Kulagina family hoping to arrange a formal PK session. Since Kulagina likes to know what kind of equipment she will be working with, they showed her some of their test gadgets, setting them out on the table before her. One of them was a plastic jelly dish and behind it was a wooden cube. Both were resting on an open book. Kulagina started moving her hands around the objects and suddenly,

> . . . the block of wood moved about one inch (two cm.) in her direction, angling slightly toward her left and rotating slowly in a clockwise direction as it did so. Both of us saw this, as we immediately confirmed with each other. Then we saw it move again in the same way. (211)

They showed her a hollow plexiglass cube containing two dice and some aquarium gravel. She tried to move the dice alone, but, though she was unable to, the cube itself moved about an inch toward her. Unfortunately, the more formal test session did not take place, apparently because the authorities forbade Kulagina to keep her appointment with Pratt and Keil. Though the informal session cannot be regarded as a well-controlled test, Pratt and Keil make the following points:

> Kulagina had not moved from the table from the time we put the objects down until they moved, and one or both of us had her under direct observation for the whole time. The objects were ours, and they were resting on our "surface," the page of [our] open book. We never observed any behavior suggesting that Kulagina was preparing a trick, and she would not have known to prepare it before we unexpectedly produced the object.

Kulagina is also reported to have caused objects to levitate and to have affected photographic materials (317).

In 1973, Benson Herbert returned to Russia. Kulagina was said to be too ill to demonstrate her powers, but she did visit him to discuss her abilities. Once in his hotel room, she became fascinated by the display of gadgets (set out on three tables) with which he had hoped to test her. After taking some medication she apparently felt better. She placed her hands close (too close, at times, for proper control) to a hydrometer floating in a bowl of water, and it moved. She then sat down some distance from the bowl and the table on which it sat. Several of those present walked between her and the table as they talked, unconciously establishing that no wires or hairs led to the hydrometer. Then they realized that she was concentrating again, still sitting down, and they fell silent. The hydrometer moved away from Kulagina to the far side of the bowl, remained there about two minutes, then moved straight back across the bowl to the side nearest her. Later a compass case zigzagged across the table toward her while Herbert had a close and clear view of her. Swift examination of the area around the case satisfied him that no threads could have been used to bring about this effect. In further discussion of ways in which such phenomena could be caused by trickery Herbert rules out supersonic vibration (which might reduce friction and make objects move more easily), magnetism, electro-statics, and gravity (119).

Keil and Fahler, during their visit, observed and filmed Kulagina apparently moving a glass that was inverted inside another inverted glass. A green wooden object was inside the inner glass. The outer glass did not move and the wooden object moved only when pushed by the inner glass. A tennis ball suspended from a steel spring inside a clear plastic cube also moved downward and toward her. (Whenever steel is involved, fraud by magnetism cannot be ruled out, but the experimenters apparently considered that their controls were sufficient to guard against this possibility.)

Kulagina has difficulty moving objects that are inside hermeti-cally sealed containers. She is reported to have affected one Russian scientist's heart rate while it was being recorded by an electrocardio-graph machine, and to have first accelerated and then stopped the beat of a frog's heart in a test tube (316). Usually under similar conditions a frog's heart will beat for about four hours.

Another Russian woman, Alla Vinogradova, also performs PK but seems to produce a narrower range of phenomena. She appears to use electrostatic forces, and sparks have been seen at her finger-tips while she is working, yet she can move objects even when she is electrically grounded (317).

Though Kulagina and Vinogradova were the first modern super-stars, no sooner had their fame begun to spread in the Western hemisphere than it was eclipsed by a veritable Halley's Comet (though less reliable) in the person of a brash young man from Israel called Uri Geller. Geller has been described by observers of many different persuasions as a showman, a miracle man, a charlatan, an innocent abroad, the puppet of extraterrestrial beings, the final and absolute proof of PK, the forerunner of a new type of humanity, the con man *par excellence* . . . the list of descriptions is lengthy.

As a youth, Geller claims, he developed both psychokinetic and extrasensory powers. Subsequently, during a time of financial crisis, he made himself available for paid demonstrations. By his own admission, he was persuaded by the manager with whom he had signed a contract to include some mentalist trickery in the sup-posedly extrasensory part of the act. Geller claims that he quickly realized the error of his ways and from then on relied solely on his own paranormal powers (104). On the other hand, H.C. Berendt, chairman of the Israel Parapsychology Society and openly hostile to Geller, claims that he has heard from former members of Geller's staff that trickery was a regular part of his performance (17). Berendt states that he invited Geller several times to take part in experiments with the Israel Parapsychology Society, without success. Geller has since claimed, so Berendt alleges, that he has never heard of the IPS.

His early history of admitted magicianship has haunted all Geller's more recent attempts to be accepted by science, and controversy still rages over him. Ignoring his extrasensory claims, which smack of mentalism, can he really bend keys and metal bars, stop and start watches, affect complex measuring equipment, and cause balances to move? Is it possible for a person to be a fraud and yet to deceive as many scientists as have seen Geller's performances, and never be caught?

The mercurial young man is so busy following the lucrative lecture and TV circuit that, as with Kulagina though for different reasons, there are far more accounts of informal demonstrations of his skill than of properly controlled experiments that might take days out of his schedule. However, Geller has been the subject of a considerable amount of literature, and though some is sensational in the extreme, some is sufficiently careful to bear close study.

One criticism that may be made of much of the work with Geller is that it has been done by physicists new to the field of parapsychology. From one point of view, this interest by well-qualified scientists not previously "contaminated" by the subject (as some critics feel long-established parapsychologists are) should be welcomed, as should the work of every new, serious, and properly qualified researcher. However, although newcomers to the field always consider themselves to be more objective than those who have been in it for years, those same newcomers are often not familiar with the history of parapsychology. In many ways, in spite of their vaunted objectivity, they are naive. They have little knowledge of the tricks of the physical mediums and magicians, the disillusions that lead to caution, the blind alleys up which researchers have gone before, even the apparent futility of trying to "prove" psi to the determined skeptic. Thus much of their fresh influx of energy and enthusiasm has to be wasted going over the same old ground yet again. Newcomers also tend to invent their own terminology. Sometimes the fresh viewpoint is helpful, but at times it leads to confusion and irritates those who are used to established terms with the same meaning.

On the other hand, Geller has attracted the interest of many physicists of good repute who have access to professional publications that would not dream of publishing work by "mere" parapsychologists—even when they are highly qualified psychologists. Their work has thus been reported to many more scientists, who may perhaps regard parapsychology somewhat more open-mindedly now that they know their colleagues have found the field a valid one for research. Others, of course, will simply write off these scientists as former colleagues who have become temporarily insane, and forget the whole thing.

Another problem that concerns some researchers about Geller is that he has received so much publicity that, to some segments of the public, he has come to be identified with parapsychology as a whole. If, therefore, he should eventually prove to be a fake, the credibility of parapsychologists in general will be severely damaged, since the quieter and less sensational research that does not involve Geller tends to be forgotten by the news media and much of the public.

Probably the most publicized work with Geller has been done at the Stanford Research Institute in California. Much of the work involved ESP and was reported in *Nature* (216). The experimenters, Harold Puthoff and Russell Targ, did not consider the controls on their PK experiments to be absolutely foolproof, but found the results interesting enough to be worth presenting in a film to the 1973 Parapsychological Association convention in Charlottesville, Virginia.

In one experiment, a precision balance that transmits the weight it is measuring onto a chart was placed under a bell jar with a weight of one gram on it. While Geller attempted to affect the balance, it moved, sometimes as though weight had been placed on it and sometimes as though weight had been removed. At the same time the chart recorder showed changes of between one and one and a half grams. "These displacements were ten to a hundred times larger than could be produced by striking the bell jar or the table or jumping on the floor" (215).

(There is an old story of a magician effecting just such changes on a balance by inserting a flea into the bell jar just before the balance was covered. He knew that sooner or later the flea would hop onto the balance, and then hop off it again. How much does a flea weigh? One hopes that the balance was properly covered with the jar before Geller was allowed access to it.)

Geller also seemed to affect a magnetometer, which measures magnetic fields (and could not be affected by fleas). Of this Puthoff and Targ report: "He did not touch the measuring head of the instrument, and the deflections of the meter were not in general correlated with his hand motions."

Since Geller is considered to have some skill as a magician, it would seem that the best-qualified person to test him would be a parapsychologist who is also a magician. Such a man is Ed Cox, whom we have met in earlier chapters. Cox met with Geller in the latter's living room to try some informal tests in 1974 (63). First Cox gave Geller a plain safety-deposit box key "much too hard to bend by hand." After some hesitation Geller agreed to work with it, and laid it on a glass coffee table, where both men took note of its straightness. With Cox's forefinger on one end of the key, Geller lightly stroked the remainder. It is logical, since he was stroking it from above, that any pressure he would apply would bend the key downward, but it started to bend *up*. Even after it started to bend, so that downward pressure on one end would be expected to cause upward pressure at the other end, Cox could not feel the key rock, so Geller's stroking must have been light indeed.

After a similar performance with a second key, Cox produced his *pièce de résistance*, a pocket watch which, he told Geller, had had its regulator altered so that it was not running. In actual fact, a piece of candy wrapper (foil and wax) had been carefully inserted into the works so that it stopped the watch and would not easily move. After holding the watch for a few moments and shaking it "slightly but not unduly," Geller announced, "It's ticking." Cox opened the two lids, one of which "is extremely difficult to open" and found that the watch was going; the regulator had moved its full length of adjustment (40°); the foil was torn in two; and part of the foil had moved about half an inch. Although he conceded that Geller's preference for handling objects on which he works makes proper control extremely difficult, Cox concluded: "I have failed to conceive of any means of deception in these tests, nor have other magicians whom I have consulted."

In England, John Taylor, professor of mathematics at King's College, University of London, had Geller hold and attempt to influence a Geiger counter. At first nothing happened, indicating that Geller did not have radioactive material hidden on his person. Then "the sound suddenly rose to become a wail, one which usually indicates dangerous radioactive material nearby" (308). The same thing happened several times, once with the count going up to five hundred times the normal rate of background radiation. Later tests showed that such an effect could not be achieved by pressure on the counter, so manipulation by Geller seems unlikely. However, it is possible that an electrical source could have stimulated the sound.

Once Taylor asked Geller to bend a plastic strip that was inside a wire mesh tube. He could not bend it, but as he attempted to, the strip became discolored *just as that type of plastic would have if it had been bent.*

Geller's alleged bending of cutlery is world-renowned. Typically he strokes a spoon or fork gently. After a while the shaft seems to soften until it is almost the consistency of chewing gum, and in extreme cases the two ends can be pulled apart (52, 116, 308). This process seems to have been shown quite clearly in photographs (325). At other times, the metal simply bends and often continues to bend after it has been examined and put aside and Geller has started to work on something else. Fact? Fiction? Who knows?

Nitinol is an alloy developed at the Naval Ordnance Laboratory (now the Naval Surface Weapons Center) where scientist Eldon Byrd works. Nitinol's major peculiarity is that it has a "memory" for the shape in which it was originally made. No matter how it is bent, it will spring back to that shape when heated.

Byrd had Geller handle a straight piece of nitinol wire while Byrd held both ends under tension. The wire had already been checked to ensure that, if bent, it would become straight again when placed in boiling water. In Geller's hands the wire quickly formed a kink, and Byrd sent for boiling water. Upon immersion the wire, instead of straightening, formed an angle. After Geller had left, Byrd had it X-rayed and analyzed; all was normal except for the bend. Chemicals and tools were later used to try to reproduce "Geller's kink" in nitinol wire, but without success, says Byrd. Later, Geller bent five other pieces of nitinol wire under unspecified conditions. Byrd concluded that the bends had to be paranormal (39).

Many people believed that this was the finest and most convincing work that had been done with Geller. However, others perceived it differently. *The Humanist*, a frankly antiparanormal publication, devoted an issue to the "debunking" of psi and included in it an article by Martin Gardner (99). Gardner made a very strong case for the possibility that Geller and one of his constant companions could in fact have substituted previously manipulated wire during the nitinol work. He pointed out many weaknesses in the experimental method and its reporting and explained how he himself had managed to produce some of the reported effects quite simply and normally. A strong case for the *possibility* of something is not proof that it actually happened, but if it *could* have happened then the scientist must accept the possibility that it *might* have happened. Gardner's case in itself includes a certain amount of unscientific conjecture, but nonetheless, it is strong enough to preclude total acceptance of Byrd's work as proof that Geller has paranormal abilities.

This is one of those unfortunate cases where a well-qualified scientist was not necessarily experienced enough in parapsychology to use his experimental opportunity to the best advantage.

In another, somewhat similar, case, the late Dr. Wilbur Franklin, then chairman of the Department of Physics at Kent State University, Ohio, reported that a platinum ring affected by Geller had two fractures, barely one hundredth of an inch apart, that appeared to have been caused by extremely different conditions. The surface of one resembled what might occur had the ring been heated almost to the melting point (1,773°C. for platinum), and the other seemed more typical of cleavage at an extremely *low* temperature (95). After further and more thorough examination, Franklin concluded that the fracture had "occurred at an incomplete braze at the point where the jeweler attached the shank of ring to the portion holding the gem-stone" (96).

Explaining that his earlier examination and statement had been made under conditions of "limited funding and short-term access to a SEM" (scanning electron microscope), Franklin added that he had found evidence of metal fatigue around the brazed area, and that it could have been fractured by bending. However, he went on to point out:

> . . . the new interpretation of the platinum ring fracture does not answer the question of whether the actual fracture involved trickery or a paraphysical influence function. In fact, there are still perplexities in comparing the microscopy of the four samples with the modalities of fracture amenable to chicanery.

In other words, he apparently did not feel that the fracture in the ring, and those in two spoons and a needle that he also examined, were identical with fractures that had been produced by "normal" bending or trickery.

Most analyses by scanning electron microscope of metal bent by Geller have indicated "fatigue," which can be brought about by repeatedly bending an item back and forth. This, of course, is an indication of possible fraud, but Geller has never been observed even to attempt such manipulation. Other researchers are pursuing the analysis of metals that appear to have been bent paranormally, but unfortunately the equipment is expensive and is frequently required for matters that most universities regard as more weighty than parapsychology.

Another claim made for Geller is that he has caused objects to dematerialize. Most of these events have been reported anecdotally, since they occurred under totally uncontrolled conditions. As an example, an Ila Zeibell claims that she placed a coin in a matchbox—both her own property—and held the box in her closed left hand. Geller did not at any time touch the coin, the matchbox, or Zeibell, yet she felt "a light tingling sensation—like ants crawling on my hand . . . and when I looked in the box the coin was gone" (342).

However, at Birkbeck College in London an apparent dematerialization did occur under fairly good (though far from perfect) laboratory conditions. Two vanadium carbide crystals in plastic pharmaceutical capsules were among several objects on a metal plate. J. B. Hasted, professor of experimental physics and head of the Physics Department at Birkbeck, held his open hand over the objects. Geller placed his hand on Hasted's for a moment, then clasped his hands above it. One of the capsules moved "rather like a jumping bean"; it was examined, and part of the crystal was seen to be missing. Later examination showed that the remaining crystal was the same one that had been placed in the capsule originally; there had been no substitution (115, 116).

Just as Ila Zeibell had noticed a tingling sensation before the coin apparently disappeared, so Hasted reported feeling warmth in his knuckles when Geller's hand was above them. He touched Geller's hand with his own other hand and found it cool (perhaps a moment for Geller's other hand to do something sneaky while Hasted's attention was away from the crystal?). Later Hasted could not decide whether the warm sensation was physical or psychological. His knuckles were somewhat uncomfortable for a couple of hours after the experience.

The verdict on Geller is still not in. On the one hand, a number of eminent scientists claim that Geller has been subjected to tests under *their* control, not his, and has performed feats for which they can find no explanation. On the other are those who maintain flatly that they know Geller has simply developed his skill at sleight of hand, substitution, and misdirection to a high art, that they can do anything he can do, and that the scientist believers allow him to dictate the conditions under which each test is run (220). Unfortunately, they also say that since their own professional secrets must be preserved, they cannot actually tell *how* Geller does what he does, so we are asked to take their word that they know—not a particularly scientific means of verification.

The scientists who believe in Geller (and there are many who do not) reply that "no one in the world could be *that* clever" (11), and that misdirection and sleight of hand are not possible when an object never leaves the hand of the experimenter involved and the procedure is witnessed by several others who are looking for trickery. On the other hand, Gardner has illustrated that people often put things down or let someone else hold them momentarily, without even thinking about it, and later maintain that they never let go of them. The continued bending of some objects after the experiment is also hard to explain, although after the experiment the witnesses' attention is usually elsewhere, and substitution might be simpler.

If Geller stood alone, we could legitimately dismiss him. If stage magician Doug Hennings can make an elephant appear to disappear before the TV cameras, then who knows what wonders magicians can perform? Geller does not stand alone. Not only is he preceded by Kulagina and the physical mediums, but he is followed by an ever-increasing horde of "mini-Gellers," people who, after seeing him perform in person or on TV, claim that they, too, can bend cutlery, keys, and paperclips without having physical contact with them.

This situation came to light during one of Geller's tours of Europe. On several TV programs, he assured his audiences that if they would place stopped watches, cutlery, or pieces of metal on or in front of the TV, extraordinary things would happen. TV studios were flooded with calls from people who claimed that objects had been affected. Most of the callers believed that Geller himself was responsible. It has even been alleged by some women that their pregnancies are due to their metal intrauterine devices having been bent out of shape during such a TV performance (308). However, researchers think it more likely that the individuals themselves were responsible—many, presumably, by normal means, but some by paranormal effects. A number of them were contacted for more information (212) and some have been willing to work in the laboratory under test conditions (88, 117, 308).

Many of these mini-Gellers were children, and some were scarcely old enough to have developed full eye/hand coordination, let alone the sleight-of-hand skills needed to fool an assortment of investigators (though this cannot be ruled out in all cases). Several could bend straightened paper clips into a tangled heap even when the clips were in a container with a hole scarcely big enough to poke one finger through. (It should be added that this feat can be achieved by normal means, given the time and patience.) Others have bent metal and plastic strips under laboratory conditions. (A weakness of most of the reports on mini-Gellers is that details on controls are not as complete as most other researchers would like.) Like Geller, a sixteen-year-old girl affected a Geiger counter so that it showed readings of up to a thousand times the normal background level, yet no malfunction in the counter could be detected.

How the "Gellerization" of previously nonpsychokinetic people occurs, if it occurs, is not entirely clear. It is possible that we have a credulity barrier preventing acceptance of the possibility of PK, and therefore blocking its effectiveness. After watching Geller perform and deciding that PK is possible, some people may be able to "unblock," particularly if, at the beginning, they believe it is Geller himself who is doing the bending (see Chapter 13).

Another case that may involve a lowering of the credulity barrier is that of Felicia Parise, a research technician at Maimonides Medical Center (126, 141, 195, 332). After taking part in some experimental ESP work at the Maimonides Dream Laboratory, Parise was among those invited to see a film of Kulagina moving objects. Inspired, she went home and started trying to do the same thing. Her persistence deserves mention; she practiced for four months, usually several hours a day. A last, just after hearing that a loved one had died (which may be significant), she succeeded in making a bottle move. Later, when more confident, she had a photographer make a movie of her moving corks and a glass vial and causing a compass needle to rotate.

Parapsychologist Charles Honorton was invited to witness her PK abilities and later persuaded her to work in a laboratory, though here she was more nervous and less successful. She also succeeded, after a very lengthy session, in moving a compass needle in the laboratory of Graham and Anita Watkins (see Chapter 6).

Unfortunately, Parise decided not to continue with her PK work. She found that it took a tremendous physical toll, leaving her barely fit for her usual work. In addition, she was deeply hurt by the constant criticism and questioning by skeptics who accused her of fraud and was distressed by knowing that in continuing she would be responsible for the success or failure of often extremely expensive experiments.

Other "applied psychokinetic specialists" of note include Matthew Manning, Ingo Swann, and Jean-Pierre Girard. A great loss to parapsychology was the death in 1975 of Pat Price, a former chief of police of Burbank, California, who is reported to have exhibited great talent at both ESP and PK.

Manning is a young Englishman who first brought chaos to his English boarding school because of the poltergeist-type phenomena (see Chapter 9) that surrounded him. For a while he showed great promise with macro-PK, bending forks and turning compass needles. Some later, more closely controlled experiments in Amsterdam were disappointing, with microdynamic and macro-PK test scores being no better than would be expected by chance (23). One possibly interesting effect was discovered after analysis of the various physiological measures taken during the series. A relationship seemed to exist between the variance of each run from chance and Manning's delta and alpha electroencephalogram waves (74), but this may not be as meaningful as it appears. Since he was receiving instantaneous feedback, this apparent correlation could actually have been due to his feelings as he discovered hów well, or otherwise, he was doing, rather than to his actual production of PK. However, more recently in the United States he has seemed to maintain a scoring rate that, though perhaps not spectacular, can usually be relied upon to be somewhat above chance. Perhaps he will prove to be an atypical poltergeist agent, one who is able to maintain and direct his abilities past the onset of maturity.

Ingo Swann has worked with parapsychologists from coast to coast. Working with Dr. Gertrude Schmeidler of the City College of New York, he was apparently successful in changing the temperature of thermistors on command (264). However, some questions about the methodology in this work have been raised (165), and other ways of using his talents are being sought. He has also worked with researchers at Stanford Research Institute. There, in one of the earliest SRI excursions into parapsychology, he seemed to affect a very well-shielded magnetometer several times, both when asked to and later when he was thinking about the apparatus and trying to describe what he had done to affect it. He feels that he gets a clear picture of the inside of the equipment, even when he is not near it, and decides which piece to "mess with" in order to bring about the effect he is seeking (217). Since he has an excellent record in testing for clairvoyance, his clear picture may well be accurate.

Another new and promising PK specialist is Jean-Pierre Girard, who has been observed apparently moving objects over a grid-marked surface while under close supervision by several scientists, though not under laboratory conditions (72). In a laboratory, he has bent aluminum bars when strain gauges, which should have recorded any tampering, were attached to the bars (76, 158). Since he seems more amenable to scientific testing than most people with macro-PK abilities, perhaps more can be discovered about his gift—whether it is the gift of PK or the gift of prestidigitation.

As we have seen, most macro-PK is open to charges of manipulation, sleight of hand, and other forms of fraud. While much of the work that has been done gives strong indications that macro-PK exists, the perfect experiment, totally controlled and without alternative explanation, possibility of fraud, or equipment malfunction (PK subjects seem to cause a lot of that) has not yet been reported. Until it is (and perhaps even after it is) the skeptics will remain skeptics and the scientists will continue to wonder. Even if such an experiment should ever be run the question of *what* is happening, and how the superstars do what they do, will call for many more years of investigation.

Chapter 6

What (If Anything) Do We Know About PK?

The student of psi soon realizes that he is like someone attempting to complete a jigsaw puzzle. He has many pieces available to him and knows that they must fit together somehow. His only problems are that there is no picture on the front of the box to guide him, and he has no idea whether all the pieces are present, how many may be missing, or even whether some of those he has may belong to another puzzle. In addition, it is not entirely clear whether the finished picture is to be two- or three-dimensional. All he can do is concentrate on the pieces he can see, keep looking for more, and hope that those available will, in the way they fit together, give some hint of the nature of the missing pieces, and therefore of the whole that he is seeking.

Having covered the ways in which PK may be shown to exist (we think), perhaps now is a good place to summarize what, if anything, has been discovered about it in terms of finding the optimal situations in which PK is likely to occur. Does it work only on the third Sunday after a full moon? Would a left-handed red-haired Irishman be better at PK than a right-handed blonde Norwegian teenager? Are such questions even answerable?

Many of the questions that one might think are obvious actually cannot yet be answered with certainty as far as PK is concerned. As indicated earlier, PK has only recently returned to fashion. For many years, the study of psi has been the study of ESP, and our knowledge of factors affecting ESP has been expanded to a far greater extent than has our knowledge of factors affecting PK.

Some parapsychologists feel that, if the two are indeed like the two sides of a coin, the same rules should apply to both ESP and PK. If this is so, then all the work that has been done on ESP can be said to apply to PK, too. However, as Gardner Murphy has pointed out:

> There is practically nothing in the literature which compares the working conditions for, say, psychokinesis and the working conditions for telepathy. We don't even know whether a person good at one type of paranormal task is good at other types of paranormal tasks,* for we have not taken seriously the notion that the interdependence of many realities is what is required. (178)

Although Murphy made this statement in 1969, little has been done since then to change the situation, and so, to be suitably conservative, a survey such as this must ignore most of the discoveries relating to ESP, even when reports concerning them are carelessly titled so that they seem to refer to psi in general rather than just to ESP (a problem that has sent the writer running up many a blind alley while doing research for this book). Most of the findings discussed here are therefore confined to work specifically related to PK.

A factor that relates, perhaps, to the personality of parapsychologists in general may add to the problems of deciding what has and has not been discovered about PK. In science, a discovery is not a discovery when it is first made. It is simply an unreplicated finding and must remain so until someone else decides to repeat the experiment. Only if he, too, gets the same results under the same conditions and reaches the same conclusions can we begin to take the conclusions as anything more than an interesting hint. (This is the theory, at least. In actual fact even in conventional psychology a great many hypotheses have been taken as confirmed on the basis of only one researcher's work.) The personality problem lies in the fact that the pressures against parapsychology in our society ensure that few conformists enter the field. Parapsychologists are as individualistic a group as can be found anywhere, and individualists do not like to follow in the footsteps of others. In the past they have, therefore, tended to be reluctant to replicate experiments that have already been designed and run by other people. Each prefers to do

---

* We do now know, however, that a few superstars *seem* to produce striking scores in both ESP and PK tests.

his own thing. As more people enter the field this tendency is becoming less of a problem, but some of the work that follows must be considered somewhat suspect in that it has not been replicated. Still, such work certainly should not be ignored, for it may well be pointing us in the right direction, wherever that may be.

The importance of replication, and perhaps of several replications, is clear if we simply bear in mind the preferential effect and the experimenter effect. Suppose an experimenter investigates the effect of weather on PK. Do storms affect results? A single experiment may indicate that storms have an adverse effect, and the experimenter may conclude that the humidity or the electricity in the air has something to do with how PK works. But wait; maybe the poor results are due to the psychological effect on a subject or an experimenter who simply does not like storms. (Incidentally, both Kulagina and Vinogradova believe that clear weather is better for their PK work. Vinogradova can work in thunderstorms if she absolutely has to; Kulagina says she cannot (317).

An Australian experimenter has indicated that the feelings of these superstars about clear weather may be right, for, in working with a random number generator, E. Andre's subjects seemed to obtain slightly higher scores when humidity was low (1). Again, however, we cannot tell whether this effect is physical or psychological.

For many years, a popular assumption has been that distance has little or no effect on psi, a belief somewhat supported by long-distance ESP tests. However, for PK no clear answer has yet been obtained. One dice test found slightly higher scores for runs when the subjects and experimenter were standing thirty feet from the target dice than when they were three feet from them. On the other hand, Kulagina and Vinogradova have clear limits on the distance at which they can work, Kulagina's being two meters and Vinogradova's two feet (317).

Quite early in the Duke dice work, in May 1936, the effects of drugs such as alcohol and caffeine on PK were questioned. For the alcohol test, three people, J. B. Rhine among them, threw eighty runs each, aiming for the six face. The lowest scorer on these runs became the experimenter, who had to stay sober so that proper records could be kept. The other two then drank 100 cc. gin, waited twenty minutes, and threw one hundred runs each. The result was a significant drop in the rate of scoring, but this was entirely due to one subject, Rhine. The other subject was "unable to retain the alcohol long enough for much of it to be absorbed" (5). Ah, the rigors of scientific endeavor!

Not long afterward, a similar test for caffeine was run. In this case it was decided that the highest predrug scorer would become the experimenter, and Rhine was the lowest scorer, though he had scored highest in the predrug tests for the alcohol experiment. Each subject drank a bottle of Coke, waited twenty minutes, and then threw the dice—again for the six-face. A second, similar session was run several days later, with Rhine and another person as subjects. The after-Coke scores were significantly better than the pre-Coke scores, largely because less decline effect was observed than in the pre-test, where all significant scoring occurred in the first half of the score sheet (240).

Both these tests were firmly labeled "exploratory" when they were originally reported; yet the results have since been mentioned by other writers as "findings." In actual fact, as the experimenters were well aware, there are many reasons why this type of test cannot be taken at face value, particularly without replication. It is obvious, for one thing, that the participants had preconceived expectations as to the effects of the drugs, for in selecting the subjects they looked for the greatest contrast with what was expected to happen. In other words, they expected lower scores after alcohol, so picked as subjects the two people with the highest scores. For the caffeine, which they apparently expected to raise the scores, they chose as subjects the two with the lowest scores. Not only does this indicate that the subjects expected to score in a certain direction, which may have caused them to do so, but it also means that one would expect a difference in scoring subsequent to the tests. If you have just scored fairly high, the law of averages suggests that your next test will show lower scores, and vice versa.

An interesting aspect of these two tests is the pretest scores of Rhine himself. In the prealcohol test, in which the highest scorers would be active subjects instead of having the less interesting job of observing and keeping records, Rhine's mean run score over eighty runs was 4.79, giving a P of about .0004. In the caffeine test, it was the lower scorers who would participate,and Rhine's mean run score over twenty runs in the first test was 3.30, and over eighty runs in the second test was 3.99. No doubt he consciously tried to score well both times, but it looks as if he really hoped to be a subject in each case and subconsciously decided to get the kind of scores that would enable him to be a participant.

Drug tests such as these actually are almost impossible to carry out under ideal conditions because the subject is never blind. Even if the drug taste is masked in some way, and some subjects are given the drug and some a placebo that has no effect, most subjects would know whether or not they had taken an active drug. The physical sensations twenty minutes after taking alcohol, if enough is given to produce a sure effect, would probably be a giveaway, and so, for many people, would the effect of caffeine.

Some later tests using caffeine and meprobamate (a tranquilizer) showed no clear scoring effects related to the drugs (30). Only one subject, who was also the experimenter, was involved, and obviously, therefore, he was not blind as to what drug he had taken. In addition, the accuracy of an experimenter who keeps his own records while under the influence of tranquilizers is open to question.

As Charles Tart has pointed out (305), the great difficulty in learning to do something is that we must have feedback as to when we are doing it right and when we are doing it wrong. Then we can immediately observe our memory of *how* we felt and *what* we did that might have contributed to the success or failure of the trial. Next time we can try to replicate that feeling, if it led to success, and see whether success follows again.

On the face of it, feedback under PK conditions is relatively simple and automatic. You release the dice and can immediately see how many of them landed with the target face uppermost. Or you watch the little lights on the machine, or listen to the tone, and know whether the random generator is producing the results that you are trying to bring about. The difficulty lies in the fact that a chance factor is always involved. The probability is one in six that the target face will be uppermost by chance, without the interference of your PK. When you are using a random generator the chance factor may be one in almost anything, but one in two, one in four, and one in five are the most common. The popular binary random generator, the electronic coin-flipper, provides a chance factor of one in two. In other words, in every hundred trials, about fifty will be hits by chance, and it is only if you obtain more than fifty percent hits that you will perhaps be giving evidence of PK.

Consequently, you will obtain many hits that have nothing to do with your PK, and yet you will have no way of knowing *which* are due to chance and which, if any, to PK. It will be extremely hard to single out any particular sensation or state of mind to identify with success, since you don't know when you are being successful. To counter this problem, these machines can at times generate targets at such speeds that your aim is not so much to influence an individual trial (which is over before you have even thought about it) as to affect a light or a sound that will remain on only as long as you are generating more than fifty percent hits. In this case it would not be the individual trial but the overall effect that gave you the feedback.

Whether or not PK can be learned is still a matter of dispute. Obviously, someone whose scores are barely above chance will get so little opportunity for feedback from his hits that he is unlikely to learn. Working with ESP, Tart has shown that `individuals who score well to start with, and therefore get more valid feedback, do improve their scores somewhat, or are at least able to overcome the decline effect. Tart suggests that the decline effect is caused by the lack of immediate feedback in ESP tests, but this would not explain the similar declines found in dice PK, where the feedback is available, unless they are caused by the incorrect feedback on chance hits mentioned above. However, it was noted long ago that the decline effect agrees with decline curves in learning and memory (229), so Tart may well be right. The large number of dice used per throw in much dice work may have led to feedback confusion and made the subjects unable to identify their "PK sensations" from their non-PK feelings.

Even the necessity for feedback is unproven, despite Tart's work. One survey of various microdynamic experiments at the Mind Science Foundation and the University of Houston (26) has shown that even those in which subjects and experimenters received feedback in the most general terms, and often on a very delayed basis, showed evidence for PK having occurred.

In 1972, Bert Camstra reported on an attempt, mentioned in Chapter 3, to condition PK (conditioning is, in psychological terms, a form of learning) by rewarding the subject every time a random number generator generated the number 99. This should have occurred by chance only once in every 99 numbers. Both the pilot and the main test showed an increase in the number of 99s generated, an apparent learning process, though a confirmation test did not show the same increase (40). Whether this last result was due to various modifications made in the test procedure or to the fact that the earlier results were a fluke is, again, open to question.

On a more anecdotal level, it seems that some superstars have developed their ability in a process that could perhaps be called learning. Russian parapsychologist Viktor Adamenko used hypnosis and yoga to train Vinogradova (144), and Parise practiced moving a compass needle for hours at a time before she progressed to larger objects. However, though many parapsychologists agree that certain mental blocks prevent us from using psi, and that training programs may help remove such blocks and allow whatever psi is possessed to operate, a distinction must be made between this and *learning* psi. Learning implies that some ability that does not exist to start with, or that exists to a very limited degree, can be brought into being and expanded. Removing blocks simply allows an already existing ability to manifest itself. Since most human abilities can be developed, it certainly seems logical that one can learn to use psi, but the concept has not yet been proven (despite the advertised claims of various commercial organizations) and we must wait, as with everything else, for more research to be done.

Much of what is known for sure (almost!) we have seen in earlier chapters. PK scores, like ESP scores, usually show a chronological decline that is the bane of every researcher. No consistent correlation between scoring rates and the number, weight, or size of dice has been found (229). Although Forwald seemed to find a connection between the atomic weight of the substance covering the dice and the distance the dice moved, this has not been confirmed by other researchers, and his results may have been a reflection of his own expectations.

Researchers have found some evidence that deliberate distraction of the subject results in psi-missing (132), but the reason may be that the subject, who is trying to concentrate on his PK task, becomes irritated at the distraction and so goes into a "psi-missing mood."

Similarly, two obvious explanations can be offered for the early help/hinder experiments indicating that if a second person is mentally trying to help the subject score well, scores will be higher than when the second person is trying to hinder the scoring process (132). The first is that the second person actually affected the dice, so that a stronger PK effect showed when he was helping, and that his PK "canceled out" that of the subject in the hinder sections, when the scores were very little above chance. The other possibility is that the subject detected by ESP which condition was in effect and scored accordingly. A third explanation will be examined in Chapter 13.

One strange finding that was mentioned in Chapter 4 and will turn up again in the chapters on healing and on poltergeists is the linger effect. A dramatic example was described at the 1973 PA Convention in Charlottesville, Virginia. Graham and Anita Watkins of Durham, North Carolina, told of their work with Felicia Parise, during the course of which Parise attempted to move the needle of a compass. The needle "moved westward approximately fifteen degrees over a period of about two minutes, with a slow, smooth motion, and remained there." A few minutes later the experiment was discontinued and Parise walked away from the compass, but the compass needle remained deflected and was "totally unresponsive" to a knife blade and a bar magnet that were brought near it.

Thinking that the needle was jammed, the experimenters moved the compass about four feet, and the needle slowly returned to its proper position and became responsive to the knife blade. It "was then returned to the original spot on the chair, and again the needle moved fifteen degrees off north and was incapable of being influenced by the metal blade." This was repeated several times. It took nearly half an hour for the needle to return to north, when it again became responsive to the metal of the knife blade (332). In other words, the linger effect operated only in the area on which Parise had been concentrating. It is also interesting to notice that during this experiment the compass was within the field of a metal detector, and when the needle moved, the sound made by the detector changed greatly. Its new sound could be replicated only by placing a two-pound roll of solder in the field (hardly something Parise could have secreted on her person without its being noticed by the watchful experimenters).

We have already discussed the preferential effect on PK scoring, and from here it is but a short step to realizing that the subject's state of mind is crucial to successful PK.

A report by Robert Thouless in 1951 gives some tentative findings (not, Thouless was careful to emphasize, "conclusions that I regard as established"), which still seem to hold good today, even though Thouless was his own subject in this work, a weakness that has already been discussed. A feeling of playfulness seems to improve scores, whereas "too strong motivation tends to result in effort, and failure results." Effort and anxiety are hindrances. Thouless found that his morning results showed a "startling superiority" over those of late afternoon, even when he did morning and afternoon tests on different days so that the afternoon sessions could not be affected by a decline from the morning. Evening scores were also better than those from afternoons. This tendency has not, as far as I have been able to discover, been followed up with attempts at replication. It should be simple for any research organization that conducts tests on a regular basis to divide test scores according to time blocks and compare them. Were Thouless's results to be replicated, they might suggest a study (unfortunately expensive) of the possible effects on psi scores of the rise and fall of various hormones in the diurnal cycle. The scheduling of tests might also be reconsidered.

Thouless included in his report a series of "thou shalt nots" for the would-be experimenter:

> One must avoid increasing the emotional tension of the subject by showing gratification at his success and disappointment at his failure. One must not introduce an atmosphere of tension by maintaining silence during sessions. If witnesses are present they must not be allowed to create tension by maintaining a suspicious attitude or by such behavior as whispering. The subject should be not required to

do large numbers of experiments at a time or to do a sufficient total number of sessions to make him exasperated by the experiment. A single experiment should not be repeated without variation through the experimental series. The satisfactoriness of an experimental design should be judged, at least in part, by the extent to which it avoids all of these unfavorable conditions. (311)

One gifted subject, Jan Merta, who has worked with the Toronto Society for Psychical Research, seemed to confirm Thouless's feelings about effort and attitude, as have many other subjects. A. R. G. Owen reported that Merta "had to be relaxed, yet he had to 'intend' the motion of his P.K. object, but he could not allow himself vehemently to 'will' the outcome" (187).

Lawrence LeShan has said that a successful subject needs "a feeling of being at home in the world, with a sense of adventure" (149), which seems to agree with the concepts of relaxation and playfulness suggested above.

Like Thouless, Robert L. Morris feels that a moderate arousal produces the best psi performance, and that excessive arousal or anxiety-provoking situations produce scores of chance or below (173).

Some work has focused on discovering what mental technique, if any, is most successful in PK. Does it help to "will" the object to move as you wish (albeit not too strongly, according to previous paragraphs)? What if you visualize it clearly? Or should you just decide what you want it to do and then "let go," content that your subconscious mind or whatever will do the rest?

Rex Stanford sought to compare visualization (in which the subjects tried to picture the die in their minds as it fell, and mentally to "see" it landing with the target face upwards) with "associative activation of the unconscious." In the latter method the subjects were told the target face, and then, for two minutes, they were asked to free associate with that number, telling the experimenter every word or thought the number inspired. Then they were told to forget about the PK task, to distract themselves, read, think, walk—do anything except think about PK while the die was actually thrown.

Each of the twenty subjects alternated between the two methods, performing thirty-six trials each. The scores from each method showed little difference. However, a word association test was also given to indicate the subjects who tended to use imagery in thinking. Analysis showed a tendency for these subjects to do better under the visualization condition than in the free association condition (282). In other words, "imagers" have more PK success when visualizing, but other techniques may work better for nonimagers.

Another attempt to use visualization as a PK technique, this time contrasted with "conscious concentration," has been made by Bjorn J. Steilberg of Amsterdam (294). Again using dice, his ten subjects alternately met two conditions: the "conscious concentration" condition (in which they tensed their muscles and focused totally on following the fall of the dice and forcing them to stop with the target faces upward), and "visualization" (in which they didn't worry about the process of the dice moving, but simply visualized the desired end result). Steilberg used the same type of word association test as Stanford to discover which subjects tended to use imagery in day-to-day thinking, but his results showed no significant differences in this respect. Overall, the conscious concentration with muscle tension produced slightly significant psi-missing, with an insignificantly positive score for visualization and a marginally significant ($P = .05$) difference between the two conditions.

Steilberg also divided his subjects' scores according to whether they were male or female and whether the die faces they were throwing for were those they preferred or did not prefer, but he found no significant differences. His work was intended to replicate some earlier studies from the Dream Laboratory of Maimonides Medical Center, where Charles Honorton and Warren Barksdale had contrasted muscle relaxation with muscle tension during a test (129). However, the results were in the opposite direction. Using as targets two colored lightbulbs connected to a Schmidt random number generator, Honorton had used the muscle tension and muscle relaxation conditions, each subdivided into "willing" and "passive" to produce four conditions. The first test showed strong PK-hitting for the muscle tension condition with most of the hits occurring in the passive concentration part. A second series showed results in the same direction for tension versus relaxation, though not significantly so, but this time the active concentration runs showed higher scores than the passive (again, not significantly).

Honorton decided to do a third series with himself as subject and Barksdale as experimenter, using just muscle tension and relaxation without the active/passive mental conditions. The results show clearly how an apparently nonsignificant score may be immensely significant when separated out. Though his overall score showed a deviation from chance of only six, when the scores were divided the muscle tension runs showed a deviation of +59 ($P = .00005$), balanced by a muscle relaxation deviation of -53 ($P = .0005$), one of the most significant examples of PK-missing ever recorded. However, as Honorton and Barksdale point out, there is no way of knowing whether the results of this last series were due to the difference between muscle tension and relaxation, or to Honorton's desire to see his original hypothesis upheld. Indeed, such an extremely significant result raises the question of whether there might have been an experimenter effect brought about by Honorton in the first series or, as Honorton and Barksdale put it, whether "the first experiments may not have involved *seven* Ss rather than six—or perhaps just *one*" (130).

The interest in a possible connection between muscle tension and PK was prompted by observations made about Kulagina and Vinogradova, as well as Ted Serios (Chapter 10). They all seem to use tremendous physical tension while doing whatever it is that they do. Perhaps the most extreme is Kulagina, who

> . . . experiences great stress, with pulse increases to a rate of 150-240, increased respiration, and pain in her upper spine and the back of her neck. She shows weight losses of .7 to 2 kilograms [1.5 to 4.5 lbs.] within one hour after her PK attempts, and a raised blood sugar level. . . . During the activated state she experiences occasional vertigo and vomiting. (317)

Though Vinogradova experiences less stress, she does have an increased pulse rate during PK work and appears to undergo a certain amount of physical tension. Parise experiences difficulty in speaking for a while after doing PK (126). She perspires freely and trembles, and her eyes and nose run. Her heart rate increases, but the pulse becomes weaker (332). She has also reported a "gut feeling, almost like fright or shock" just before the object moves (195). Cox has noted that the degree of exhaustion after PK varies more with the individual subject than with the amount of physical effort that one would expect to be required for the specific task (65). In other words, he believes it is not *what* is being done that produces stress, but *who* is doing it.

It has been suggested that Kulagina *must* exhibit stress because, in the materialistic philosophy of the USSR, there has to be a physical explanation for psi, and so her psychological "set" is toward sending out energy. Parise, as we have seen, was inspired to attempt PK after seeing a movie of Kulagina. It is possible, therefore, that she suffers stress because Kulagina was her model. On one occasion she reportedly produced a psychokinetic effect without stress. "She waved her arm in the direction of the compass and jokingly said, 'Abracadabra!' The compass needle immediately deflected ninety degrees" (126). However, it was also reported that at the time she was in a hurry and did not want to work on PK but was being "prodded" by the experimenter. Obviously, therefore, a certain amount of mental stress was involved. Whether this had been converted to physical stress we do not know. We also do not know whether a person who expects to produce PK without stress would be able to do so.

Mental stress, mental states in general, alpha states, meditation, all have been considered important in improving ESP scores. Properly controlled experiments have shown that some claims are excessively optimistic, but progress is being made. What about PK?

A study by Francine Matas and Lee Pantas, then at the FRNM, gave indications that after meditating for fifteen minutes, regular meditators scored higher than nonmeditators, but they did not test the same meditators when they had not been meditating (155). We cannot tell, therefore, whether the significant difference in scores ($P = .003$) was due to the mental state induced by meditation, to some kind of difference in personality that both aids PK and attracts one toward meditation, or to the stronger motivation of those who spend time meditating regularly, and who are therefore anxious to prove its effectiveness. Nor can we forget, as usual, a possible experimenter effect.

William Braud and Janice Hartgrove (27) attempted to avoid the problem of possible personality variables by testing a group of meditators and a group of people who did not meditate but were attending a lecture for those interested in learning to meditate.

Since both groups were interested in meditation the experimenters reasoned that their personality factors should not be significantly different. They found no significant differences between the PK scores of the two groups—a result that could indicate that the type of personality, not the act of meditating itself, caused the differences in the Matas and Pantas work.

People seeking an "ideal" mental state for ESP have begun to notice a similarity between what is required for ESP and what is involved in the functions of the nondominant cerebral hemisphere.* To oversimplify, while the dominant hemisphere (the left in most right-handed people) seems to function in a logical, linear, mathematical way, the nondominant hemisphere is nonanalytical and much involved in imagery, spatial concepts, music, and other such pleasantness. As usual, the question posed, this time by Ken Andrew of the Mind Science Foundation in Houston, was, what about PK? Does the same thing hold good as for ESP?

Andrew had one group of subjects attempt to influence a random number generator while listening to and performing complex mental tasks demanded by a tape designed to evoke dominant hemisphere functions. The other group listened to a tape of music and other relaxing sounds designed to evoke nondominant functioning while performing their PK task. Near significant hitting ($P = .02$) was attained by the "nondominant" group and significant missing ($P = .01$) by the "dominant" or analytical group (2). Two more experiments by Andrew and his colleagues showed similar results except that the "dominant" group scored near chance rather than missing significantly (29). It was suggested that nondominant hemispheric activity (the fun stuff) "seems to facilitate PK performance," whereas activity by the dominant hemisphere "seems to interfere with good PK performance and yield either chance performance or PK missing."

However, Murphy's Law may well be in operation again. The results could be due to hemispheric activity, but they could equally

---

* The dominant hemisphere is commonly referred to as the left hemisphere, and the nondominant as the right. Since approximately 10 percent of the population is left-handed, and lefties may have either hemisphere dominant, this designation has a .05 chance of being incorrect, and is also somewhat irritating to some lefties. As a lefty myself, I acknowledge that the terms "dominant" and "nondominant" are not entirely accurate, but I prefer them over "left" and "right."

well be due to the fact that the type of situation in which the dominant activity group were placed is not enjoyable. Hemispheric activity apart, very few people *like* having to "count letters in words, [solve] math problems, [solve] reasoning and logic problems, and listen to linear prose," all of which they were asked to do. Such a situation is not generally enjoyable, and the subject is likely to be irritated at whichever experimenter got him into such a mess. He may, therefore, at a conscious or subconscious level, decide not to produce high scores as a way of "getting back" at that experimenter. In contrast, the nondominant activity was rather enjoyable and likely to produce just the kind of mood in which psi flourishes.

Another point to be remembered from earlier chapters is that psi-missing is as clear an indication of a form of psi as is psi-hitting, and in the case of Andrew's first experiment the missing was even more significant than the hitting. This would appear to indicate that psi can work, albeit negatively, when the dominant hemisphere is active—a result that is somewhat contradicted by the near-chance results of the "dominant" groups in the later two experiments.

Another way of searching for the right mood or thought pattern for PK has been to use EEG's (measures of brain wave activity) to discover whether certain types of wave are more conducive to PK than others. Though public superstition has it that alpha waves are the answer to all psi problems, no clear-cut answers have yet been found in the laboratory, for results vary from test to test and often seem to contradict each other. We have seen that muscular activity seems necessary to many people when trying to produce PK, and muscular activities muddy EEG readings to the point where they may become useless. Also, EEG activity seems to vary too much among individuals to allow firm conclusions so far. There are hints that alpha states may be involved, but whether they occur during or before the PK peak we cannot be sure. Once again, the verdict is not yet in.

Frustrated again in our search for clear-cut pointers toward reliable PK scoring, we may wonder whether perhaps there is a "PK personality." Is the PK person somehow strange, weird, perhaps not normal? No, reassures a 1950 *Journal of Parapsychology* editorial: "We have gone far enough to be reasonably certain that there is no close association of psi with any familiar kind of abnormality or subnormality" (164).

The article goes on to suggest that personality and psi may not even be directly related at all, but that personality "could be related to something secondary to the functioning of psi itself, to traits or states that inhibit or qualify" psi.

Certainly attempts to correlate psi and personality, and particularly PK and personality, have produced more tantalizing hints and anomolies than success.

In 1958 Robert Van de Castle, in the process of reporting some experiments of his own, made what is now a classic survey of experiments that attempted to relate PK and personality (318). He points out that some have indicated the possibility of a correlation between PK scores and "expansive" and "compressive" subjects. (Whether one is expansive or compressive is judged by one's use of space available in drawing. Basically, expansiveness "conveys an atmosphere of freedom, courage, adventure, and may be a symptom of vitality and of healthily developed extraversion. . . . Compression conveys a feeling of discomfort, of being shut in, of pressure and compulsion." The differences were not significant, but the tendency was found in several studies, including that made by Van de Castle himself. Steilberg's study of conscious concentration versus visualization also divided subjects into expansives and compressives and also produced no significant differences. Expansives, however, usually rate high in spontaneity, and studies of spontaneity and PK have been made. The famous Rorschach (inkblot) test can usually identify people high in spontaneity, and Van de Castle found that his most spontaneous subjects scored well above chance, with less spontaneous subjects PK-missing.

In a German study by John Mischo and R. Weis, subjects were asked to influence a random number generator while calm and again while presumably in a state of intense frustration (just after being asked to complete a task that was almost impossible). Two personality questionnaires were also given. While the subjects were calm no significant differences in their scores appeared, but in the frustrated state they showed a very different picture. Subjects who were rated high on calmness and sociability scored well; those who were high on depressivity, neuroticism, and inhibition scored low (168).

Since neuroticism, compressiveness, and inhibition (the opposite, in many ways, of spontaneity) go hand in hand, as do expansiveness and spontaneity, one gets the impression that, though these tests are not replications of each other, they do point in the same direction. PK-missing seems to be more common among those tending to neuroticism and PK-hitting among those who are fortunate enough to be able to approach life in a spirit of "high adventure." However, such personality variables, though fairly constant in themselves, cannot be said to be constant as predictors of constant PK performance. The most expansive subject may have his off days, his psi-missing moods, and even the most consistent psi-misser gets above-chance scores from time to time.

Stanford has also pointed out (282) that one personality may function well with one type of task or experimenter, while another, who may do badly under those same conditions, may do very well in a different test situation.

Obviously personality, while it may provide clues, is not the answer.

One thing that we do know is that the act of "doing" PK is essentially unconscious. For many years, the unconsciousness of psi was considered an annoying complication that could foul up laboratory tests, and emphasis was placed on bringing PK under conscious control. More recently researchers have turned their attention to making use of and experimenting with the unconscious aspects of psi. An example is Stanford's work with "associative activation of the unconscious," described earlier in this chapter. It will be remembered that under one condition the subjects were told to free associate on the target number for two minutes in order to get the unconscious "primed" toward that number, and then to distract themselves and forget about the test completely while the die was being thrown. In his discussion of this study Stanford commented that some subjects found it very hard to distract themselves, particularly when they had produced few associations to a number and so felt they had not done as well as they should have.

"Thus," he says, "their reported inability to get their minds off the die-face number on such trials might have interfered with their success."

This certainly seemed to be the case, for subjects scored far higher on die faces for which they had produced a larger number of associations.

Not long afterward, Stanford presented to the world of parapsychology his theory of psi-mediated instrumental response, hastily abbreviated to PMIR by all but a few hardy souls. (We will discuss PMIR in more detail in Chapter 13.) To summarize and oversimplify two very comprehensive papers (283, 284), Stanford suggests that psi is *so* unconscious that in everyday life we use it at times when we are quite unaware that we are doing so. This theory is backed by a number of very convincing experiments, some using ESP (291, 292) and some involving PK (40, 293), in which the subjects did not know what their task was, or *even that they were involved in a psi-related task at all,* and yet performed at rates well above chance when good performance would result in their being placed in a more pleasant situation than would chance scores. In one case, half the subjects knew the task involved PK and half did not. The second group performed far better than the first.

Finally, evidence is accumulating that PK is *goal-oriented.* In other words, PK is not involved in *how* something is done, only in the fact that it gets done. The scores of Schmidt's subjects seem to be unaffected by whether they are asked to affect a very simple PK machine or a very complicated one, though if PK were process-oriented the extra complication should have made the task more difficult (268). Cox disconnected the part of his ion machine in which he expected the PK to occur, and his scores continued just the same.

The usual fact that an increase in radiation is required to affect the noises of a Geiger counter seems irrelevant; if the PK subject is told to affect the Geiger counter, he can in some way do it directly without radiation. It is true that Ingo Swann likes to understand the machinery with which he is working, and feels that he "gets into it and messes with it." However, Swann seems to be the exception, and, in fact, this procedure may be his own personal supportive ritual rather than an integral part of the PK process.

As would be expected from the unconscious, which is not normally process-oriented, in PK "the goal's the thing" and the end, not the means, is important.

Chapter 7
Healing as PK

It is worth considering how far PK may be involved in the psychogenetic causation of organic effects. Among the case records a fair number of outstanding instances are reported in which something that looks like a PK effect occurs. . . . There are instances in which the patients are very young children to whom the suggestion theory is less applicable, and even some domestic animals which, it is reasonably certain, are not merely responding to suggestion in the ordinary sense of the term.

Back of these challenging problems of medicine is a whole array of unexplained cases of biological effects that seem to involve a psychokinetic principle.

J. B. Rhine (194)

If PK is goal-oriented, few goals can be more worthwhile that that of healing.

Outside the laboratory, the healing touch has been the subject of folklore for hundreds of years. Women have been burned alive because they seemed able to heal (or cause) the ills of their neighbors. Shamans and witch doctors were, and still are, the main source of healing in many cultures. When the Western "age of reason" turned its attention to alleged healing phenomena, accounts of successful cures by touch were dismissed out of hand as sheer nonsense. Perhaps, it was suggested, some primitive knowledge of herbal cures, anatomy, or the art of massage had helped a few patients respond under the ministration of rural "wise ones," but apart from that their claims were obviously false or due to sheer good luck.

Later, as we gained an understanding of psychology, we realized that perhaps some rituals and ceremonies might have an effect on psychosomatic ills, and it became easy to explain away so-called miraculous cures in this way. There could not, we were told, be any other way in which such untrained healers could bring relief.

Nevertheless, the desire for good health, for relief from major or minor ills, is so universal that books on healing are sure sellers—there is even available a book on healing that describes all the other books on healing (207). Every new "cure" or "healer" that comes along is sure to find adherents, and events advertised as public demonstrations of healing are assured of large audiences.

Such demonstrations vary in method. Some healers prefer to use direct contact, a "laying on of hands" method. Others feel that they can send healing to everyone in the room with them, even if several thousand people are present and none of them is touched by the healer. Still others believe that prayer and concentration from a distance work as well as direct contact, and they may never even see those who ask them for help by phone or mail.

Some talk of an energy flow and believe that they are directing a form of energy into the patient so that his body can use it to bring about a cure. Some feel that the source of such an energy is God and that they are simply channels. Others, less modest, maintain that they themselves accumulate and disseminate the energy. Those healers who are also spiritualists often claim that the spirits of long-dead doctors work through them to help the living. All can point to ex-patients who will bear witness to the fact that they were ill when they first came into contact with the healer and were cured just after contact with him.

The medical profession in general is skeptical. It is known that about 85 percent of all illnesses will get better regardless of whether or not they receive treatment. The body has an incredibly efficient system for self-healing and, given time and rest, can deal with most things. It is probable that many of the minor cures claimed by healers would have occurred anyway in the normal course of events.

The psychosomatic effect is important, too. How many of us have visited a doctor with a complaint, only to find that we started to feel better even before the resulting prescription had been filled? One reason for this is that some minor ailments *could* be symptoms of something more serious. Before consulting a doctor we are likely to dwell on the worst possible outcome, and the symptom seems to get worse, so we worry more, and so on. After the doctor has reassured us that nothing serious is wrong, we relax; the body is free to get on with the business of healing, and we start to feel better almost immediately. A visit to a healer may have a similar psychological effect, resulting in a similar physical effect.

The psychological effect of some healers can be so great that patients will *feel* cured when they are not. It is not unusual for a reporter to follow up a case in which a patient stood up at a public demonstration of healing and claimed a cure, only to find a week or so later that he is as sick as he ever was.

Some illnesses may, even after many years, go into spontaneous remission. In other words, they stop getting worse, and sometimes get better, for no apparent reason. Treatment has not been changed; the patient is unaware of anything different that might have caused the remission, yet it happens. This may happen without the intervention of any healer (as far as anyone knows) and so when a sudden cure does seem to be effected by a healer there is no way of guaranteeing that it was not, in fact, spontaneous remission. The medical profession, preferring to deal with something familiar, tends therefore to label all inexplicable cures as spontaneous remission rather than give credence to unconventional healers.

Physicians also point out that many people are *not* healed by these healers, and that some patients spend more money chasing after healers who promise near-miracles than they would seeking help from a more conservative physician. Believers in unconventional healing may also stop using regularly prescribed medication, discard braces or crutches, or postpone surgery or diagnosis. Any of these actions may aggravate a condition that could normally be cured fairly easily.

Something that occurs to very few physicians is the possibility that PK may be real, and that perhaps, just perhaps, some unconventional healers really may be using PK to help sick or injured bodies heal themselves.

There have been very few well-controlled attempts to study this possibility using human subjects, because recovery from any illness is such a personal phenomenon, influenced by individual body chemistry, attitudes of mind, and so on. Most researchers doubt that the dispute over whether healers actually do anything to bring about healing (other than provide psychological support) will ever be solved by observing the healing process in individuals. However, one fascinating attempt to study the effect of laying on of hands was carried out by Dr. Dolores Krieger, a professor of nursing at New York University (143).

From 1971 to 1973, Krieger conducted a pilot experiment, a full-scale study, and a replication, in which the hemoglobin values of ill people were checked before and after the laying on of hands by a healer. Control groups of ill people who had not been subject to the laying on of hands were also checked at comparable times for changes in hemoglobin values. Krieger's hypothesis was that the hemoglobin values would change after the laying on of hands, but would not change significantly in the control group. She was right. In the first two studies the difference in "before" and "after" hemoglobin values had a probability of one in a hundred, and in the third experiment, one in a thousand.

Having found strong evidence that a healer could effect physical changes, Krieger wondered whether "ordinary" people could bring about similar changes. She selected thirty-two nurses, each to work with two patients; sixteen were in the experimental group and sixteen were controls. At the beginning of the study no significant differences existed between the two groups in hemoglobin values, sex, and average age. The differences in the hemoglobin values before and after therapeutic touch, as Krieger calls it, were analyzed. The differences were so great that they would happen by chance only once in a thousand such cases. In contrast, comparable blood samples taken from the control group showed no significant differences, making it appear that the therapeutic touch really does have *some* effect on hemoglobin values.

Krieger felt that a healer must be "self-actualized"—Maslow's term (154)—in order to be effective, and so all the nurses involved in the experiment took a test designed to measure self-actualization. All scored quite high (that is, appeared to be inner-directed, independent, self-supportive, expressive of feelings, self-accepting, had a high sense of self-worth, and possessed a positive capacity for intimate contact).

It would be interesting if Krieger were to run another test on nurses both high and low in self-actualization to discover whether the hemoglobin values of the two subject groups varied to the same extent or whether the low self-actualization group of healers had less effect.

Obviously, the patients in the experimental group may have gained some psychological benefit from experiencing the laying on of hands, and this in itself could have brought about some physical changes. Avoiding the problem of psychological effects is so difficult that many researchers feel that conducting experiments *in vivo* (on the living individual) can never provide complete evidence for or against the efficacy of unconventional healing. They prefer the idea of experiments *in vitro* (literally, in glass, or in the bottle) in which enzymes or isolated processes are used as targets.

In vitro studies are not always easy to do, for skilled "healers" often are not willing to "waste their time"—as many of them put it —on laboratory experiments. They prefer to work with people. However, over the years a few reports of experiments on healing have trickled into the parapsychological journals and conventions.

Most of these, including Krieger's work, were inspired by one pioneer, a biochemist at McGill University in Montreal named Dr. Bernard Grad. Grad met a man who believed that he had healing powers. His name was Colonel Oscar Estebany, and when he had been an officer in the Hungarian cavalry he had noticed that lame horses seemed to recover after he had held their injured legs in his hands for a while. As a refugee in Canada, he was eager to cooperate with interested scientists to find out whatever he could about his strange gift.

Because Estebany believed he had treated thyroid disease successfully, Grad's first experiment was with goiters (enlarged thyroids) in mice (109A). Seventy mice were put on a goiter-inducing diet. An experimental group was treated regularly by Estebany; one control group received no treatment; and members of another control group were placed in treatment cages slightly heated to reproduce the temperature of the cages warmed by Estebany's hands. The thyroids of the two control groups increased in size significantly faster than those of the group being treated ($P < .001$. In a later experiment Estebany treated pieces of wool and cotton, which were put in the experimental cages. Similar material, untreated, was placed in control cages. Again, the goiters of the experimental mice grew significantly more slowly than those of the control mice ($P < .001$).

The most famous experiments that Grad conducted with Estebany were actually just pilot projects, with less stringent controls than were used in later work. Nonetheless, they were very impressive and certainly not sloppy in design.

In the first pilot, forty-eight mice were anesthetized and small sections of skin were removed from their backs. Exact measurement of the size of each wound was made by covering the wound with transparent plastic and tracing its outline onto the plastic. The outline was then transferred to paper and cut out. The pieces of paper for each group of mice were weighed on a highly sensitive balance scale.

The mice were divided into three groups. The *E* or Estebany group was "healed" by Estebany twice a day for fifteen minutes, five days a week and once on Saturdays. During healing, Estebany held a special treatment cage, holding eight mice in separate compartments, on his left hand while holding his right hand above (not touching) the wire mesh that made up the top of the cage. When not being treated the mice were kept in ordinary laboratory cages.

The second, or control, group of mice was not treated, but was transferred to treatment cages for the same amount of time as the *E* group, so that they experienced the same amount of stress from being handled and moved into different cages.

Another group, also untreated by Estebany, were subject to a third condition. When they were in the treatment cages the cages were slightly heated to the temperature that the *E* group cages reached when being held by Estebany. This procedure was designed to test whether the mere warmth of the healer's hands might affect the rate of healing.

The wounds of all forty-eight mice were measured again on the first, eleventh, and fourteenth days after wounding. On the day of the wounding and the day afterward there were, not surprisingly, no significant differences among the sizes of the wounds in the three groups. On the eleventh day there was little difference between the control and the heated groups, but the wounds of the *E* group were significantly smaller ($P < .001$). By the fourteenth day the wounds of most of the *E* group had healed to pinpoint size, while those of both other groups again were significantly larger ($P < .001$).

Grad repeated the experiment and obtained similar results. In reporting this work, he pointed out that, since they were pilot projects, he had not applied strict double blinds, but that "crucial procedures were always handled in such a way that the person carrying them out did not know on which group he was working, although others did."

Later Grad teamed up with Drs. R. J. Cadoret and G. I. Paul of the University of Manitoba to carry out a more stringently controlled experiment, using three hundred mice and elaborate controls. Again three groups were used. One was treated by Estebany as before. One group was held, in a manner similar to the *E* group, by various volunteers—different every day—who were not healers. The control group was not treated at all.

Each group was subdivided so that half its mice were treated in cages inside heavy paper bags. The bags were closed with staples so that the healers' hands were not in direct contact with the cages. The cages of the other subgroup were placed in open paper bags and the treaters could put their hands inside the bag but they could not look at the mice or cage.

On the fifteenth day the mice in the group *E* open-bag subgroup had healed significantly more than those in the other two open-bag groups ($P = .01$). These in the *E* enclosed bag had also healed more than the other closed-bag groups, but not significantly so.

However, although the wounds of both *E* subgroups continued to be smaller than those of the other two groups, the difference did not continue to be significant. As planned, the experiment was stopped twenty days after the wounding had been done.

One weakness of this experiment is that the healing abilities of the "nonhealers" were actually an unknown quantity. Since some people find, on taking part in PK tests, that they have PK abilities that they had not previously suspected, the same thing may occur with healing. It is possible, then, that some of the nonhealers who intended to act as controls *may* actually have had a healing effect, and that it may have developed through use during the course of the experiment, decreasing the difference between that group of mice and the *E* group.

The care and feeding of mice is time-consuming and can be expensive. Also, they are nervous beasties, easily panicked by the requirements of a laboratory experiment of this type and susceptible to many contagious diseases. (One roomful of mice did have an unusually large amount of sickness during this experiment, which may have made the results less reliable.) For example, Grad reported that the mice in the closed-bag subgroups "bit frantically at the bag." He had found earlier that mice need to be calm during healing if it is to be effective, so the attempt to discover just *how* Estebany's healing reached his subjects, and whether it could be made less effective by a paper barrier, *may* have shown that healing doesn't work through paper, or it may simply have shown that you cannot be healed when you're in a state of panic.

Looking for less highly strung subjects for his experiments, Grad settled next on barley seeds and attempted to discover whether their germination and growth would be affected if Estebany "treated" the first water they received. After some preliminary investigation he carried out six separate experiments. Equal numbers of barley seeds were planted in pots and watered with saline solution (to give them a slightly hostile environment to overcome). In five experiments, half the pots were watered with solution that had been treated, half with untreated solution. Next they were dried for forty-eight hours, and from then on were watered regularly. Measurement of plant growth was calculated in three ways: number of plants per pot, mean height of plants per pot, and yield per pot (total of all heights of all plants in the pot). A strict system of controls was used so that no one knew which of the numbered pots were experimentals and which were controls. The sixth experiment investigated whether significant growth differences would be observed between two groups of seeds prepared in the same way but neither of which was given treated saline solution. This experiment yielded no significant differences, but the others did.

The first experiment produced the most significant results, with more plants per pot almost every day *and* significantly greater height and yield for the treated pots every day that measurements were taken. Later experiments seemed to indicate that treatment had not affected the *number* of seeds that germinated. Although in one experiment there were more plants in the treated group (significantly more on three days), in another there were fewer, and the other two experiments produced little difference. However, in *all* the experiments the height of the treated plants was greater than that of the controls, significantly so on several days, and the yield was greater for treated plants in all except the last experiment (significantly greater on some days in the third experiment, all the time in the fourth [108]).

Whether the first experiment was more successful because during treatments the water was uncovered, while for the others it was covered, cannot be stated for certain; it is interesting in view of the fact that open-bag mouse healing had been more successful than closed-bag healing. Both results give some support to the idea that healing is less effective when it has to pass through a physical barrier, though, as we will see later, healing mice through a glass window has seemed to be effective. However, the lesser success of the later experiments may have been due to a decline effect of some kind, or to a psychological barrier on the part of the healer, who was aware of the physical barrier.

A similar experiment carried out by Enrique Pauli, S.J., showed no overall significance. Pauli had a Buenos Aires sensitive "treat" the water, which was then stored for a month before being used in a plant growth test. The overall results were not significant (196). A comparison between the results of recently treated and month-old treated water might be interesting, since Dr. Robert Miller of Atlanta feels his experiments have indicated that water so treated loses its "energy" over a period of time (166).

Both Grad and parapsychologist Douglas Dean, then at Newark College of Engineering, were intrigued that treated water could apparently have an effect on plants that was different from the effect of untreated water. In an attempt to find out more, Grad decided to compare treated and untreated water on a spectrophotometer, which measured the amount of light in a specific wavelength that is transmitted (and therefore also the amount that is absorbed) by a solution. Since every substance absorbs and transmits the various wavelengths differently it is possible to judge whether or not two solutions are identical, provided thay are of identical strengths, by spectrophotometry.

Grad found that, though the treated and untreated solutions were the same throughout most of the spectrum, the treated solution transmitted one area of the infrared range less well (that is, it absorbed more of it) than the control solution. Because at that time spectrophotometry had so many variables that it could not be considered entirely reliable, Grad did not pursue this matter further, but four years later Douglas Dean obtained from Grad six bottles of water for a similar experiment. Three had been treated and three had not, but Dean did not know which were which; they were identified only by letters. He took the bottles to an award-winning specialist in atomic spectra, and she, using new and more efficient equipment, found the same difference in the infrared range that Grad had found. She also found two other points in the spectrum where the treated and untreated water seemed to differ, and this was confirmed by another chemist (71). The results mean that the structure of the water molecules had probably been changed slightly in a way that would normally be achieved when the water was heated, except that this change had lasted for a considerable time, an occurrence that would not be expected with a normal heating process. There is no indication of how this change was accomplished.

Another attempt to harness and investigate Oscar Estebany's talents (he was also the healer for Dolores Krieger's first experiment) was made by Sister Justa Smith, then of Rosary Hill College, Buffalo, N.Y. Sister Justa is an enzymologist, and she used solutions of trypsin, an enzyme involved in digestion, for her research. Each day of the experiment, a portion of the solution was divided into four parts. One stoppered flask was treated by Estebany for up to seventy-five minutes. Another was exposed to ultraviolet light, which slows the activity of trypsin, and a third was placed in a high magnetic field. The fourth was a control, heated to the same temperature as that produced by the healer's hands, but otherwise not exposed to any changes. Sister Justa's conclusion at the end of the experiments was that treatment by Estebany increased trypsin's activity as much as did exposure to a magnetic field of *13,000 gauss* (the magnetic field of the earth is about 0.5 gauss). In spite of this, measurements taken near his hands while he was giving treatment did not show any increase in the magnetic field around them (277, 71).

A later Grad experiment used the fermentation of yeast as the function to be affected by healing treatments. Five sets of three bottles were used. In each set one bottle was treated by a male and one by a female, and one was untreated. Three bottles in a sixth set were not treated at all. The solution from each bottle was then added to a controlled amount of yeast, and the rate of fermentation of the yeast was measured at regular intervals by measuring the rate at which carbon dioxide was produced. In four out of five experimental sets, significantly greater fermentation occurred in the treated solutions than in the untreated, "three being significant to the level of ($P <$ .0005)." In the control set, in which no bottles were treated, very little difference was found among the three bottles, making it fairly clear that *something* had indeed happened to the treated solutions, although nobody knew quite what it was (109).

At the 1971 Parapsychological Convention in Durham, North Carolina, Graham and Anita Watkins reported on another experimental use for mice in healing research. They measured the speed with which "healed" and not healed mice recovered consciousness after being anesthetized in etherizers. Each trial used two mice. A previously prepared random number list decided whether the first mouse to lose consciousness would be the experimental or the control subject. A "healer" then tried to treat the experimental mouse, and the attempt was counted as successful if the experimental target mouse awoke before the control mouse. The report showed that three experiments had been carried out, using eleven healers, a total of 768 trials, or thirty-two runs. The first seven runs in the last experiment had controls so strict that the healers complained that they could not concentrate their attention properly because they frequently had to switch from one side of the laboratory for one mouse to the other side for the next mouse. The results of these seven runs were at chance, but for the first two experiments, and the last part of the third, the results were reported as positive; the treated mice had recovered faster than the controls.

Incidentally, in this experiment the subjects who did the healing did not all claim to be healers; some were subjects who had done well in other forms of PK experiment, and others were members of the staff at the Institute of Parapsychology (331).

Another experiment with yeast was reported at the next PA convention, this time by Erlendur Haraldsson of the ASPR and

Thorsteinn Thorsteinsson of the University of Iceland. They mixed yeast and nutritive solution before subjecting half of 20 test tubes in each experiment to a ten-minute treatment by a healer who was not allowed to touch them. All 20 tubes were than stored for twenty-four hours, after which the growth of the yeast was measured by a light-absorbency test. Twelve such sessions were held, using seven healers. The overall scoring was slightly positive; of 120 pairs of test tubes, 58 showed more growth in the experimental tubes; 33 showed less; and 29 showed an equal amount of growth. What was particularly interesting in these results was the fact that three of the seven healers were responsible for nearly all of this effect, and these three were in fact involved in healing, two as "mental healers" and another as a conventional physician. The other "healers" in the experiment had not been involved in healing in any form until they took part in the experiment. The level of success for the three "real healers" was such that $P = .00014$, whereas, if scored separately, the four nonhealers' results were only at the chance level (114).

Clearly, some people *are* able to have an effect on living organisms by doing something that they call "treating" or "healing," but none of these experiments gives any indication of what is actually happening to bring about these changes. Is the effect a form of telepathy in which the healer mentally "encourages" the enzyme, yeast, or living system to do its thing? Is there some kind of physical force that, by PK, actually surrounds the treated subjects?

Some researchers feel that the telepathic explanation is the most likely one (142), but further work with anesthetized mice seems to suggest the existence of something that not only affects the "patient" at which it is aimed but also demonstrates the linger effect, seeming to affect succeeding patients placed in the same location. In other words, it continues to work even after it has been "turned off" by the healer.

Graham and Anita Watkins had noticed that, during their work on mouse resuscitation, healers were not successful if the side of the room in which the target was located was switched frequently. To see whether the healing effect did indeed "linger" they had the healer—who could not be seen by them—work on resuscitating mice on one side of the room for half a run. Then, instead of switching to those on the other side of the room as was standard procedure, he would leave. The experimenters continued to anesthetize pairs of mice and time their recovery just as in the standard procedure they had developed. In the two series in which this was done the mice on the side on which the healer had concentrated recovered significantly faster than the controls *even after the healer had left.* It was as though he had affected the entire area in which the mice lay, which in turn affected the mice.

It is unlikely that the effect was brought about by factors in the environment, because the experimental mice were not on the same side of the room all the time; the experimental side was frequently switched between runs, but remained constant *during* each run (333).

A more recent method of attempting to discover whether a person can influence another individual's body, and hence perhaps his well-being, by PK has been termed *allobiofeedback* (25). In biofeedback a person receives feedback as to whether he is able to change his *own* physiological activity—brain waves, heartbeat, or whatever. In allobiofeedback procedures a subject tries to affect the physiological activity of *someone else,* a target person, while the subject receives feedback to show him how he is doing. The term comes from *allo,* which is Greek for *other.* Both William Braud and Charles Honorton have been working in this direction and feel that allobiofeedback is directly related to healing.

In a typical experiment, the target person sits very relaxed in a quiet, preferably soundproofed, room with sensors attached to his fingers. The subject, or agent, is in another room where he can see continuous readings showing the target's galvanic skin response (GSR). Other physiological activities can be used, but GSR is the current favorite. At times selected by a random number generator, the agent tries to increase or decrease the target's GSR. The target may or may not know *what* is being attempted, but he does not know *when* it is being attempted.

In pilot and confirmation experiments of this type, Braud found that seventeen out of twenty targets showed greater GSR during "increase" periods than during decrease periods (25). It is just possible that the subjects knew by ESP what the agent was trying to do and that their bodies cooperated so that the results would have been obtained by percipient ESP rather than PK. Another possibility, though a very unlikely one, is that the subject affected the equipment so that it gave an increased or decreased reading regardless of whether the target's GSR had actually changed. However, on the whole, this type of work does strongly suggest that in one way or another one person can affect another's body by psi—strong evidence that healing by psi is a possibility.

It seems quite apparent that there is, indeed, some kind of healing effect that is independent of psychological factors, since in many of the experiments reported here the experimental and control "patients" were treated in exactly the same way as far as any psychological effect might be concerned. Even if we were to accept the very slight possibility that seeds and yeast could be affected "psychologically" by extra attention and affection, Grad's barley seeds were all treated in the same way; it was only the water used in the initial watering that was treated. Until the experiment was complete *no one* knew which seeds had received the treated water and which were controls. Similarly, the yeast he used was added to the treated and untreated water only *after* the solution had been treated.

The Watkins experimental and control mice were treated identically to the extent of being anesthetized at the same time in the same etherizer. No one knew which would be which until after they were unconscious. The healer did not touch them, but was in another room behind a one-way mirror so that he could see them but the two experimenters handling the mice could not see him. They did not know which mice were experimental and which were controls, that being decided, in the later tests, by random number lists known to the healer but not released to the experimenters working with the mice until the experiment was over. (It is possible of course that an experimenter effect was in force via "blind PK," but then, it always is.)

Although we can see that there probably is a healing force, and that it does seem to linger in one area, there is at this point little more that we have discovered about it. The type of function that would affect trypsin is not the same as would increase hemoglobin. The growth of barley seeds and the fermentation of yeast are in many ways very different, and the healing of wounds and recovery from anesthesia are yet more variables. Still, all these things seem subject to the "healing force," whatever that may be. If it exists, then we must learn how it can be used and how to avoid its abuse by charlatans more concerned with healing their bank accounts than their patients.

Part 2

Further Afield

Chapter 8

Physical Mediumship

*If a table moves when no one is touching it, this is not obviously more
likely to have been effected by my deceased grandfather than by myself.
We cannot tell how I could move it; but then we cannot tell how he could
move it either.*

F. W. H. Myers (180)

ESP and PK are often said to be the main subjects of study in
parapsychology. However, the third important area of research, one
that is often forgotten or dismissed as unscientific, is survival
research. As we saw in Chapter 1, survival research attempts to find
a scientifically acceptable answer to the question, "Is there a *something* that survives man's bodily death?"

It is ironical that survival work now constitutes such a small part
of parapsychology, because it was a desire to study purported proofs
of survival that led to the formation of the first formal parapsychological organization, the Society for Psychical Research, in London
in 1882. The SPR was formed by a group of people who felt that a
formal study of mediumship should be made, since for some time
spiritualism had been sweeping across the Western world and an
ever-growing number of people claimed that through them the
spirits of the dead could be contacted and would as proof of their
continued existence send messages, play musical instruments, tilt
tables, materialize flowers, levitate the medium, and even materialize themselves in a form recognizable to their loved ones on this
side.

This chapter can give only a brief and incomplete summary of the subject of mediumship, with emphasis on the physical aspects, but the field is complex and has a history that fills many volumes presented from many different points of view.

Spiritualism as an organized force had started in 1848 in a small community called Hydesville, near Rochester, New York. There lived the Fox family, which included two young daughters, Kate and Maggie. Their peaceful existence began to be plagued by raps and bangs from the cellar, which the family somewhat fearfully attributed to the devil. Flippant young Kate took things less seriously, and one day demanded, as tradition tells us, "Here, Mr. Splitfoot, do as I do," and snapped her fingers.

She then found that however often she snapped her fingers, the sounds of that many raps would follow. A code was quickly devised to communicate with the "intelligence," which claimed to be the spirit of a dead peddler who had been murdered and buried in the cellar of the house. Word of the events soon spread, it was found that the girls could elicit the raps even away from the house, and before long they made their first public demonstration in Rochester.

Psychologically and sociologically the atmosphere in America was right for something like this, and within months spiritualist circles spread across the country and on to Europe. Most mediums discovered their abilities when they attended the circles of other mediums and were told that they, too, had mediumistic tendencies. They would then form their own circles, and "discover" more mediums, so that the movement spread with astonishing speed.

Of course, the Fox girls were not really the first to experience this kind of phenomenon, though they seem to have been the catalyst that led to its dramatic spread in semiorganized form. Spontaneous and inexplicable raps have been reported for hundreds of years, and the Fox girls were not the first to devise a code by which the sounds could be made to communicate. Such phenomena are often followed by the mysterious movement of household objects, and are then referred to as poltergeist phenomena (Chapter 9).

However, in the spiritualist movement of the 1800s it was usually the table around which the medium and her (or his) circle sat that moved, and it moved most genteelly, with just a slight tilting or levitation to prove the power of the spirits—nothing large enough to frighten away the eagerly anticipatory sitters (who, as time went by, were more and more often expected to pay for the privilege of participating).

In the early stages of spiritualism, messages were obtained by the sitters asking a question and then saying the alphabet. When the appropriate letter was reached a rap would so indicate, and the process would start again to find the next letter until the answer was complete. When table-tilting became the vogue, the tilting of the table would indicate the correct letters. Later the planchette and similar board devices with the letters printed on them were developed. They were often kept out of sight of the medium, but the raps would still sound, or table tilt, when someone pointed to the correct letter. In another form of seance the medium would hold the pointer, glass, or whatever was to indicate the correct letters, but would be blindfold so that, in theory, she could not be aware of what was being said until the message was completed.

Mental mediumship did away completely with such lengthy proceedings. The medium would go into trance (as she usually did for the raps and table-tilting) and would be "taken over" by a personality claiming to be a spirit. This entity would then act as a control, passing on messages from other spirits and describing their appearance so that the sitters would have "evidence" that their loved ones had survived on the other side. This was done verbally, with the medium doing the speaking or, occasionally, writing.

As time went by, physical mediumship developed beyond raps and table-tilting, and the phenomena became quite sophisticated. So did the methods of producing such phenomena by fraud. In fact, as investigators' sophistication also increased, the vast majority of the physical mediums were found to be using trickery to achieve their results. Only a few names stand out in the history books as being worthy of continued interest.

Perhaps the greatest was Daniel Dunglas Home, or Hume as he was called in his earlier days. Home, born in Scotland in 1833, was taken to the United States as a child and adopted by an aunt, though his parents were apparently still living. In his autobiography (125), he tells of some apparently telepathic phenomena in his youth followed by the onset of typical, meaningless rappings a few months after the death of his mother. The raps were followed by movements of furniture, which his religious aunt ascribed to the devil. She held Home's recently acquired Methodist beliefs to be responsible for the introduction of Satan into her abode and, according to Home, ordered him from the house. By now he was using the alphabet system to communicate, he believed, with his mother and others. Word of his abilities had spread, and he had no difficulty finding friends willing to allow him to stay with them—and, of course, demonstrate his mediumship.

This was to set the pattern of his life. He did not accept money for his sittings, so he could not be said to be a professional medium. However, he spent most of his life being supported by friends who, in spite of his charming personality, would probably not have been so generous had it not been for his abilities. It could, therefore, be said that he depended on his mediumship for a living even though he was not technically a professional.

By 1855 when Home first visited England, his fame had spread. He conducted seances before many members of Europe's royalty, and was investigated by noted physicist Sir William Crookes. Crookes has been criticized for his credulity when investigating Florence Cook, a charming young medium whose attractiveness is alleged by some to have blinded Crookes to her opportunities for fraud. However, he conducted some carefully controlled tests with Home, including one in which a spring balance was used to support one end of a board, the other end of which was on a table. Home placed his hand on the part of the board that was on the table and, according to Crookes, the spring balance showed a far greater pressure increase than would have been physically possible for Home to exert, even if he had been exerting pressure. According to observers, he was not (44).

Another typical Home effect was to make an accordion play while held by only one end—the end away from the keys. Hereward Carrington was an early researcher and writer who wrote much about fraudulent methods used by mediums. However, of Home's accordion playing he wrote:

> I have described several methods by which this accordion test might be accomplished by fraud . . . but I may say that a careful study of

the evidence in the Home case has convinced me that the accordion could not have been played by any such means in these seances. (44)

Home even let go of the instrument entirely and placed it, in good light, in the hands of the person next to him. It continued to play. At times it was placed in a cage under the table, where investigators could and did look at any time. There was just room between table and cage for one of Home's hands to fit into the cage so that he could hold one end of the accordion. At times he removed the hand, and the accordion continued to play within the cage—which, incidentally, was electrified to prevent tampering.

Home was later involved in a sleazy court case involving money given to him by a wealthy widow. He lost the case, but even at that time no doubts were cast on his abilities as a medium. He died in 1886 after a long period of illness, never having been detected in fraud.

Another well-known medium was William Stainton Moses, a minister who was reported to have brought about such phenomena as "apports" (in which objects believed to be elsewhere appeared in the locked seance room), levitation (a favorite of Home's, too), unexplained lights, musical sounds, and the introduction of various perfumes to the room. The weakness of the Stainton Moses phenomena lies in the fact that he sat almost exclusively in a small private circle with two close friends, the Stanhope Speers (actually his employers, since he was private tutor to their son). There are a few reports by others who visited the circle, but Moses was not studied at length by any major psychical researchers, and we cannot be sure that the Speers were truly skilled and objective observers. On the credit side is Moses' character, generally accepted as being as spotless as could be required of any well-educated and high-minded man of the cloth. However, a man's character when conscious cannot always speak for what happens when he is in trance and either his subconscious or another entity altogether is in control of his actions.

And then there is Eusapia Palladino. A peasant woman, Palladino was undoubtedly a vulgar cheat, and yet she was also, perhaps, an extraordinary medium. Born in Italy in 1854, Palladino, like Home, lived with an adoptive family. Her mediumship seems to have begun with the movements of objects and developed quickly, producing raps and levitations at regular sittings. Soon there was a "control," John King (a popular name, he seems to have controlled a wide variety of mediums) who could move objects, play musical instruments, and, in all, achieve thirty-nine different effects (251).

Two things worked against Palladino. First, she was coarse and ignorant—deliberately ignorant, having resisted efforts to educate her in her youth. In those days, scientists, especially British scientists, were educated gentlemen, elite, accustomed to observing all the niceties of proper etiquette, and neither Palladino nor they were particularly at ease in each other's company. Second, at least when in trance, and perhaps when out of it, Palladino would cheat whenever she got the chance. Unlike Stainton Moses, the case for her paranormal abilities is supported not one whit by her character but rests solely on whether she was under perfectly controlled conditions at times of paranormal occurrences.

In 1894, French scientist Professor Charles Richet arranged for Palladino to visit his home on the Isle Roubaud. Since his was the only house there, he and the scientists who were with him could be reasonably sure that Palladino had no confederates around. Even so, the seance room door was locked, and the window shutters left open just enough to allow the participants to dictate to the notetaker who sat outside. Palladino's hands and feet were supposedly held by the investigators at all times, but on reading some of the reports one is struck by how often the investigators changed from controlling one limb or part of the body to another. We read:

> 12:35. R. held both arms and one hand of E. [Eusapia], while M. held both feet and her other arm. R. then felt a hand move over his head and rest on his mouth for some seconds, during which he spoke to us with his voice muffled. The round table now approached. R.'s head was stroked behind. R. held both E.'s knees, still retaining one hand while M. held the other, and the round table continued to approach in violent jerks.
> 12:49. A small cigar box fell on our table, and a sound was heard in the air as of something rattling. R. was holding head and right hand; M., holding left hand, raised it in the air holding it lightly by the tips of its fingers, but with part of his own hand free. A saucer containing small shot (from another part of the room), was then put into this hand of M. in the air. A covered wire of the electric battery came on

to the table and wrapped itself round R.'s and E.'s heads, and was pulled till E. called out. Henceforth R. held her head and body, M. kept one hand and both feet, while L. held the other hand, and in this position E. made several spasmodic movements, each of which was accompanied or followed by violent movements of the neighbouring round table. (100)

In other words, between 12:35 and 12:57 (the 12:57 note starts immediately after the passage above) Richet alone held (1) both arms and one hand, (2) both E's knees and one hand, (3) head and right hand, and (4) head and body. Remembering that the other investigators must have been changing their holds accordingly, the whole procedure sounds more like a wrestling match than a properly controlled seance. However, to be fair, it was the first of the Isle Roubaud sittings, and perhaps it took a little experimentation before a routine system of controls could be developed by a team of scientists who may not all have worked together before.

Five days later, the fourth sitting, with Richet, F. W. H. Myers, and Sir Oliver Lodge, was held. The Polish psychical researcher Dr. Julian Ochorowicz took notes. At one point it sounded as though the door was being unlocked, though Palladino's hands were held and a clear space "of several feet near door was plainly visible." The key appeared on the table and then disappeared again. The locking sounds were heard again, and the key appeared in Richet's hand.

So impressed were Myers and Lodge with the phenomena produced by Palladino that they persuaded Professor Henry Sidgwick and his wife, Eleanor, senior and skeptical researchers of the SPR, to visit France for more investigation. By this time the Sidgwicks were thoroughly tired of physical mediums, having spent long hours investigating many only to find them fraudulent. However, they dutifully made the trip and contributed their expertise to the proper control of the medium. One trick used by many mediums, including Palladino, was to have an investigator control each hand at the start of the seance, but gradually to bring both hands together during the spasmodic movements that seem necessary to many physical phenomena. A sudden jerk would then free one hand for a brief moment, after which the investigator would, he thought, reestablish control, not realizing that he was now holding part of the same hand that was being controlled by his colleague.

Palladino in the meantime had one hand free, though seance notes would record that she was under complete control.

The Sidgwicks were acutely aware of such tricks, and when Mrs. Sidgwick controlled Palladino's left hand she was "constantly verifying that there had been no substitution" (100). With Palladino's hands and feet controlled, sitters' hands, faces, and heads continued to be patted, notes sounded from a piano well behind Palladino, and once a melon that was behind her appeared on the seance table.

The reports that resulted from these sessions stimulated considerable controversy, with those who had not been there alleging, as so often happens, that those who had been there must have missed something, some way, in which Palladino had deceived them. Though the Sidgwicks' notes were positive, they maintained a publicly skeptical attitude.

Later Palladino visited England, where the disparity between her and the English researchers became very apparent. Her performance was unimpressive and conditions were deliberately relaxed so that she could cheat. She did and was caught and denounced.

In America her reception was similar. She was again caught cheating after conditions had been set up to enable her to do so, and she was condemned as a fraud. It had actually been known from early in her career that Palladino would cheat if given a chance. Nevertheless, each new "unmasking" was hailed by those involved as a triumph over earlier researchers who had failed to discover how she achieved her effects. Whether some of these failures to discover fraud were because the phenomena were genuine we do not know, but certainly some astonishing effects were obtained when Palladino was in her prime and at ease among *sympatico* continental researchers. The key is the question of whether those researchers were so sympathetic that they allowed themselves to be hoodwinked—and that question can never be answered.

There have been other great mediums. Stanislawa Tomczyk was studied at length by Ochorowicz. Early in this century, she was said to have been able to move balls, depress scales, and stop pendulums much as Kulagina is reported to do (298).

In the 1920s and 1930s Willy and Rudi Schneider were perhaps the most famous physical mediums. Willy, the elder of the two, caused movements of bells, toys, musical instruments, and the usual paraphernalia of the physical medium, but under what appear to have been well-controlled conditions (328). Younger brother Rudi's major claim to fame is that something he did interfered with an infrared light beam, yet the photographs taken at the same moment (the cameras were triggered when the beam was broken) showed nothing. Allegations of fraud were inevitably made against him, but, in a study presented before the PA in 1968, British researcher Anita Gregory said that she could find no allegations that seemed to be upheld by facts. Even a photograph that was said to show that Rudi had an arm free during an allegedly well-controlled seance was, in Gregory's opinion, "almost certainly a fake—a compositive picture: the medium's legs point in another direction from the back, an anatomical absurdity. There is also clear evidence of retouching on the supporting plates" (110).

How psychical researchers regard physical mediumship appears to depend greatly on where they live. British and American scientists seem to have far less success in finding genuine phenomena than their continental European counterparts. Or, depending on your point of view, they have far more success at controlling conditions and detecting fraud.

Frank Podmore, a superb investigator but one with great bias against physical effects, admitted that some of Home's phenomena were not normally possible under the conditions that existed. Rather than consider a paranormal explanation, however, he suggested that the witnesses were hallucinating (205). Later he admitted that this explanation was unsatisfactory, but said that it was still more satisfactory to him than any other (42).

A contemporary writer who presents the continental viewpoint is Rene Sudre. Of British researchers he writes:

> ... they have always rejected physical phenomena which do not accord so well with the religious needs of their nation. God knows how they discouraged all the great mediums who were brought to them from the Continent! They subjected them to precautions as irritating as they were useless; they created around them a sterilizing atmosphere, and they were perpetually "exposing" them, as they called it, that is to say revealing the fraud which was always assumed. (298)

Later Eric J. Dingwall, who from his approach to psi might be a reincarnation of Frank Podmore had he not been born while Podmore was still alive, was to tell with relish how he had attended a sitting where effects were achieved that Sudre dubbed "impossible." Dingwall reproduced the effects, under the same conditions and without resort to the paranormal, within half an hour (77). The obvious inference is that Dingwall considers it to be Sudre who is too credulous, not the British who are too skeptical.

Certainly there was chauvinism in early British attitudes. Most of the early SPR people were from Cambridge; all were well educated, wealthy, and upper-class (the three went together almost automatically in those days). They tended to feel that scientists educated or raised elsewhere were just not quite as objective or as capable as "our own people." Nothing was known of the experimenter effect in those days, so the British group had no idea that their disgust at the coarse Palladino and her unmistakably sexual writhings during trance could completely sabotage their entire experiment. (It is probably significant that the most successful Palladino sittings were those at which all the investigators were males, with whom she felt more at ease, and several were from continental Europe. Skeptics, of course, might well say that such sessions were more successful because the males could not entirely keep their minds on the required controls when those controls required that they hold the arms, legs, or even body of an apparently orgasmic female.)

The distaste of some of the experimenters was probably not entirely personal. Experience had taught these people that the vast majority of physical phenomena was produced by fraud. Time and again they had set out with high hopes of finding genuine phenomena, only to be disillusioned once again. Their cynicism is easy to understand. Their training in rigid standards of evidence is to be applauded. It is perhaps only their understanding of the psychology of their frequently temperamental subjects that can be faulted, and that in itself may have caused them to be disappointed more often than might otherwise have been the case.

The continentals, on the other hand, were (and in some cases still are) considered by many people to be too ready to accept explanations considered "occulty" by their Anglo-Saxon colleagues. For example, the idea that physical phenomena were caused by "rigid rays," rods, or "pseudo limbs" exuded from the medium's body was put forward by Ochorowicz (299). The theory is dismissed out of hand by most British and American parapsychologists, yet it is discussed with enthusiasm by Sudre, who in fact uses it to dismiss Rhine's dice work:

> The more one accepts the idea of the temporary formation of an organ to carry out certain actions, the more difficult one finds it to accept the idea of a force which can influence the falling of several dice so that a previously determined score is obtained. (300)

That many of the marvels of mediumship *could* be caused by normal means, and therefore by fraud, cannot be doubted. A number of mediums demonstrated elongation, in which they seemed to grow noticeably taller than their normal height, and described the feat as paranormal. We read, for example, that Home elongated himself by "as much as nine inches or a foot" (102), and on several other instances by six to eight inches (45). This may sound truly paranormal, but the *Guinness Book of Records* contains the following entry:

> By constant practice in muscular manipulation of the vertebrae, the circus performer Clarence E. Willard (1882-1962) of the U.S. was, at his prime, able to increase his apparent stature from 5 feet 10 inches to 6 feet 4 inches at will. (111)

Allowing for the awe-struck state of Home's sitters there may well have been a certain amount of exaggeration of the amount of "growth" involved, and if Willard could do it by muscular manipulation there seems no reason why Home and his contemporaries could not have done the same.

Materialization mediums are often considered by spiritualists to be the cream of the profession. To be able to materialize the face, or even the whole form, of a spirit entity, so that it can move among the sitters, claiming recognition from loved ones and acknowledgement of its reality from all—of such are mediumistic ambitions made. Unfortunately, materializations are delicate. They cannot be exposed to light, nor can they be touched. Those that are touched have a mysterious tendency to turn immediately into a mass of cheesecloth—to the utter bewilderment of the medium, of course. So many such tales are told that it is difficult to give credence even to those cases that have not been completely exposed. Materialized "controls" have been observed to be *exactly* the height of the medium or of the medium when on her knees (the medium, meantime, being supposedly hidden behind a curtain in her "cabinet"). A dark sock with two "eyes" attached was once taken by several sitters to be a superb materialization of an African face. One could go on and on, and, indeed, few if any materialization reports safely rule out trickery by the medium or a confederate. The subject of materialization is not a favorite one of parapsychologists.

Apports and teleportation, in which solid objects are supposed to be moved across large areas and into or out of enclosed spaces, are another problem. Most of the great mediums produced apports (though Home did not, and affected to despise as frauds those who did). Some reported apports have appeared in locked rooms when they were "known" by the sitters to have been elsewhere at the time the room was locked. After seeing the heights to which magicians can rise it is hard to take apports seriously, yet they must be considered, for the very good reason that they still seem to occur in poltergeist cases, in which the participants are neither magicians nor professional mediums who might have been practicing on the sly.

Since we know that incredible things can be achieved by sleight of hand, it may be convenient to ignore Crookes, Myers, and the other researchers who swore that objects that appeared during seances *could not* under any circumstances have been brought in surreptitiously by the medium or a confederate. But what are we to think about teleportation of an entire person?

Podmore reports, without comment, on a case in which Mrs. Guppy, a well-known medium of the time, appeared on a seance table in a locked room, pen in one hand, account book in the other, with the ink on the pen still wet and the word *onions* "scarcely dry" as the last entry in the account book. She claimed that her last memory was of sitting at home three miles away. The narrator comments, "The possibility of her being concealed in the room is as absurd as the idea of her acting in collusion with the media." (*Media* is used here as the plural of *medium*.)

The account says that the suggestion "I wish she would bring Mrs. Guppy" was first made by a visitor, not by the mediums who were holding the seance and who might have planned the event. On the other hand, the mediums originally at the seance were Messrs. Herne and Williams, and they and Mrs. Guppy were involved in three other similar cases in the early 1870s. The possibility of collusion among the three cannot be ruled out. However, it is hard to understand how Mrs. Guppy could have been hidden in the room, for she is reported to have been "one of the biggest women in London." The incident was widely reported and attested to by all eleven people present at the time (203).

In his book *My Story,* Uri Geller also claims to have been teleported. The noted Edinburgh parapsychologist John Beloff commented in his review of the book:

> . . . it is all too easy to laugh this sort of thing out of court as just another tongue-in-cheek tall story; but why, one wonders, should Geller risk telling a story implicating his friends which he fully realized could only strain the credulity of his supporters and wreck the credibility of the rest of the book so far as his critics are concerned?

Of teleportation in general, Beloff adds, "All this, of course, is the purest Arabian nights; nevertheless, we must remember that the word *impossible* does not belong in the vocabulary of parapsychology" (11).

Levitation is another highly questionable mediumistic feat. When a group of awe-struck people in a dark room suddenly hear a voice that seems to come from the ceiling, and are instructed to feel the medium's boots as they pass over their heads, it is hardly surprising that they should conclude that the medium is indeed floating above their heads. It is something of a let-down to realize that in fact the medium may be practicing ventriloquism by "throwing" his voice so that it only *sounds* as if it comes from above, and that his boots may be on his *hands* as he walks around the table, leaning forward over the heads of his sitters. Nevertheless, this is a very real possibility.

Home is reported to have floated out of one upper-story window and into another before three witnesses, but whether he really floated or whether he climbed is another of the infuriating questions to which we will never have a final answer (206).

Few mediums could lay claim to such exotic phenomena as those claimed for Home and Palladino. However, even the rankest amateur could produce raps; they are probably the commonest mediumistic phenomenon. It is said that when Maggie Fox was old and alcoholic she "confessed" that all the Fox sisters' raps were caused by the girls cracking their toe joints, but that she later recanted her confession. Certainly some percussive sounds are not hard to imitate, but it is difficult to account for the variety of sounds produced by some mediums.

In the 1890s the Russian Society of Experimental Psychology studied an eighteen-year-old girl called Nikolaefe under what seem to have been very tight conditions. They reported loud raps sounding as though they were on soft furniture, on wood, like "the scratching of dogs' feet" some fourteen feet from the medium, and as though they were moving all around the room striking the furniture, sometimes sounding quite violent, even though the medium could be seen quite clearly, sitting motionless (197).

Further support for the idea that some mediumistic raps are not produced normally comes from Dr. Joel Whitton, a Toronto physician, who has analyzed the raps produced in seance-type situations during experiments by members of the Toronto Society for Psychical Research. We will come back to these experiments later in this chapter, but for the moment it is enough to say that Whitton, following on earlier work by Dr. Alan Gauld (103), found that the "acoustic envelopes" of allegedly paranormal raps differed considerably from acoustic envelopes of raps produced normally at the same table and made as similar as possible to the allegedly paranormal sounds, under conditions that were also kept as similar as possible (same number of hands resting on the table at the same pressure, and so on). An acoustic envelope is, roughly, the shape obtained by making a diagram of the vibrations involved in a noise and then drawing an outline around it. From this one gets the "shape" of the sound. Specifically, the sound vibrations died away, or were damped, much more quickly in the allegedly paranormal sounds than in the normal sounds (339, 340). If further analyses confirm those by Drs. Gauld and Whitton, they would seem to provide evidence that, though raps obviously *can* be caused fraudulently, some are quite probably paranormal.

After raps, perhaps the most popular physical phenomenon of mediumship was table-tilting. Again, the question is not *whether* the tables move, but *how* they move. Basically, in all these phenomena, one must ask two questions. First, "Is this produced by normal or paranormal means?" If normal explanations are ruled out, then the second question arises: "Is this caused by discarnate entities or by PK on the part of the medium or the sitters?"

A type of event that is not confined to mediums is one in which a clock stops, a picture falls, or something similar and unexpected occurs, and it is later discovered that a loved one died at precisely that moment. Such occurrences are often taken as proof of survival after death, because it is assumed that the spirit of the deceased caused the event to happen in an effort to communicate. However, it is just as possible that the living person present during the event actually became aware of the death telepathically, or by clairvoyance, and was so shocked, at the unconscious level, that his PK caused the event.

Similarly, someone may "ask" a dead person to show proof of his continued existence, and something strange may immediately occur. Of such a case the renowned astronomer Camille Flammarion, who was very interested in parapsychology, asked, "What is there to prove that the personality of the experimenter was not able to produce the phenomena unconsciously? The action of the deceased is indeed very *probable*, but is it certain?" (91).

Before getting to the question of spirits or PK in table-tilting it should be pointed out that we know that table-tilting is often produced normally, if sometimes unconsciously, by muscle power. This was shown very early in the history of physical phenomena by physicist Michael Faraday. In 1853 Faraday used sheets of cardboard soft-glued together to show that the sitters' hands were not just following the table's movements, but were moving *farther* to the left, for example, than did the table. He then showed the sitters how they could become aware of whether or not they were exerting pressure on the table. Under these conditions the table did not move, and Faraday concluded that mechanical muscle power was responsible for all table-tilting (112).

The same conclusion was reached by a group of "four medical men" who found that if all sitters expected the same direction of motion, the table moved, but if half expected one direction and half

the other, then no movement took place (202). Several other investigators came to the same conclusion. The possibility that Faraday's
subjects might be concentrating so hard on not moving the lightly
glued-together stacks of cardboard that they could not get themselves into the right state of mind to produce paranormal
phenomena does not appear to have been considered.

Interest in table-tilting declined after these denouncements, and it
was not until the middle of this century that researchers began to
look into the subject again.

In 1948, Haakon Forwald began to work with a small group of
friends in Sweden, trying to bring about movements of a table. At
times they used a table supported from a helical spring; at other
times they used an ordinary table. Since no one person was known
to be the medium (though Forwald suspected himself) all sitters had
to control each other—not a very easy task. Nonetheless, many
possibly paranormal phenomena were recorded by Forwald. For
example, of a sitting on October 20, 1949, he wrote:

> It [the table] soon started sliding movements over the carpet, raised
> on two legs and a couple of times even on one leg. Two persons
> simultaneously tried to press the table down to the floor, but felt a
> considerable counterforce. Once when the table stood on one leg in
> 20-30 degrees inclined position Mr. C. pressed down so that he felt
> pain in his hands, but did not succeed in getting the table down on the
> floor. I saw that he pressed so hard that his hands were trembling. I
> was anxious for the table, the legs being very weak. It is absolutely
> sure that the remaining participants could not have compensated the
> force from the hands of Mr. Carlsson. This should have demanded a
> force in the direction of the table surface much higher than the table
> leg could have withstood. In fact, I did not observe any deformation
> of the leg—it was just to my left—and light was good enough for
> observation. It therefore must be taken as absolutely sure that a
> considerable force acted on the table from beneath. That is to say, so
> was the immediate impression. There was nothing to see under the
> table that could have produced such a force. . . .
>
> During the experiment we were talking together, inspecting the
> hands of each other and so on. The phenomena being so strong we
> meant that the table possibly could completely rise from the floor
> with our hands lying on its surface. We expressed this desire and the
> table seemed to strain to demonstrate such a rise. It went up on one
> leg and made turning movements as if to screw itself up from the

floor, but as far as we could see it did not succeed in getting up the fourth leg. (93)

Forwald communicated with J. B. Rhine about these experiments and as a result gave up his table-turning for the work with dice mentioned in Chapter 2. No doubt this was a wise move, given the climate of the times (which inclined strongly toward quantitative work) and the difficulty of controlling against "fraud by foot" in the raising of the table. However, it is rather ironical that, by the time qualitative work came back into fashion in the early 1970s, Forwald was retired and not inclined to return to his research. (He died September 16, 1978.)

Further table-tilting work was done in the 1960s by a group in Exeter, England, led by K. J. Batcheldor (9). Before long the group joined forces with Colin Brookes-Smith, who began to develop ways of recording contacts with the table. At first, using electrical grids connected to recording equipment, he tried to record when members of the circle touched the table. By this time it had been realized that once people believed paranormal events *were* occurring, paranormal events were more likely to occur. Accordingly, one person was chosen, by the drawing of a card, to be the "aide" who might occasionally and surreptitiously press a thumb against the table edge in order to "prime the pump." Both raps and table movements were obtained.

It should be mentioned that the underside of the table was not completely covered with the electrical grids. It was therefore still possible for unrecorded cheating to occur. In addition, many parapsychologists question the propriety of having an atmosphere in which it is known that at least one person has permission to cheat. However, in favor of some kind of paranormal happening, it should be said that Brookes-Smith's apparatus soon revealed more than one type of contact. Fingers and thumbs were shown by the recording equipment to have a distinctive signature that differed from some of the other effects obtained. The latter could not be replicated normally. Further study may indicate that these unexplained contacts relate to paranormal effects (33, 34, 35).

The Exeter group placed considerable emphasis on a friendly, informal atmosphere. They sang songs, joked, talked, and relaxed completely, rather than sitting in tense silence waiting for something to happen. This attitude makes strict controls far harder to enforce, but it also seems to be more successful in bringing about results. For that is how "Philip" came into existence—though *existence* is hardly the right word.

In the early 1970s members of the Toronto Society for Psychical Research began to try to "create a ghost" (191). Their belief was that the phenomena of a seance were not spiritualistic, but psychokinetic in nature. Accordingly, they invented a character, Philip, agreed on a fairly detailed life history for him, made sure that it was fictional, and proceeded to meditate together regularly, hoping that Philip would manifest. At first they failed. Then in 1973 they began to consider Batcheldor's experience. They relaxed, sang songs, told jokes, and were quickly rewarded by raps, which started as "the 'feeling' of raps" and swiftly grew louder (190). Before long Philip was communicating merrily, giving one rap for Yes and two for No, beating time to songs, and generally acting just like the rather roistering knight he was supposed to have been. Later the table around which they sat began to move. Again, a "cheating pump primer" is sometimes used by the group, and controls against fraud are not rigid. However, the table has been known to flip right over on occasion, even under the bright lights of a television studio (188).

At one time the group visited Cleveland, Ohio, and there a heavy table with squeaky castors moved without squeaking. They also experimented with metal, slinging a steel plate from the ceiling and obtaining from it "a curious 'pinging' sound which *cannot be duplicated by actual knocking*—it is more like the noise that hot metal makes when cooling rapidly" (189). The Whitton work on the "acoustic envelopes" of raps mentioned earlier also stands in their favor.

The Toronto people occasionally get letters saying that they are dealing with a mischievous spirit that is pretending to be the Philip they created. While this possibility cannot be completely ruled out, those involved feel fairly strongly that they are dealing with psychokinetic events. They point out that when *they* are uncertain of the answers to questions, the raps are hesitant. In addition, during a test at Kent State University they were asked to guess which of ten numbered containers held a steel ball; the other nine held marbles. Their guesses were inaccurate in the extreme, but the numbered box selected (in writing) by the *majority* of the group would also be the one "chosen" by Philip, regardless of the location of the steel ball. In other words, it seems likely that Philip's answers were from the minds of the sitters.

(It should be remembered that those "four medical men" of 1853 noticed that the table did not move when half the sitters expected it to move one way and half the other. Their conclusion that the sitters were responsible for the movement was probably correct. However, they thought only of physical pressure as being the cause of table movement. It seems possible that it was psychokinetic, not physical, pressures that canceled each other out and left the table motionless.)

These experiments show very clearly why many parapsychologists do not care to get involved in survival research. They feel that ESP and PK between them provide alternative explanations to the survival hypothesis, and that, therefore, though survival may well be a fact, it is not a fact that can be proved according to scientific criteria. Others, such as W. G. Roll and Gerald F. Solfvin at the Psychical Research Foundation, are more optimistic and persist in their search, but they look mainly in directions other than physical mediumship (309).

If more great physical mediums were available today, perhaps the general attitude would change. It seems probable, however, that belief is a major requirement for good PK effects. We saw how often PK blossomed only after people had seen Geller or Kulagina perform. The Toronto group found their phenomena fading fast after one member remarked to Philip that the group could get rid of him quite easily; they had to work on restoring their "belief" in the group's abilities. Today fewer people believe in spirits, so there are unlikely to be many great mediums. Geller believes in extraterrestrial beings and achieves the same ends. Perhaps if he believed in spirits, he would be called a medium. Perhaps it is not true that there are no great mediums. Maybe the early chapter on superstars was really about great mediums and actually only the semantics are different.

What would poor Eusapia Palladino have thought about being called an "applied parapsychology specialist"?

Chapter 9

Poltergeists: Noisy Spirits or Angry PK?

Poltergeist phenomena may not represent odd exceptions to the laws of nature but lawful processes which have so far escaped our attention. If poltergeist phenomena say anything, I suspect that this is not about spirits, demons, or ghosts but about human personality.

William G. Roll (255)

PK may be beneficial in healing, or even in providing "proof" of survival to the bereaved, but when it appears as poltergeist activity it presents nothing but problems.

For example, in February 1958 a family in Seaford, Long Island, was plagued with poltergeist disturbances. All over the house screw lids were popping off bottles and the contents were spilling, objects were moving around, and furniture was falling over. Later several figurines flew through the air, crashing against furniture. This happened again and again, until they were broken. Other objects, too, were seen to move when no one could have moved them. Police, parapsychologists, the Long Island Lighting Company, the fire department, the building department, RCA, and an assortment of engineers all investigated the house while the phenomena continued, but no "normal" explanation could be found. W. G. Roll, who was involved in the investigation (255), decided that the thirteen-year-old son of the family was the poltergeist agent, or center of the activities, but this did not mean that he accused the boy of trickery. A number of events had taken place that the boy could not have caused by normal means. Eventually, after about five weeks, the events stopped as mysteriously as they had begun.

It used to be that we would speak of a *poltergeist* as the cause of such events. The word comes from the German for noisy or boisterous spirit, and one can easily see why it was so named. More recently, however, parapsychologists have come to the conclusion that poltergeist effects are not the result of a prankish or insane ghost charging around the house trying to upset people. They have observed that one person is usually at the center of such events, and after close observation of a number of cases, most researchers have come to believe that poltergeist phenomena are caused by PK on the part of a living individual.

This is not to say that the poltergeist agent is deliberately or consciously causing the chaos around him. Indeed, he is often as disturbed and frightened as the rest of the family. The PK seems to be operating at the unconscious level, to the total bewilderment of all concerned. Because the word *poltergeist* has ghostly connotations, many researchers now prefer the term *recurring spontaneous psychokinesis,* usually abbreviated to RSPK.

A French police officer, Emile Tizané, has analyzed hundreds of poltergeist cases occurring between 1925 and 1950 and categorized the various types of phenomena as follows:

A. Bombardment. Often a house becomes the object of a real hail of projectiles. Stones fall on the roof, break panes, and penetrate through openings. Phenomena rarely occur in the interior of the house once outside bombardment from the exterior begins.

B. Bangs against the doors, the walls, or the furniture are heard, sometimes at the same place and sometimes in all parts of the house.

C. Doors, windows, and even securely closed cupboards open by themselves.

D. Objects are skillfully dislocated or thrown. Fragile ones are often unbroken, even after a jump of several feet, while solid ones are sometimes completely destroyed.

E. Bizarre cracks and noises are sometimes observed.

F. Displaced objects sometimes do not show a "regular" trajectory. They behave as if they had been transported and may even follow the contours of furniture.

G. In some rare instances, foreign objects penetrate into a closed space.

H. When handled by observers, the objects give a sensation of being warm.

I. Objects seem to form themselves in the air. (314)

One well-observed set of RSPK events was the Saucie case. (Poltergeist cases are usually named for the community in which they occur, though occasionally for the name of the family involved.) Saucie is a Scottish village in which eleven-year-old Virginia Campbell was staying with her brother and sister-in-law. The first strange event was a series of thumping noises, which started November 22, 1960. The noises seemed to follow Virginia around and stopped when she was asleep. The family called in their minister, an apparently careful and skeptical observer, but, though he watched Virginia closely, he could not see that she was in any way causing the sounds. Later he saw a heavy linen chest float, slightly off the ground, for a distance of about eighteen inches and then float back to its original place. The following night the family doctor also saw the chest move. Though the noises stopped when Virginia slept, the movement of objects continued. The doctor and a colleague saw her pillow rotate while her sleeping head rested on it, and the pillow also "rippled" in a peculiar motion which could not later be reproduced by the observers. At school, Virginia was noticed by the teacher to be desperately trying to hold down the lid of her desk, while the lid rose and fell three times. Another desk, luckily empty, floated out of place as the teacher watched. Such disturbances continued until December 2 and then stopped. Fortunately, both family and school, including her classmates, kindly downplayed these events and did not hold Virginia in any way responsible for them (185).

In 1965 a fifteen-year-old boy, Heiner S., was working in a store in Bremen, Germany. Unhappy at home, he had been forced into an unhappy apprenticeship. At first he vented his displeasure by breaking a large number of empty bottles which he was assigned to collect. He was given a lengthy psychological examination, which Dr. John Mischo, in a paper read at the 1968 conference of the Parapsychological Association, described as "traumatic" (167). After this Heiner seems to have stopped deliberate destructiveness, but apparently the impulse could not be contained. Throughout the china section in which he worked, objects were said to leap to the floor whenever Heiner was on the premises. A police investigation discovered no physical cause for the damage, and during a stay in a psychiatric clinic Heiner continued to be the center of mysteriously moving objects. In a new job, as apprentice to an electrician, his talents turned to loosening screws. The foreman discovered that screws newly inserted in concrete were almost immediately loosened. Accused of deliberate mischief, Heiner stood about three feet from the wall while witnesses watched two screws that had just been inserted and checked for tightness. Both were loose within two minutes (14).

Other poltergeist cases have included lights, sometimes in swift flashes, sometimes holding quite steady and warming the surface on which they shone, and the inexplicable ringing of bells.

Poltergeist cases are not new. However, in earlier, more superstitious times, only the most analytical of minds thought of conducting any investigation of them. For the most part, a house in which objects and furniture flew around unaided was considered to be haunted, possessed, or bewitched. All three explanations seemed perfectly logical, so there was no need for further inquiry. In societies so inclined one might start looking for a handy witch to be held responsible and burned, but that was as far as most investigations went.

(Lest we feel too smug in our modern enlightenment, it should be remembered that when a poltergeist case was reported in Bridgeport, Connecticut, at the end of 1974, three people tried to burn down the house involved because they believed that this was the only way to destroy the evil forces involved.)

Toward the end of the last century, more exact observations began to be made when poltergeist phenomena occurred. A report in the *Atlantic Monthly* told of an eighteen-year-old servant girl, recently off the boat from Ireland, who was pursued by ringing bells, raps, and flying kitchen utensils. Witnesses took careful note of what she was doing at the times of the events, and whether her hands were occupied at the time. (In 1868, when the events occurred, a servant's hands usually were occupied!) The wires were detached from the ringing bells, but they continued to ring. A journal was kept to discover whether the phenomena were affected by the weather, and the girl's bed was mounted on glass to insulate it. This last did stop the nocturnal raps, which started again when the glass was removed. The observers concluded that the force responsible for the events must be electrical in nature. However, in

1911 W. F. Barrett suggested that the cessation might have been the result of suggestion rather than insulation (7).

Another fairly old but carefully observed case occurred in Vienna in 1906 in a blacksmith's shop. Here, in addition to the blacksmith, were two apprentices, aged fifteen and eighteen. One notable fact in most poltergeist cases is that, although objects may fly through the air at great speed, and sometimes strike surfaces with such force as to be completely shattered, people are not hurt. The Vienna blacksmith case is one of the exceptions.

When Mr. A. Wärndorfer, a member of the Society for Psychical Research who investigated the case, arrived at the shop, the smith was wearing a stiff hat for protection, and he displayed a lump on the back of his head that had been caused by a flying piece of iron. An apprentice had been struck on the face and later, as Wärndorfer watched the two boys working on a piece of iron, "their hands and evidently their attention being fully occupied," the younger one was struck quite hard on the temple by a metal measuring instrument. The blow drew blood.

One of the boys was later alleged to have confessed to causing the disturbances by trickery, but to Wärndorfer he denied having made such a confession. In addition to the many objects reported by others to have moved, Wärndorfer says that he personally saw "between sixty and seventy objects flying, or rather arriving" in ten or twelve visits, with, "on the 'best' day twenty-three objects flying about in less than half an hour." Because of the nature of the place, many of the moving items were pieces of metal and tools—in fact, at one point the tool boxes were moved outside the shop for safety. The smith's smoking pipes were also favorite objects, however, and so many were broken that he gave up smoking at work. Wärndorfer also described the movement of a painting of the Virgin Mary:

I saw . . . after a few minutes the picture *fluttering* to the middle of the shop. . . . It did not *fall*, but behaved rather like a sheet of paper; it did not break on the floor.

Both boys were eventually dismissed, whereupon the phenomena stopped (329).

All this is hard to believe. That objects should not only fly through the air propelled by no apparent force, but move in impossible trajectories, sometimes zigzagging as they go, sometimes turning corners, sometimes approaching something at high speed and then dropping gently to the ground just before contact—the whole thing is impossible, and there has to be a normal explanation for each and every case. So one would think.

Such a thinker was Frank Podmore, whom we met in the last chapter. Podmore regarded poltergeist cases as the result of mischief on the part of "tricky little girls or boys," combined with hallucination and imagination. In a survey of well-known cases, he dismissed out of hand all that did not include dates—because, he said, this omission indicated that contemporary notes were not taken, and the reporter's memory might have been at fault if he had not written the account at the time of the events. Podmore also dismissed all second- or third-hand reports that contained any information not contained in the first-hand reports. Thus, if a member of the family involved wrote only a brief account of a disturbance, but in conversation gave far more information to a literary-minded friend, who then wrote a fuller account, the extra details in the second-hand account were dismissed by Podmore as embellishment (201).

No doubt Podmore's criticisms have been very helpful in guiding contemporary researchers as to what *not* to do when reporting cases of RSPK, but overskepticism can indicate as much bias and lack of acceptance of reality as can overcredulity. It is interesting to speculate on how Podmore would have reacted to the more recent, carefully observed cases discussed in this chapter.

A modern explanation for RSPK is that the phenomena may indeed occur, but are often due to a combination of tidal movement, weather conditions, and local geology. This theory maintains that tidal pressures may travel inland, affecting the water table, underground streams, and fissures. This in turn would cause houses built in affected areas to shift as the tide changes. Movement might not always be smooth, but jerky, causing objects to fly off shelves, doors to swing open, and furniture to move (145).

This may be a logical explanation for some events. However, a number of quite evidential cases, including the Vienna disturbances and the Rosenheim case, have occurred many miles from tidal waters. Experiments have shown that the rise and fall of the tides affect water levels for little farther than three miles from the sea. Calculations by other researchers have shown that the kind of force required to explain many of the phenomena reported could not possibly come from such minor geophysical events (53).

More recent investigations have found poltergeist events clustering during hours when the subject is both awake and at home, and, in a few instances, such as the Saucie case reported by A. R. G. Owen, occurring in more than one place depending on the location of the subject. Since tidal rhythms change slightly every day but are always in the same location, the tidal explanation is therefore hardly sufficient to dismiss all poltergeist events.

It is true that physical causes must be ruled out before we can propose a paranormal explanation. For this reason, local utility companies are frequently called in to investigate disturbances. Maps and plans may be consulted to discover underground streams. Gas and water pipes are checked. Electrical faults may be sought, particularly when the phenomena include light flashes or ringing bells. In some cases, the most sophisticated detecting apparatus can find no physical cause for poltergeist events, even while it records the fact that the events really are happening.

In 1967 a law office in Rosenheim, Germany (mentioned also in Chapter 4), was hit (almost literally) by an outbreak of poltergeist phenomena that seemed to center around a nineteen-year-old employee, Annemarie. The local police made an extensive investigation, but could find no deception. The main effects in this case were electrical: lights would sway, fixtures were unscrewed, bulbs would explode when Annemarie was near. Pictures moved and, in some cases, rotated 360 degrees around their hooks. Phone bills climbed, though no additional calls were being made. Testing equipment was installed and showed that "the time announcement number (0119) was often dialed four or five times a minute. On some days this number was dialed forty to fifty times in a row." At one point, four nine-digit numbers were dialed at a time when no one was touching the phones.

Comments Hans Bender, one of the world's foremost authorities on RSPK:

> The PK required to do this would involve a mechanical influence applied to certain springs at certain time intervals, which would require an intelligence that had an exact technical knowledge and was able to estimate intervals in the range of milliseconds. (13)

One difficulty with using electrical measuring devices in these cases is that the equipment itself is automatically no longer reliable. If PK phenomena are real, then the dials of the equipment may as well be moved by PK as by genuine electrical surges from within the wiring system. It is possible that this happened in Rosenheim, for it is reported that the investigating electrical engineer sometimes recorded deflections of "up to fifty amps on a voltage amplifier" at times when the events were happening. Such surges, had they really gone through the wiring of the building, should have blown the fuses, yet the fuses remained intact (139).

While some scientists are searching for a normal, physical cause for a poltergeist outbreak, others look for a cause of another kind—trickery.

In every case quoted so far, adolescents have been present. Although this is not a universal constant, a poltergeist case without an adolescent is fairly rare. While the scientist knows that *any* situation appearing to involve the paranormal must be examined with the utmost care, members of the lay public are doubly quick to charge fraud when a youngster is involved, particularly when he or she seems to be in the center of the trouble. Police investigators often take the same tack. Unfortunately some family members may take the opposite position and be too gullible, assuming that no one in the family would play such tricks. When the parapsychologist arrives on the scene, he must be able to sift the chaff from the grain in all the stories he is told and endeavor to gain the confidence of family members while remaining objective and alert for clues.

It is important to know where all family members are at all times and at what times they move from one room to another. Most researchers decide fairly quickly who is the apparent agent in the case and try to keep that person under fairly constant observation. At the same time, objects must be examined for threads or other devices with which they might be moved from afar, and noises must be investigated promptly. If it is possible to install recording equipment, particularly a videorecorder or closed-circuit TV, this may be of tremendous help, but unfortunately it is seldom possible.

Suppose that an army of engineers has discovered no physical cause for a disturbance, and careful scrutiny by investigators, police, reporters, and others has turned up no trickery. Perhaps, indeed, certain events have occurred when they all feel certain that trickery *could not* have been the cause. What then? Suppose they accept the fact that objects are being moved by means not presently known to be physical, then what *do* they think happens?

In the list of phenomena at the beginning of this chapter, the penetration of a closed space by foreign objects and the apparent formation of objects in the air were mentioned. A survey by Roll of 116 major cases since the seventeenth century found such events occurring in 18 (16 percent), including 5 since 1950 (256). Obviously such phenomena closely resemble the teleports and apports discussed briefly in the last chapter. Because of this, and because physical mediumship is believed by many people to involve movement of objects "by the spirits," it is easy for those in the spiritist tradition to claim that poltergeist phenomena are indeed caused by mischievous or angry spirits. However, we have already seen that not all physical mediumship seems to be brought about by spirits, but that some effects may be due to PK.

Roll found that in 92 (79 percent) of the 116 cases he examined one person (or, rarely, two) was clearly associated with the phenomena, strong evidence for living persons as poltergeist agents. Some of the remaining 21 percent may not have been reported as being associated with specific individuals only because, as we have mentioned, early observers were little interested in scientific observation. However, some cases do not *seem* to fit into the RSPK model.

Although most parapsychologists now look first for PK by a living person as an explanation for poltergeist cases, the discarnate entity hypothesis is not totally dismissed by all of them.

Dr. Ian Stevenson, head of the Division of Parapsychology at the University of Virginia School of Medicine, has suggested that those who do dismiss the spirit hypothesis entirely may be premature. He has devised a table showing differences he would expect between phenomena caused by PK from a living person and phenomena caused by spirits, saying that it should be possible to divide poltergeist cases into the two categories by analysis of the types of events occurring in them (295). However, many well-known cases include events from both categories.

Stevenson feels, for example, that a living agent would cause objects to have simple trajectories and to land with some force, whereas discarnate intervention would be responsible for more complicated trajectories and for objects to land gently. Yet in the Vienna blacksmith case both types of trajectory and landing were reported.

A fact that speaks against discarnate involvement is that although exorcisms and similar rituals were used in 30 (26 percent) of the cases covered in Roll's survey, the phenomena ceased just afterward in only 4 of these. Nor can we rule out a possible psychological effect on the poltergeist agents in the 4 cases in which exorcism was successful.

One recently reported case seems to have involved both poltergeist-type activity and events that might be described as a "haunting." Investigation after the fairly typical poltergeist outbreak showed that events had also occurred in parts of the building not occupied by the poltergeist family, and occurrences continued to bother subsequent tenants after the family had moved. They started not long after the death of a man who had openly stated his desire to "come back and haunt" the grandmother in the poltergeist family, with whom he had had a continuing feud (156, 279).

One cannot help suspecting discarnate involvement when poltergeist activity does not seem to depend on the presence of any one individual. Such a case was investigated by Roll in Indianapolis. Movement of objects sometimes occurred in the presence of the mother only, sometimes when just the grandmother was in the house, and sometimes when both were around. Whether, as the family suspected, a discarnate spirit was harassing them, or whether both the adults were poltergeist agents independently, is still a matter for conjecture. The case is also unusual in that both women (between whom there was considerable tension) suffered "bites" or skin punctures that they claimed were not self-inflicted (254). Such cases are rare.

Another series of disturbances that might be said to indicate spirit intervention is quoted by Camille Flammarion in his book *Haunted Houses*. Though it is old, we are told by Flammarion that the case was "scrupulously studied" by F. W. H. Myers and Mrs. Sidgwick of the SPR, and anything that bore scrutiny by that pair of inquiring minds may be accepted as fairly well authenticated.

In Swanland, near Hull, in England, a carpenter's shop in which three apprentices were working became plagued with flying pieces of wood. The original account was given by a Mr. Bristow, who was working in the shop at the time. He tells us that the disturbances continued for six weeks, with pieces of wood following strange trajectories and at times displaying apparent intelligence: ". . . it is remarkable that in spite of innumerable attempts we could never catch a piece in movement, for it cleverly eluded all our strategies. They seemed animated and intelligent."

Bristow adds that the disturbances did not seem to be connected with any one individual:

> . . . the three of us, who were present the first day of the manifestations, worked repeatedly and alternately outside during the period that they took place, and more than once we were all absent. It was the same in the case of the other workmen, who were all absent successively during the six weeks' haunting. In spite of that the phenomena never ceased.

When they did cease, it was under strange circumstances. Sometime before the disturbances began an apprentice in the shop had died of tuberculosis. His uncle, a co-owner of the shop, was rumored to have failed to pay off some debts of his brother, the boy's father, also recently deceased. This man became very upset at the disturbances. Then, Bristow tells us, "One day we heard that he had paid his brother's creditors: the manifestations *stopped immediately*" (92).

The explanation that comes immediately to mind is that the spirit of the dead apprentice had returned to raise a ruckus until his uncle paid off the family debt. However, Bristow's last sentence reports that the manifestations stopped not when creditors were paid, but when the carpenters *heard* that they had been paid. Surely a spirit would have known immediately that the debt was paid and would have stopped his temper tantrums forthwith. We can wonder, therefore, whether this was indeed a discarnate poltergeist or whether perhaps the anger over the unpaid debt might have been that of the apprentices and other workers, who felt that their former fellow employee had been posthumously betrayed. Though we cannot rule out discarnate intervention, it does seem possible that the disturbances may have emanated from the living carpenters rather than from the discarnate one. The PK activity of one apprentice may have triggered a similar latent ability in others, just as Geller is said to trigger spoon- and key-bending in others, enabling the disturbances to keep going even when whoever originated the events was absent. (Alternatively, it may be that the linger effect can explain RSPK events in the absence of the poltergeist agent.)

Certainly the workers had a reason for feeling angry at one of their employers, and, as apprentices in those days were often little better off than slaves, it is probable that they were unable to express their resentment openly. In fact, one of the keys to most poltergeist disturbances seems to be the presence of someone who, because of either circumstances or personality, cannot give vent to his anger and resentment in a normal manner.

Normally, when having such feelings, we have a strong desire to throw things, punch things, or in some other physical way act out our emotions. Society tell us that we may not do this, and most of us do not. However, it is as though the poltergeist agent cannot stop himself. If he cannot throw things normally then he will unconsciously throw them paranormally.

When commenting on the psychological makeup of a poltergeist agent involved in one of the cases studied by Roll, Dr. Gertrude Schmeidler, professor of psychology at City College of New York and a past president of the Parapsychological Association, wrote:

> The best working hypothesis seems to be that poltergeist phenomena come when there is strong unconscious hostility with a brittle pattern of outward good behavior. Violent resentment is ordinarily held down under, but sometimes involuntarily explodes. The personality associated with this should then show unstable repression, a shifting balance between hateful forces struggling for expression and virtuous,

hampering control. The violence should seem spontaneous and depersonalized, as if the person were innocent of it. (263)

The phenomena often begin at about the onset of puberty in the agent, and not infrequently a traumatic change has occurred fairly recently in the adolescent's life. It is also interesting to note that many poltergeist agents are living with adults other than their biological parents at the time of the disturbances.

Virginia Campbell of the Saucie case, for example, had lived most of her eleven years on an isolated farm run by her elderly parents in Ireland. Shortly before the poltergeist events started, she had been sent to live with an adult brother and his wife in Scotland. Her mother went to work in another town, and her father stayed in Ireland to sell the farm. One can imagine that the changes in location, culture, and family all at the same time must have been very upsetting for the child.

In the Bremen case, Heiner, an illegitimate child, had been rejected by his mother; his grandmother grew too feeble to look after him, and he was forced into an apprenticeship he hated. We are also told of the lengthy and traumatic psychological examination that seems to have triggered the poltergeist outbreak as it stemmed the normal breakages.

Again, the Irish maidservant in the *Atlantic Monthly* case had only recently come from Ireland into what seems to have been a fairly wealthy and probably cultured American milieu—another traumatic change.

Is a thirteenth birthday traumatic? Perhaps, if a longed-for present is not received, or if heavy emphasis has been placed on the importance of becoming a teenager. W. G. Roll investigated the Newark case, which began on the thirteenth birthday of Arnold, a boy being raised by his grandmother. During intervals when Arnold went to stay with an uncle no RSPK events were observed, but between May and November 1961 sixty-four incidents were noted while he was at home. Most of them occurred during the week following the onset of the disturbances. They included a saltcellar that seems to have turned a corner in flight, numerous movements of glass bottles and an ashtray, and the tipping over of large appliances such as a TV set, radiogramaphone, washing machine, and refrigerator.

Though the boy was later seen trying to fake a paranormal event in the Parapsychology Laboratory at Duke University, a number of the early events were witnessed by neighbors and investigators and do not seem to be explainable by fraud. Psychological testing showed a high degree of repression and denial of emotions in Arnold and considerable stress in his relationship with his grandmother. The phenomena stopped when the Board of Child Welfare placed Arnold in a group home (253).

The Newark case is extraordinarily similar to poltergeist events that were reported in 1909 involving Elwin, an eleven-year-old boy also living with his grandparents. Over twenty "credible and disinterested" witnesses testified that the occurrences were due to "some unseen inexplicable agency." A picture that would have had to be lifted to come off its hook slid slowly to the floor without breaking; knives and forks rose up from the draining board and dropped to the floor; furniture was overturned; and food moved. A Dr. Gilbert took Elwin into his home for study, whereupon the phenomena ceased. While there this boy, too, was seen to fake the movement of some objects, causing the doctor to conclude, against the evidence of the twenty witnesses, that Elwin had caused all the disturbances by trickery.

Commenting on this type of situation, W. F. Barrett, a renowned and astute parapsychologist of his time, remarked:

> If, upon the cessation of the disturbances, investigators appear on the scene and ask for something to occur in their presence, and are sufficiently persistent and incredulous, they may possibly see a clumsy attempt to reproduce some of the phenomena, and will thereupon catch the culprit child in the act. Then we hear the customary "I told you so," and forthwith the clever investigator will not fail to let the world know of his acumen, and how credulous and stupid everybody is but himself. (6)

Given an adolescent who has suddenly become the center of attention from reporters, investigators, and particularly family members who, he may feel, do not usually pay enough attention to him, such attempts to keep the disturbances going by fraud are, though regrettable, not hard to understand. When they are detected, however, it does make doubly difficult the task of the investigator who must decide which of the earlier events may have been caused by fraud and which, if any, could only have been genuine.

One of the best investigated and witnessed poltergeist cases on record is the Miami case. The locale was a warehouse containing novelties and souvenirs—ashtrays, ornaments, mugs, and so on— and in January 1966 an unusual number of breakages began to appear. Because the warehouse was a large, fairly open structure, and disturbances seemed to take place only during working hours, close observation was much simpler than in most poltergeist cases. The investigators, J. G. Pratt of the University of Virginia and W. G. Roll, were called in quite promptly and received cooperation from warehouse employees, police, and press, so they were able to set up carefully controlled conditions.

A total of 224 incidents were reported, all occurring in the presence of Julio, a nineteen-year-old Cuban refugee who harbored considerable resentment against one of the company owners. In all, at least twenty objects moved in the presence of investigators when no one else was near the object involved. Sometimes whole boxes of items would fall from their positions in spite of the fact that vigorous shaking of the sturdy shelves left everything firmly in position. An ashtray positioned behind a cowbell fell to the floor while the bell remained in place. Everyone present was within Roll's view, and the ashtray would have to have moved around or over the bell to have fallen as it did. Some types of items and specific locations seemed to become favorite targets. When they discovered this, the investigators replaced fallen objects with similar items, which they endeavored to keep under observation and checked regularly for threads or other evidence of trickery. One such object was a spoondrip tray that had been placed, under Pratt's supervision, about ten inches back from the edge of the shelf after another had fallen from the same place. It was checked several times by both investigators, and about four hours later it, too, fell and broke. Julio was in plain sight at the time, separated from the tray by a tier of double shelves. No one else was anywhere near the tray.

A professional magician visited the warehouse but was quite unable to explain how the objects, particularly fairly large boxes, could have been moved by fraud. The case came to a close when Julio was dismissed from his job (259).

Based on this and other cases he has studied, Roll and his colleagues have conducted a series of complex analyses. In addition to checking the types of objects moved and the timing of the events, they have examined the actual trajectories of the objects from various viewpoints and made some interesting discoveries.

If an object has been moved once, as mentioned in the Miami case, it or its facsimile is more likely to move again than another object that has not been moved. If something is replaced immediately after it has been moved it will often move again at once, as though some energy were still attached to the object, via the focus effect, or to the area, via the linger effect (135).

If the agent is taken to be the physical center of the events, and a diagram of all object movements relative to his position is made, it is apparent that most of the movements are in a clockwise or counter-clockwise direction, rather than directly toward or away from the subject, suggesting a rotating energy (254, 257, 258). Roll suggests that many attributes of RSPK phenomena might be explained if they were caused by two nonsynchronous sources of energy within the body. These would cause what is described as a rotating beam of energy, which fits the facts noted in these studies of object movements (256).

Many events occur near the poltergeist agent, and as the distance from him increases the number of events attenuates. Roll has found that this decrease best fits the mathematical model known as the exponential decay function. This model is usually associated with changes from one form of physical energy to another—for example, a transformation from light in one medium to heat in another—and so may provide a clue as to how poltergeist phenomena occur, and perhaps what happens in PK in general.

A slightly different form of poltergeist case from those mentioned above is that in which stones and other missiles are apparently thrown from outside a building. In some cases they smash windows; in others they seem to enter the building in the absence of any opening for them to enter; and in others they just *appear* in a room, as though thrown from outside, but no source can be found. Sometimes stone-throwing is the only disturbance that occurs, and sometimes it is just one phase of an outbreak that includes other forms of poltergeist activity.

Such a case occurred in the family of Mr. J. Bisschof, a senior official of the Dutch government in Java, in 1893, and was witnessed by several apparently reliable witnesses.

The disturbances started with stones that seemed to be thrown from outside and continued with objects falling from shelves and tables inside the house. Called to investigate, the family doctor invited the son and daughter of the family to spend the night at his house. When they arrived, five stones that the doctor had previously marked and hidden flew "across the room and through the windowpane." That evening "thirteen windowpanes were smashed, a toilet-set, a washbasin, a chamberpot, and various articles of lesser value were broken. Inkstands and heavy paperweights made of lead were hurled through the windows, returning to the room after a time, one phenomena being more unbelievable than the other."

Later the twelve-year-old girl, Betsy, became the target for an assortment of annoying and sometimes revolting substances that were smeared across her face. Seeking relief, she spent a night at a neighbor's house, where she was repeatedly soaked with water from an unknown source. That night, while she was asleep, a champagne cup and a box of pills that had been *locked* in two separate places appeared in her bed. (This, of course, was not witnessed by Bisschof himself.)

The disturbances began while the boy's mattress was being repaired and he and his sister, as a result, had had to share a bed. It has been suggested that the tension leading to the RSPK might have been caused by sexual exploration. Resulting guilt feelings might account for the increasingly unpleasant forms of humiliation suffered by Betsy, who may have been unconsciously attempting to punish herself (343).

In a 1970 symposium on "The Future of the Poltergeist," A. R. G. Owen, author of *Can We Explain the Poltergeist?* opined that poltergeist activity represents an unusual form of nervous tension release (185). Because it is a release it is self-limiting, just as steam escaping from a kettle under pressure soon lowers the pressure enough to stop the forceful escape. Owen also feels that the tendency for poltergeist agents to be within a few years of puberty (nine to twenty years seems to be the usual range) points to a biological basis for RSPK.

Dr. Joel L. Whitton has suggested that a poltergeist agent may be unconsciously recreating stressful situations from infancy. A baby hears noises around him, sees things move, appear, and disappear, without having any understanding of what is causing these events, so they may sometimes come to be associated with fear or other stress. When, as a near adult, he is under stress, he may unconsciously use PK to recreate the effects he associated with that kind of stress as an infant (338).

This theory is somewhat supported by the large number of cases that involve bottles, food, and eating utensils, all of which might relate to the powerful oral needs of infants. In the Miami case, for example, of sixty-one objects named in the report by Roll and Pratt, thirty-six were connected with drink (mugs, glasses, and pop bottles), and ten incidents involved ashtrays. Objects connected with smoking may represent oral needs, *or,* if the resented authority figure smokes, they may represent that person. The Vienna blacksmith, for example, was forced to stop smoking in the shop because so many of his pipes were broken.

A connection between poltergeist events and eruptions in the central nervous system (CNS) has been suggested (256). One form of such eruption is epilepsy. In a study of one poltergeist agent who was also an epileptic, Gerald Solfvin and Roll remarked, "In many respects, the classic poltergeist agent begins to look like an ideopathic epileptic whose massive brain discharges are somehow transformed into RSPK" (280). Many parallels have been noted between epilepsy and RSPK. Epileptic discharges may occur in more than one part of the brain, and frequently are not synchronous. As mentioned earlier, it has been suggested that the pattern of object movements could be explained if "energy waves are radiated from two positions on the agent's body and if they were nonsynchronous" (256).

Epileptic outbreaks can be detected by EEG measurements, but so far attempts to measure the EEGs of the apparent poltergeist agents during poltergeist outbreaks have been made in only two cases. In neither case did any RSPK events occur while the apparatus was in use.

Recently, two more RSPK cases have been reported in which the agents had histories of epilepsy or "fits." Roll and his staff are attempting to investigate further, making use of portable EEG equipment.

It has also been suggested that poltergeist agents, as a group, have a high tendency to hysteria (186), an element of personality that they may hold in common with many mediums. In fact, it seems that poltergeist phenomena may sometimes accompany the development of mediumship or other forms of psychic sensitivity. We saw that D. D. Home's family was disturbed by rappings and movements of furniture just before his mediumship developed, although he had had a few isolated psychic experiences previously.

The development of the teenage Fox sisters as mediums was also preceded by raps that were amenable to a code with which they answered questions. In such cases not all answers are accurate, but some are not only correct but seem to be telepathic. In 1877 W. F. Barrett investigated a poltergeist-disturbed home in Derrygonnelly, Ireland. He reported:

> I mentally asked it, no word being spoken, to knock a certain number of times and it did so. To avoid any error or delusion on my part, I put my hands in the side pockets of my overcoat and asked it to knock the number of fingers I had open. It correctly did so.

Barrett repeated this experiment four times, obtaining a correct reply each time (6). Whether a living person or a discarnate entity was responsible for such raps, he, she, or it would have to have used ESP to know Barrett's questions and the answers, as well as PK to cause the raps.

In his book *The Link* (153) Matthew Manning tells of major poltergeist events that plagued him, his family, and his fellow students at boarding school before he developed his claimed ability to bend metal, though, as we saw in Chapter 5, this ability does not seem to have endured.

Manning is an exception in that his poltergeist events seem to have continued for a considerable period. Most poltergeist outbreaks last for from five to eight weeks. (The Cure d'Ars was another exception. His RSPK lasted for thirty years, according to contemporary accounts.)

If poltergeist events are indeed a way of releasing nervous tension, it is logical that they should die out as the tension is released. They may also fade because the events themselves lead to changes in family attitudes, sometimes even to a change of residence—either for the agent himself, who may be sent to stay with relatives, or for the whole family. Thus the situation that gave rise to the stress may change. Alternatively, the family problem may be solved in the normal course of events, as usually happens in nonpoltergeist families. If this tension release does not occur, and if there is indeed a connection between epilepsy and RSPK, then treatment for epilepsy, particularly new forms of relaxation training, may also be helpful in ending poltergeist outbreaks (280).

Though the researcher may regret the passing of an opportunity to investigate a fascinating phenomenon, the other individuals involved are usually only too happy to see the end of it and to return to their normal routines undisturbed by flying furniture or mysterious noises.

Chapter 10

Modern Media and PK

Thoughtographs raise questions about the external world and the mind's relationship to it in perhaps a more insistent way than many other data of psychic research.

Jule Eisenbud (83)

One feature frequently claimed in early physical mediumship and habitually disdained by skeptics was so-called "spirit photography." Typically, a photograph of one or more people, or even of an empty room, would be taken, and the resulting negative would show an additional vague figure or face somewhere in the background. In the early 1860s, when the first spirit photographs appeared, families were large and lives were short, so someone could always claim that the image resembled a deceased relative or friend. Sometimes, in fact, eager folk claimed to recognize apparently identical oval blurs as the faces of fathers, mothers, and infants alike, according to who they most wished to see. Word would spread; others would flock to the studio of the photographer/medium; and, of course, his profits would increase greatly.

In those days, photographers used glass plates and long exposures and had plenty of opportunity for deliberate or accidental fraud, as doubters soon pointed out. At the simplest level, a gauze-wrapped confederate might sneak into the room and stand unnoticed behind the official subjects of the photo as they all "watched the birdie." Double exposures could also be used, though unless done with great skill these were wont to leave the pattern of the carpet or furniture showing through the subjects' suddenly transparent legs or skirts. Another device was to insert a plate that had been tampered with between the photographic plate and the lens. The introduction of unorthodox or unevenly mixed chemicals during the processing could also produce apparently paranormal effects, and, as each new fraud was publicized, ambitious photographer/mediums seemed to stretch their ingenuity to ever greater heights in order to evade detection. The fad began to fade in the mid-1870s, and, for many years, spirit photography was the subject of great contempt. Nonetheless, some effects that were achieved remain difficult to explain.

A photographer named Beattie, who had been active in exposing (!) spurious spirit photographers, found an assortment of blurs and shapes that he could not explain on some of the photographic plates with which he was experimenting. Few people paid much attention because, although "a few [bore] a remote resemblance to the human figure . . . the majority [were] shapeless and unrecognizable" (204). Those who were interested only in spirit photography easily explained away Beattie's plates as being the result of light inadvertently admitted during processing. However, when one considers that the photographic process may be affected by PK from the mind of the living, rather than by spirit intervention, it is no longer essential that the images obtained resemble the human face or figure in order to be acknowledged as paranormal. The light in the darkroom explanation remains a possibility, but Beattie seems to have been an experienced photographer who did not obtain such results except when conducting certain experiments. In addition, he had earlier been committed to the theory that spirit photography could not exist, and his sudden change of attitude seems hard to explain.

Fascination with the psychic photograph continued to wax and wane, and a number of experimenters have worked with it, apparently becoming more and more convinced that many of the paranormal effects were produced by the mind of the medium.

T. Fukurai of Japan was testing a subject for clairvoyance early in this century when he accidentally stumbled on what appeared to be a paranormal effect. His subject had attempted to guess the undeveloped image on a photographic plate, but later it was found that another plate, not involved in the experiment, had become imprinted with something that Fukurai took to be the result of her concentration. He coined the term *thoughtography* and followed this new experimental path, having his subjects attempt to produce Japanese characters on photographic plates that were flanked by other plates. They were, apparently, successful in making the characters appear on the target plate without affecting the plates sandwiching it—even when all were tightly wrapped and enclosed in containers (83, 98).

Fukurai's work was not duplicated, and once again psychic photography became unfashionable until, in the 1960s, word spread that an elevator operator called Ted Serios could produce psychic photographs. Then, in 1967, a book about him, *The World of Ted Serios,* was published (80). The author, Dr. Jule Eisenbud, told an extraordinary tale. Serios, given to heavy drinking and almost completely unreliable in his behavior, could apparently produce images on Polaroid film (so removing the problem of possible dark-room tampering) almost at will. Eisenbud had contacts with many academic, scientific, and professional people who had taken part in sessions during which Serios, liberally primed with alcohol, "did his thing."

His thing, in the main, consisted of getting drunk, concentrating on a camera, and signaling when he wanted the person holding the camera to press the button, or pressing the button himself in the less controlled sessions, in which he was allowed to hold the camera. In addition to the alcohol he often seemed to need a psychological prop that became known as a "gismo." This consisted of a cylinder about two inches long and one inch across, usually made of black paper taken from a Polaroid pack but sometimes made of cardboard or other material. As a rule it was open-ended, but sometimes experimenters would cover the ends with tape. Serios liked to sight through it at the camera lens, feeling that it helped focus his concentration, but it quickly became the focus of bitter controversy.

When the camera button had been pressed, the film was allowed to develop in the usual Polaroid way, and Serios was not allowed to handle either film or camera. Each print was immediately coated, dated, numbered, and signed by an experimenter. Both cameras and film were supplied by Eisenbud or other experimenters, not by

Serios, and Serios was not allowed to handle the film prior to the camera's being loaded. At frequent intervals the experimenters inspected the cameras and took control shots to make sure that both camera and film were operating normally. Distance and shutter settings were securely taped so that they could not be surreptitiously changed during the sessions.

The resulting pictures varied. Sometimes, as one would expect, they showed Serios' face, since the camera pointed toward him when the button was pressed. Others showed totally black or totally white surfaces ("blackies" and "whities"), neither of which would normally be expected and neither of which could always be adequately explained under the circumstances in which they were taken (82). Most extraordinary of all, and the center of the storm of controversy that raged around Serios and Eisenbud for years, were the photos in which images, sometimes blurred, sometimes clear, would appear. Most often the images would be of structures, rarely of people. Sometimes Serios would be shown a picture and asked to reproduce it. At other times, the target picture would be in an envelope in which it had been sealed by the experimenter before he arrived for the session, so that Serios would have to use ESP to discover it. Often the images obtained did not clearly resemble the targets for which Serios had been asked to aim, but at times they did. Even the fact that he could produce any image at all was enough to boggle many a previously boggleproof mind.

Some pictures of recognizable structures showed them from angles, or in combinations that were physically impossible to obtain. Others resembled target pictures in a symbolic way or appeared to have other symbolic connections with subjects that had been discussed at the session or with things that were uppermost in the experimenters' minds *but had not been discussed in front of Serios.*

Once Serios forecast *before* the session that the target to be chosen by a witness would resemble a design of flowers and leaves that he showed Eisenbud. It did not, but the witness did have with him, in addition to the target picture, a painting, part of which closely resembled the design that Serios had forecast. A stylized version of these flowers appeared repeatedly in the paranormal pictures that Serios produced later that day (86).

Serios has also produced images on videotape, which, when transferred to movie film, show that images build up and dissolve, sometimes in as little as one-twelfth of a second, sometimes taking as long as two-and-a-half seconds (81).

In an attempt to discover *how* Serios did what he did, Eisenbud took him to a lead-lined room and had him work on film that had been shipped to Colorado from Berkeley, California, in lead-covered containers. Working from within the lead-lined room, while experimenters outside held cameras up to the lead-impregnated glass window, Serios obtained three apparently paranormal pictures, each on a different roll of film. In one of the three, the "gismo" was being held by the experimenter outside the glass, proving fairly thoroughly that (1) what caused the images was not stopped by lead, and (2) the gismo was not the source of the image (86).

This last point is important, because Serios and Eisenbud have been attacked violently by people who allege that thoughtography is patently impossible, and therefore the images produced must be the result of fraud. It is alleged that Serios somehow introduces an image to the camera via the gismo by sleight of hand, and a number of magicians have stated that they can produce similar results in this way. In Serios' defense, it should be pointed out that he has produced paranormal effects *without* the gismo, and in fact did so for some time at the start of his thoughtographical career before the gismo was introduced to keep his hand away from the camera lens.

It is possible that some "blackies" might have been fraudulently obtained by Serios squeezing the gismo over the lens to cut out all light at the moment the shutter was opened. However, in most experiments each observer was given a specific task, and when the gismo was held by Serios one person was usually assigned to observe it carefully. Again, at times both camera and gismo would be held several feet away from him. Gismos were frequently checked before and after each shot, as were Serios' hands in the better-controlled sessions.

Not only did Eisenbud request help from scientists and magicians alike in making the sessions as fraudproof as possible, but parapsychologists Ian Stevenson and J. G. Pratt invited Serios to visit them at the University of Virginia in Charlottesville for two test sessions (296, 297). The sessions did not go as well as they had hoped. Partway through the first series Serios left abruptly, behavior not uncommon to him, and at the time of the second session he was in a "negative phase" in which he produced few paranormal effects, though there were some of interest.

The difficulties of working with anyone as temperamental as Serios under controlled conditions are extreme. He is a maverick, given to taking off on impulse, unable to work without alcohol, easily discouraged by allegations of trickery. In fact, Stevenson and Pratt felt that just such an allegation had induced a depression during his second visit to them in 1968.

At that time Serios and Eisenbud were becoming embroiled in controversy that has continued intermittently ever since. Their opponent is a magician whose stage name is Randi and who claims that he can do anything that Serios can do, using sleight of hand. Contrary to common belief, most parapsychologists are eager to uncover fraud, and Randi's offer was received with interest. Unfortunately, according to Eisenbud, Randi has never made himself available for such a test *under the same conditions that prevailed during the sessions with Serios.* There is no question that the effects Serios produces *can* be produced by sleight of hand. The important question is whether they can be produced by sleight of hand under those same controlled conditions. And that question has not been answered. Beyond this, allegations and counterallegations have been made as to whether or not Serios did at one time confess in front of Randi that he achieved his results by trickery—a charge that apparently was not made until nearly seven years after the alleged confession.

All in all it seems that the question of Serios' authenticity should be considered without regard to Randi's involvement, and the entire question comes down to whether or not, *at any time* when paranormal photographic effects seem to have been obtained, the conditions were sufficiently controlled to obviate all possibility of fraud. On the one hand are those who believe that human vision, even in the full light used for the Serios sessions, is never good enough to detect skilled sleight of hand reliably. They feel that the jury is still out, or that the whole thing is impossible. On the other hand are those who feel that the fine motor control necessary for skilled sleight of hand is unlikely in the inebriated state in which Serios works best, and that in any event such trickery could not apply in the type of phenomena that Serios produces. In fact, a letter signed by five doctors and a photographer, all of whom had worked with Serios and Eisenbud, states that a magician told them that conjuring techniques could not apply to the Serios work (97). Such witnesses feel that thoughtography either is a fact or at least has been supported by so much evidence that further investigation is well worth the time, trouble, and money involved.

As in the case of so much else relating to PK, the evidence is inconclusive. In the meantime, we can ponder on the fact that Serios,

> . . . over a peak period of a year, produced three dozen pictures at distances [from the camera] ranging from one to over sixty feet. These were observed on twelve separate occasions in nine locations by one or more of a dozen investigators besides [Eisenbud]. Of the pictures produced in this way, moreover, several were target hits. (84)

(Target hits are pictures in which a definite resemblance exists between the photographic image and the target picture the investigators had asked Serios to attempt to reproduce.)

From time to time, one hears anecdotes about another form of apparently paranormal photographic effect—the existence of people who seem to be extremely difficult to photograph. A far larger than normal number of photographs of them do not "come out." Some brief examples will have to suffice to illustrate this point, since as far as I know it has not been formally investigated and is not supported by any laboratory evidence.

In an article on thoughtography C. T. K. Chari tells of an experience of his nephew, who attempted to photograph the spiritual leader Sai Baba (see Chapter 11):

> . . . the *Swami* repeatedly predicted that his image would *not* appear on the developed plates. These predictions were fulfilled too often to be attributed to chance. My nephew showed me his "fogged" plates. Unfortunately this is not evidence in a controversial field: I did not witness the conditions myself. (50)

Author Alan Vaughan, himself a sensitive, tells of several similar events in his book *Patterns of Prophecy* (326). In one, Vaughan was taking part in a panel discussion, sitting between parapsychologists Charles Honorton and Gertrude Schmeidler, when a friend took a number of photographs. Though Vaughan was in the middle, the same distance from the camera as Honorton and Schmeidler, they were both in focus while Vaughan was out of focus in every picture. It seems unlikely that he moved at the exact moment of every shutter opening when his companions remained still.

Vaughan also mentions that sensitive Eileen Garrett once told him that she had failed to show up at all in a photograph that was intended to be of her, as did another medium who sat for photographs at the Conan Doyle Museum in London.

According to Vaughan, Serios himself once achieved such a disappearance when he was the subject of a television documentary film made by a German company. On film, as Serios began to try to produce the photographic image, the image "began to blacken from around the outer edges. With a few more attempts, the image was blackened out altogether, and then, finally, there appeared in flashes another picture—a close representation of a target picture in a sealed envelope that he was attempting to reproduce."

Photographic film is not the only material used by modern media that the mind may be able to affect. It has been suggested that PK may be responsible for a comparatively recent phenomenon in which "spirit voices" are alleged to be recorded on tape under conditions in which, it is claimed, no other form of electronic skulduggery or accident could be responsible for the mysterious sounds.

Among the first people to notice and work with the phenomenon (separately) were Allila von Szalay (10) and Friedrich Jurgenson, an artist living in Sweden. Jurgenson tape recorded bird songs one day and decided, on playing back what he had taped, that in addition to the bird songs there were voices where no voices should have been. After further experimentation he concluded that the sounds were communications from spirits on "the other side."

The late Dr. Konstantin Raudive, a psychologist, took up the challenge of this new discovery, and his book on the subject was published in English in 1971 (224). Since then, though comparatively little notice has been taken of the phenomenon in the United States, "Raudive tape recording" has been almost as much the rage in some parts of Europe as table-tilting was a century ago.

Two techniques are used. One may simply run a tape recorder in the presence of two or more people. They may talk or be silent as they choose. Perhaps significantly, in view of the atmosphere needed to create "Philip" (see Chapter 8), Raudive preferred to make his sessions very personal. He used a microphone to introduce the people present at the sitting to those from the other side who he thought might be present, taking it for granted that such beings *were* present and would be willing to talk. The important thing during the actual session is that everyone know or, better, make a note of exactly what he says. When running this kind of experiment it is best to have a tape recorder beside each person, so that individual utterances, however quiet, are sure to be picked up.

The alternative (which I believe to be a rather questionable method) is to tune a radio to a spot on the band where there is no broadcast, just "white noise," and connect the tape recorder to the radio. Whichever method is used, it is claimed that on playback there seem to be extra voices on the tape.

Obviously the radio method offers little control. At the time the set is tuned, it may *appear* that one is between stations. However, it is almost impossible to find a point on the band where someone is not broadcasting somewhere in the world. At times, changes in atmospheric conditions can bring in surges of sound from very far away, and radio transmissions can drift from their appointed wavelengths. One now famous recording made by Raudive, and interpreted by him as involving a name familiar to him, was later recognized by others as part of a broadcast from Radio Luxembourg, a pop radio station popular throughout Europe. To avoid this problem, Raudive sometimes used a diode instead of a radio. A diode is simply what used to be called a "cat's whisker" in early radio work, and, as many people can testify, it does indeed pick up radio broadcasts. Raudive supporters maintain that the form of diode he used had an antenna far too small to pick up anything, but I suspect that those familiar with the vagaries of broadcasting will look somewhat askance at that assurance.

One weakness of the theory that radio transmissions can explain most of the Raudive effects is that the messages heard, although always very brief, frequently seem to pertain to the conversation or circumstances of the group involved in the taping session.

Jurgenson acknowledged that radio transmissions were often involved, but he maintained that the messages heard on the tapes were not the original broadcasts, but had been modified by spirit intervention. In other words, he felt that the spirits used the power and modulation of the radio waves but remodulated them to adapt them for their own purposes.

The radio broadcast explanation is less likely when only tape recorders are used, but it cannot be entirely ruled out. Almost any electronic equipment can, under some circumstances, pick up radio broadcasts. In rare instances, even peoples' dental fillings have picked up pop music! In the United States particularly, experimenters should be wary of overenthusiastic interpretation of results they may obtain from taping sessions because of the proliferation of citizens band radios. If a CB operator is broadcasting as he drives past your house you may pick him up loud and clear on radio, television, tape recorder, public address system, or even on an electric organ. Since not all CB conversations are loaded with "ten-fours" and "good buddies" it may not be possible to identify a CB conversation if it turns up on your tape.

The Raudive messages usually consist of only a few syllables and are quite faint. Picking out the relevant sounds and interpreting them takes considerable practice, and this is another source of controversy. Raudive, who died in 1974, maintained that the messages were polyglot—that is, comprised of different languages even within the same phrase. Most of the languages he identified were Eastern European (he himself was Latvian though the later part of his life was spent in West Germany). Some critics feel that many of the sounds are simply scratches in the tape or white noise from the radio or tape recorder, subjectively interpreted to be consistent with whatever is going on at the sitting, a task much easier for one who has a wide range of languages on which to call in searching for meaningful words to fit the sounds.

Several tests (15, 87, 150) have compared the interpretation by different people of the same sounds. D. J. Ellis of Trinity College, Cambridge, used only the clearest voices, those that would probably have been rated A to $A++$ on Dr. Raudive's rating scale, and even so the variety of interpretations is very wide. One phrase will often call forth a range of ten or more different word combinations, all of which vary again from the interpretation originally assigned to the sounds by Dr. Raudive. Raudive's own interpretations and tests seem to have been somewhat dogmatic. As Ellis describes it (87), the phrases were presented to the listener only *after* he had been told of Dr. Raudive's interpretation.

> The listener is not even asked to say whether this is correct, but merely to indicate how well he can hear the voice. Agreement is taken to imply verification of the particular interpretation given, disagreement as showing that the listener is hard of hearing!

The difficulty of properly interpreting sounds without their context was shown clearly in experiments conducted by Charles Tart (306). Using a technique developed by John Lilly, Tart made a tape recording of the word *cogitate* spoken only once. He made a loop of the tape, so that the one word was repeated over and over again without a break, and he asked students to listen to it and write down any words that they heard that were different from the first word. Result? As he put it:

> My student hear anywhere from one to forty different words each in twenty minutes! One or two out of three or four hundred manage not to hear anything but "cogitate" in twenty minutes. Those who have heard many other words often disbelieve my statement afterwards that only one word was exactly repeated: they *know* they heard other words.

Against this criticism that the sounds may not be voices at all, Hans Bender points out that use of visible speech diagrams has proven *some* words to be objective acoustical events, but admits that many of the sounds cannot be identified in this way (16).

Another hypothesis very hard to guard against is that the sounds heard are spoken unconsciously by one or more of the people taking part in the session. A tape recorder beside each person may help provide a check, but a sound that appears only on the tape recorder beside one person may be interpreted as a recording of something he muttered, or it may be regarded as a paranormal effect, so this type of control is not foolproof.

Bender reports situations in which the sounds obtained on tapes made by Jurgenson relate strongly to situations involving Bender and his colleagues, including one in which a woman's voice was obtained when there were no women in the house where the sitting was being held. His interpretation is not that spirits are involved, but, as with thoughtography, that the sounds are caused by PK from one or more of the sitters.

Another theory suggests that PK *and* spirit intervention may be involved, with the PK supplying the power and the spirits modifying it to present the chosen words—a solution that sounds rather like a politician trying frantically to answer yes and no to the same question on election eve. It is conceivable, however, that if spirit survival and contact are facts, spirits may need to use human "mind power" to affect matter, just as they are alleged to use the energy of the medium to bring about more conventional seance effects.

Some researchers feel strongly that they have received messages via tape from entities that have properly identified themselves as having been related to those present at the sitting involved. However, when we remember Serios' apparent ability to perceive a target by ESP and then transmit it to photographic emulsion, we can see that it would be equally possible (if possible at all) for someone to use ESP unconsciously to pick up information about recently dead friends or relatives of those around them, and then transmit this to the tape. The "Philip" group has recently been working with electronic voices (249) and attempting to get Philip to respond to them. They seem to have got something on the tapes, but what and how is still uncertain.

Bearing in mind Philip and other information from previous chapters, it would seem that the PK explanation is very likely for those few cases in which (1) the sounds are *clearly* voices and not artifacts of white noise, (2) the possibility of broadcast excerpts is absolutely eliminated, and (3) there is total control to prevent unconscious utterances by those taking part in the sittings.

Chapter 11
Miracles as PK

Religious communication is basically psi communication, pure and simple: it is neither sensory nor motor; it is unequivocally extrasensorimotor. . . .

All the physical miracles, whether in the healing of disease, the miraculous movement of objects, or the control of the elements, had to be manifestations of PK. . . . It looks as though the insightful founders of religion were in their time almost as observant of the way psi operates as the psi-researchers have been in the laboratories.

J. B. Rhine (233)

In the early 1940s a few people began to wonder whether, in addition to working in the laboratory, parapsychologists should not be turning their attention to members of so-called primitive cultures (many of which are far from primitive in substantive matters) and to religious leaders reported able to work miracles.

Were such people in some way different, perhaps closer to nature and so able to perform feats that modern man could not? Could it be that, as one John Layard suggested,

> . . . primitive people with relatively undifferentiated egos are in touch with collective powers to a far greater extent than modern man, and that native magicians and others with special gifts in that direction develop and foster them by means of a definite technique . . . that in favorable circumstances that relatively close connexion between the primitive mind and natural forces may be such that some kind of contact may indeed be established on the lower levels of consciousness by means of which a certain measure of control may become operative? (146)

Terms such as "undifferentiated ego" have long ago left the modern psychological lexicon along with many other purely Freudian terms, but by definition it is probable that the truly advanced spiritual leaders, as well as tribal man, have "relatively

169

undifferentiated egos." They are not, ideally, concerned with self but with mankind and man's relationship with the Ultimate. In the same way, though often at a different level, primitive tribe members are supposedly more concerned with the tribe as a whole, and with the universe, than with individual well-being and status.

Obviously, exceptions occur at both levels. The adulation of his followers has fed the ego of many a potential spiritual leader until it attained a size far greater than his holiness deserved. Likewise, observers have discovered that many primitive tribes are far from idyllic and have their share of egotistical members. Nonetheless, both groups seem more likely to be able to break the bounds of sensorimotor self than are most members of modern society, centered as we are in self, ego, and "me/you" rather than "us." We might perhaps expect, then, that these two groups, the spiritual leaders and the tribal primitives, would be the source of far more spontaneous psi phenomena than is modern man.

Anecdotal evidence has supported this expectation. The tribal "applied specialist in parapsychology" is usually the "clever man," shaman, or witch doctor of the group. The shaman is expected to use his gifts for the good of the community—or of whoever will pay him, depending on his orientation. He uses ESP to answer questions, find criminals and lost objects, and predict the future. ESP may also provide communication with other communities, according to some reports. PK may bring rain or sunshine. A shaman's tent may shake, rattle, and roll as he, hands and feet tightly bound, communes with the spirits, though who can tell whether the commotion is caused by the spirits or the shaman's PK? (A shaman may, of course, be another Houdini, able to escape his ropes and cause all the rumpus in a nonparanormal way. However, some reports by anthropologists and others seem to indicate not all "clever men" are frauds (131).

In the late 1940s and early 1950s, Lyndon and Ronald Rose tested a number of Australian aborigines for both ESP and PK. Though the accumulated ESP scores were significant, the PK results, after 3,504 runs, were at chance (320). The Roses pointed out that the aborigines believe that "mind over matter" is the sole prerogative of "clever men" and that it would not be possible for an ordinary person to manifest it. This belief, as we have seen, may cause blocking and an inability to achieve success in PK tests.

Robert L. Van de Castle has done numerous psi tests of the Cuna Indians of the San Blas Islands. Like the Roses, he has concentrated more on ESP than on PK, but the PK tests that he did revealed no significant scoring. Van de Castle felt that the noncompetitive society of the Cunas made it difficult to induce his subjects really to try to succeed at their dice placement task. They, too, regarded PK as possible only for *neles*, or shamans. Unfortunately, the *neles* themselves were always "too busy" for Van de Castle to test them.

At first glance, the lack of success encountered by the Roses and Van de Castle when testing for PK seems to scuttle the theory of psi among preliterate people with "undifferentiated egos," at least as far as PK is concerned. However, with all due deference to these researchers' work, it seems fair to point out that the theory has not really been given a chance, and perhaps it can never be tested properly. For one thing, truly primitive societies are disappearing quite rapidly. For another, when they can be contacted and persuaded to participate in controlled experiments, the milieu immediately becomes alien to them. Substituting pictures of jaguars, canoes, and other objects familiar to them for the ESP symbols, as did Van de Castle, is a step in the right direction, but the entire procedure of scientific control is likely to create a dissonance that will not bode well for high scores. As Van de Castle explained,

Subjects had a great deal of difficulty in grasping the requirements of the testing situation and did not seem to comprehend readily what the task involved. They would stare at the playing card designating the target side continuously and seldom even glanced toward the platform to observe where the dice had fallen. Cunas become extremely embarrassed if they become the center of attention, and they were frequently uncomfortable during the sessions because others crowded about them and considerable laughter would frequently emanate from the bystanders. It was not possible to avoid this latter problem because no privacy exists on the islands. If testing was carried out inside a hut, the villagers would gather about and peek through the slotted walls while making joking remarks. (319)

Another point also militates against high PK scores in such societies. If subjects are selected from volunteers, they are likely to be individuals who volunteer as much to become the center of attention as for any other reason. Such people can be presumed to be far more egotistical than those who do not volunteer. Thus, though the experimenter may have picked a society in which he believes the social situation is conducive to psi, he will probably get as volunteer subjects those whose personalities are the least suited to it, if the undifferentiated ego is relevant. If in some way he is able to pick subjects regardless of whether or not they volunteer, then, as Van de Castle points out above, he runs the risk of embarrassing them.

The problem is not much simpler at the other end of the spectrum—the attempt to study the miraculous abilities of religious leaders and their devotees.

Many religions promise their adherents some form of miraculous power if they follow the rules properly. Buddhism speaks of six "superknowledges" attained through meditation. In yoga, with its Hindu background, we are told that the yogin who is close to complete liberation attains "victory over matter, compounds, molecules, atoms, and ultra-atomic particles." The absolutely liberated yogin has yet greater powers; even, we are told, the ability to change destiny (169).

Jesus told his followers, "He that believeth on me, the works that I do shall he do also; and greater work than these shall he do . . . " (21) and set them examples that may well be forms of psi.

Many teachings of the various religions seem to tie in with traditional ideas of what helps psi performance. Few of these ideas have been confirmed in the laboratory so far, but there are some interesting hints. Rex Stanford's subjects who could focus their minds ("let thine eye be single") on the target number (282) seemed to do better than those who could not. Meditation, in at least one of its many forms, is taught by every religion, and we have seen some connection between meditation and PK scores, though the exact connection is unclear. Those who cannot still their minds ("take no thought for the morrow") but are constantly thinking and worrying may have less success with ESP.

Lawrence LeShan's subjects who had "a feeling of being at home in the world" (Chapter 6) surely are those who "trust in the Lord," regardless of what definition they give to the word *Lord,* a concept to which we will return in later chapters.

Basically, investigators of such promises and examples look at two kinds of religious leaders—past and present. The past religious leader is, or was, the founder or highly enlightened follower of a religion, and all his or her paranormal acts are deemed to be miraculous. Those who examine them more closely risk being accused of blasphemy. On the other hand, the contemporary religious leader is generally far too involved with his spiritual teachings to spare time for controlled experiments. At least that is what he says. In addition, religions almost universally condemn the use of paranormal powers for the sake of show, as in the case of Jesus on the mountaintop being tempted to demonstrate his powers.

However, some amusing paradoxes have been noted. While refusing to demonstrate for researchers, many contemporary leaders happily produce manifestations such as "sacred powders," flowers, and sometimes even jewels when faced with a large and admiring crowd. Budding yogins are advised to ignore all signs of psychic development lest they be distracted from their main task, which is reunion with God, yet, if someone does start to show paranormal gifts he is immediately revered as a holy man. Christianity as a whole frowns on most production of paranormal events by the living (an attitude not quite as safely grounded in the Old Testament as some believe), but makes an exception when the event involves healing, and allows such events, when posthumous, to be used as evidence in favor of canonization.

When he tries to study scientifically the abilities of such exalted people, the would-be experimenter inevitably appears as the crass materialist with no comprehension of the finer things of the spirit. (This is a somewhat misleading impression. Taking the deeper meaning of the word *religious,* I would say that the percentage of parapsychologists who are religious is considerably higher than the percentage of the population in general.) Nonetheless, let us risk universal condemnation by taking a look at some religiously oriented events that may relate to PK.

We have already looked at healing as a form of PK, and Jesus seems to have practiced a variety of forms of healing. Sometimes He used the healing touch, and sometimes He simply talked to the sick person. In the case of the centurion's servant (18) He even healed at a distance without seeing the patient at all. Several of the disciples practiced healing successfully, as did Paul (22). In the case of saints and those being considered for canonization, cures may apparently take place even after the healer is dead.

Another biblical miracle is the stilling of the storm (19). This may have been a fortunate coincidence; storms do flare up and die down again with startling swiftness on the Sea of Galilee. However, a belief in man's control over the weather is widespread, even in the Western world.

Shortly before this chapter was written a dire shortage of snow afflicted Colorado, and one community hired a group of Indians to perform a snow dance. The performance was followed by four inches of snow—not enough for the ski resorts, but snow nonetheless—in an area where snow was in extremely short supply. The Indians may not have brought the snow, but a reasonably hardheaded business community was willing to pay them to try. Scarcely a summer goes by in which we don't read of rain dances being performed in one drought-stricken area or another. Though follow-up reports of rainfall are less frequent, such attempts demonstrate a considerable level of belief in weather control—a function that has been claimed by shamans and witch doctors for centuries.

In *Africa Dances* (107) Geoffrey Gorer tells of a visit, on a "particularly fine and cloudless afternoon," to a "convent" of worshipers of the thunder fetish. He recounts that, though the sun continued to shine, his party was treated to the full visual and audio effects of an approaching thunderstorm, the lightning and thunder getting closer and closer "till they seemed simultaneous and the thunder gave that peculiarly unpleasant crack which it does in the tropics when the storm is nearly directly overhead."

Three of the inhabitants of the convent were out of sight in a nearby hut, supposedly in trance, but it seems unlikely that they could have produced such violent results by fraud.

The miracles of the loaves and fishes (20) are frequently dismissed by biblical authorities. Some claim that the food involved was "spiritual food." Others suggest that the eventual over-abundance of food was due to the fact that many people had food with them, and once their consciences had been prodded by the sight of others offering to share, they, too, made their supply available to others. A third explanation, that the food actually was materialized, is usually considered only by those who accept every word of the Bible as literally true—people who, strangely enough, frequently consider psychic phenomena to be the work of the devil.

However, the multiplication of food is a miracle attributed also to a number of medieval mystics, including St. Teresa of Avila, St. Clare of Assisi, and St. Pius V. Herbert Thurston, S.J., an eminent and generally extremely objective student of mysticism and religion, comments,

> . . . the fact is that prodigies of this type are of frequent occurrence in our hagiographical records. For some, of course, the evidence is very inadequate, but others are well attested. Prosper Lambertini (Pope Benedict XIV) . . . fully recognizes the supernatural character of these multiplications where proper precautions are taken against errors of malobservation, etc.

Writing of Father Angiolo Paoli (1642-1720), Thurston quotes an account of a long walk on which Father Angiolo started out carrying "a few scraps of bread, hardly enough to give seven or eight people." During the course of the walk, the original author, a Father Magginie, comments, "We, who kept our eyes upon him the whole time, knew that he never stopped in the street to receive a fresh supply from anyone whatever." Yet, "he satisfied from fifty to sixty poor beggars who all went away contented with the alms they had received" (313).

Flowing robes can, of course, hide much, and admiring acolytes are notoriously credulous, so no final conclusion can be reached as to the source of Father Angiolo's generosity.

Thurston also mentions occasions on which mystics prayed over the food supply of their monasteries and these mysteriously lasted far longer than logic dictated that they should. A similar event forms the basis for the celebration of Hanukkah, which recalls an occasion when, after the temple had been defiled by the troops of Antiochus Epiphanes, only enough uncontaminated oil was left to burn for one day and yet, when lit, the lamp burned for eight days.

Levitation is another "spiritual" ability. St. Teresa's levitations were attested to by several witnesses including a Sister Anne who saw her "raised about half a yard from the ground without her feet touching it," and said that she had "put my hands under her [St. Teresa's] feet . . . for something like half an hour." Far from wishing to use such phenomena as evidence of her piety, St. Teresa ordered Sister Anne to say nothing of what she had seen. For herself, St. Teresa seems to have resisted the apparent levitations:

> Occasionally I was able, by great efforts, to make a slight resistance, but afterwards I was worn out, like a person who had been contending with a strong giant; at other times it was impossible to resist at all; my soul was carried away . . . and now and then my whole body as well, so that it was lifted up from the ground.

Some mystics obviously had illusions of levitation, as in the case of St. Mary Magdalene de'Pazzi who, while anchored firmly on the ground by her two feet, was heard to shout loudly when answering someone standing near her and then to mutter to herself, "They can't hear me down there; it is too far off." Nevertheless, on the subject of levitation Thurston concludes:

> I have taken note of the names of something over two hundred persons alleged to have been physically lifted from the ground in ecstasy. In about one-third of these cases there seems to me to be evidence which, if not conclusive, is to say the least respectable.

As to whether such events were caused by God, angels, spirits, or the devil, he remains uncertain:

> . . . it seem to me that in the present state of our knowledge we cannot even decide whether the effects observed do or do not transcend the possible range of what may be called the psycho-physical forces of nature.

Many signs of sainthood attributed to medieval saints—elongation, materialization, levitation, and ESP, for example—were reproduced by the mediums mentioned in Chapter 8, and some continue to be attributed to some Eastern religious leaders even today.

Several Western parapsychologists have visited India in recent years, trying to discover whether the "miracles" attributed to such gurus as Sai Baba are genuine. For the most part the reports have been inconclusive because, although investigators were able to observe and interview their subjects, they were not able to test them under controlled conditions. However, repeated requests for controlled tests sometimes seem to provoke such leaders into some kind of demonstration, even though uncontrolled. When pressed on the subject by Erlendur Haraldsson and Karlis Osis, Sai Baba once responded to Osis, "Look at your ring."

Osis found that the stone of his ring, which had been firmly embedded in the gold, had disappeared even though the frame remained unbent and the prongs that stuck out over the stone to hold it in place were unbent. Haraldsson and others had noticed the stone in the ring shortly before Sai Baba drew attention to its absence, and the guru, sitting several feet away, had not touched Osis in the meantime. Except for a chair, the room was bare of furniture, yet the stone could not be found. "This," commented Sai Baba, "was my experiment" (113).

The investigators were justly impressed. It should be noted however, that the ring had originally been presented to Osis by Sai Baba himself, so the possibility of its being some kind of trick gadget cannot be ruled out entirely.

Sai Baba seems to materialize objects more often than to dematerialize them. His specialty is *vibuti,* a powdery, grayish substance sometimes called holy ash, which seems to appear "just below and at his palm and Sai Baba seemed to grasp it into his fist with a quick downward movement of his hand, as though to prevent its falling to the ground."

The production of *vibuti* is reported to be an almost daily occurrence in Sai Baba's presence. He is almost as casual in his production of jewels and other small objects.

Haraldsson and Osis were able to sneak a look at a discarded robe of Sai Baba's and to talk with someone who had examined one still in use. Neither robe had pockets or hiding places; the sleeves were "about the same length and width as those of our Western jackets" and, perhaps most important, neither showed signs of having been soiled as would be expected if the ash, or other greasy substances sometimes "materialized" by Sai Baba, had actually been hidden in them.

Certainly Sai Baba's unwillingness to participate in controlled tests is questionable, but then he is a busy man, and religion, not science, is his main interest. No doubt he is aware that, were he ever to agree to controlled tests and not be caught in fraud, he would be descended upon by every parapsychologist possessing the fare to India and would never be free of them again as they attempted to study everything from his brain waves and blood pressure to the magnetic energy around him and the exact chemical content of *vibuti*. (I am sure this last test must already have been done, for most people are given some of the stuff during audiences with Sai Baba, but I am unaware of the results.) On the other hand, if he does indulge in fraud, he must be aware that discovery would ruin his reputation forever. Either way, there is little incentive for him to take part in parapsychological experiments.

Sai Baba has attracted so much attention from Westerners, including many skeptics, that it is hard to believe he would not have been detected in fraud if he indulged in it. However, it is sadly astonishing how long a skilled sleight-of-hand artist can perform without detection even by sophisticated observers in an uncontrolled situation. This became apparent when another spiritual leader, though of lesser fame, was filmed in India by researchers Ed May and K. T. Jahagirdar. Mrs. Bengale, like Sai Baba, seemed to produce quantities of sacred powder, though in her case it was red and known as *kum-kum*. (That fact led May and Jahagirdar to title their report "From Where Does the Kum-Kum Come?"—a welcome respite from the self-consciously polysyllabic titles preferred by many researchers.)

Mrs. Bengale's movements, when she produced the *kum-kum*, were so swift that it was hard to follow them with the eye, but a number of trained and supposedly sophisticated observers had been unable to observe any fraud on her part. In addition, she was quite willing to be filmed while in her *kum-kum*-producing trance. Alas, when the film was run at one-third normal speed, it revealed that before every handful of *kum-kum* appeared Mrs. Bengale dipped her hand into her flowing sari (160).

Dr. Ramakrishna Rao is presently director of the FRNM Institute for Parapsychology, on leave of absence from his position as professor in the Department of Psychology at Andhra University in

India. He has been similarly disappointed in his study of Indian mystics, writing,

> . . . I attempted to study a number of yogis, swamis, babas and psychic healers reputed to have paranormal powers. We had hoped that at least some of the many claiming to produce such "supernatural" phenomena as materialization of objects, for instance, would be able to do so to our satisfaction and under our conditions. We collected information concerning several dozens of such men and were able to work with a few. Our experience has been quite frustrating. We found some actually cheating, some using sleight of hand and none demonstrating psi to our satisfaction. The only phenomenon we found to be of some interest is healing through prayer. Some authentic cases of cures purported to have been effected by the healer without any normal means came to our notice. But to our disappointment, there was no noticeable improvement in any of the experimental cases we sent to the healers. (222)

One cannot help but wonder about the *purpose* of the manifestations by such people if, at any time, they are genuine. Certainly they serve to "show us a sign," but a sign of what? Do the objects produced by these gurus help people in their search for inner growth, closer contact with the divine, or whatever their religious goals may be? Do the objects themselves have miraculous powers, as is sometimes claimed?

There is a story, told by Madame David-Kneel (69), of an Eastern merchant. Each time he went on a trading mission to a certain holy city his mother asked him to bring her back a holy relic. Each time he forgot, and each time, upon his return, she became angrier and angrier. At last, when halfway back from the city, he realized that he had forgotten yet again. Hardly daring to face her, he sat at his campfire and wondered what to do. Then his eye fell upon the jawbone of a dog, long whitened by the elements. He pulled a tooth from it, wrapped it elaborately, and in due course presented it to his mother as a holy relic. All in his home village were duly awed and frequently came to gaze upon the tooth and pray to it. Some considerable time later, to the merchant's amazement, the bone developed the faint glow associated with holy relics.

As such tales clearly illustrate, Eastern philosophers are aware that miracles, if and when they occur, are due less to the intrinsic virtue within an object itself than to the reverence subsequently paid to it. One can only conclude, therefore, that because the object in some way *absorbed* so much of the awe and the prayer, it began to reflect it back. The story is almost certainly apocryphal, but it nevertheless serves as an illustration of how an object, or a location such as a shrine, may come to have apparently miraculous properties. It is probably a result of what we have been calling the linger effect. Sometimes the source of the healing power, or whatever it is, may be the holy person who once sat there or is buried there. It may be that the object or place absorbed his "vibrations"—for want of a better word. Or the object may, like the dog's tooth, have no such origin, but may simply reflect the love and reverence that have been directed toward it by worshipers over the years. Or again, it may be that a *belief* in the powers of the object enables the petitioner's PK or powers of self-healing to work, a matter to which we will return in Chapter 13.

To discuss the possibility that biblical miracles (including those reported in the Old Testament and those performed by the human disciples as well as those of Jesus) may be psychic phenomena should not in any way be taken as sacrilegious or as bearing on the divinity or otherwise of Jesus, for two reasons. First, as we have seen, Jesus promised that His followers would be able to do the same works that He did. Second, He was after all human. If it were sacrilegious, as some have suggested, to claim to do the same things that Jesus did, then eating, drinking, walking, and talking would be sacrilegious. If psi is due to a normal law of nature, then its use is hardly evil, blasphemous, or demon-inspired. Some schools of thought hold that miracles are the result of divine intervention to suspend temporarily the laws of nature, and that those who do anything similar in this day and age are using power from the forces of evil. However, St. Augustine, whose piety and devotion to Christianity are hardly in doubt, remarked that the inexplicable happens, "not contrary to nature, but contrary to *what we know* as nature" (italics mine) (262).

Perhaps some people have an instinctive knowledge about the laws of nature that they are able to put to use without necessarily knowing how they do it. It may be that the great religious figures were more fully aware of what they were doing and how, but that does not necessarily mean that they were using any kind of power that is not available to everybody else.

What seems more likely, as St. Augustine suggested, is that miracles, and probably psi, relate to a law or force of nature that we do not yet understand. The fact that we do not yet understand the laws we are studying does not mean that they cannot be used. Electricity served mankind for many years before we knew exactly what it was—and how many of us even now use it without that knowledge? A young child may spend all day happily sledding down a steep hill and yet have no idea of the laws involving gravity, friction, and the construction of snow crystals that are responsible for his happiness. Exactly that same combination of gravity, friction, and crystals may be responsible for a broken ankle or worse.

In the same way, psi could, perhaps, be used for harm or help, either consciously if it is ever harnessed or unconsciously by those who know not what they do. Of itself it may be neither good nor evil, but, like electricity or nuclear fission, can be used for good or evil according to the bent of the individual using it.

Chapter 12

Straws in the Wind . . . or Vagrant Chaff?

There are many modern magical practices in use today by various societies, and the efficacy of these practices ought to be tested. . . . If anthropologists interested in areas such as we are here to discuss would, as a standard procedure, administer an appropriate . . . test, then by examining those practices which do yield parapsychological results and comparing them with unsuccessful modern ones, perhaps there, too, we can extract parapsychological principles from anthropological studies.

Robert Brier (31)

If parapsychology has one thing in common with most other fields of human endeavor it is politics—right-wing and left-wing politics. On the right are the conservatives, concerned, quite rightly, with upholding the scientific standards of the field and repelling the tide of popular occultism that has been surging across the Western world for the past fifteen years or so. On the left are the adventurers, those researchers who will leap from lab to anywhere, look for any connection with psi in any area of interest and call it parapsychology, claiming as they do so to be in the service of holism.

To a certain extent this dichotomy is represented by the British versus continental approach to mediumship discussed in Chapter 8. However, in that instance both sides would probably have claimed to be the conservatives, the British because of their demands for ever stricter controls and the continentals because they began to consider the PK hypothesis while the British were still involved in the survival question, with its inevitably religious (and therefore nonscientific) connotations.

Today, though, the lines are drawn somewhat differently. As parapsychology has moved from seance to science and adopted the experimental methods of other, more established disciplines, acceptance of parapsychology by other scientists has become extremely important to many researchers. Without such acceptance, parapsychologists will meet with opposition from colleagues and have difficulty obtaining funds or facilities; parapsychology will be ignored or derided in psychology classes; and progress will be slow or nonexistent. Accordingly, the conservatives have proceeded to adopt the methods and language of the sciences from which they seek acceptance. The result is a standard of experimental method and criticism that is entirely admirable and that was largely responsible for the acceptance of the PA by the American Association for the Advancement of Science.

All well and good. However, since anything to do with psychical phenomena is regarded by some people as "occulty" or superstitious nonsense, some (though not all) conservatives seem to feel it vital that they should avoid any possibility of contamination or guilt by association with anything that could be considered superstitious, occult, or nonscientific in any way. Like the magician drawing his protective pentacle around him, some parapsychologists draw uncrossable boundaries between what they consider to be parapsychological science and superstitious antiscience. Therein lies no little danger.

While the most commonly used experimental subject is now the average college student, researchers always urgently need special subjects, those who can score better and more consistently than can the average person. By drawing uncrossable boundaries, conservatives may be cutting themselves off from a potentially rich source of such subjects. As Robert Van de Castle, then of the University of Virginia, expressed it in 1971:

> I think we should take a look at our attitudes in dealing with people who claim psychic gifts. Too often, we seem to come on as "snobs." There are several organizations in this country whose membership consists of people with a strong interest in psychic matters. Many of these members are making continuing efforts to develop their psychic abilities through prayer, meditation, dream exploration, sensitivity

training, and various other techniques, and they report numerous instances of apparent psi phenomena.

Generally, the response of official parapsychology is extremely cool to these "occultists" and we strive to maintain a respectful distance so that we won't be contaminated. This attitude may be working to our disadvantage. Such organizations could provide a large source of interested and highly motivated subjects for research efforts if the prospective experimenter were willing to explain his purposes in terms that would be congruent with the interests of the group. The image we convey seems to be that of sterile scientists who must wear antiseptic rubber gloves because some form of germs might be contracted from these people.... It seems strange that we favor college sophomores who may be uninterested or only slightly interested in psi to serve as subjects while we deliberately ignore these large numbers of people who have made psychic concerns an important part of their lives. (321)

Gardner Murphy made much the same point when speaking of Mrs. Piper, an extremely gifted sensitive, who was studied at length by the ASPR:

... how was she recruited? She was recruited through the American spiritualist movement. If William James had been afraid to make contact with this type of movement, a very important period in the history of psychical research would have been lost to us. (177)

Mediumship has long since been banished from the pale by many parapsychologists, often quite rightly. Yet if a few occurrences during seances *were* genuine, can we learn nothing from a study of the field? If a belief in the spirits helps a person manifest PK, may this not be a way of encouraging his or her abilities so that they may be studied?

When the scientific/nonscientific boundary is drawn, on which side lies healing? Is it scientific when Colonel Estebany treats enzymes and occult when he treats people, because healing in people is difficult to measure scientifically? Should we, because of this problem, dismiss the whole thing?

The superstars—where do they fit? Should they be banished? Studied? The controversy is often bitter.

What of the methods of shamans and witch doctors? The teachings of religious leaders? Even if, as we have seen, we cannot test the leaders themselves, can parts of their teachings perhaps be applied and tested? How about the "secret laws" of the mystery schools and other frankly occult groups?

Parapsychologists do tend to be more open to superstitions from other cultures than to superstitions from our own. In 1973 at a major international conference on Parapsychology and Anthropology (3) participants repeatedly emphasized that anthropologists should bear parapsychology in mind when studying "magical" practices in various societies. Since that time an increasing number of anthropologists have been taking an interest in psi.

Such suggestions are acclaimed by the left-wingers (who do not consider themselves left-wing at all); they believe that all these fields make claims that may relate to parapsychology. Why, they ask, do we have to risk damage to our careers and reputations if we study them—and particularly if we study them by immersion, trying to get a subjective understanding as well as an objective view of what is going on? Perhaps other cultures and beliefs do have something to teach us, so why may we not learn? Dice and cards, random number generators and sterile labs are so soulless and mechanical that they make it impossible for the human psyche (from which psychic) to function, they claim.

If parapsychology is to preserve its newfound scientific status, the boundaries must obviously be drawn, but they should remain crossable. Writing of just this problem, J. B. Rhine commented, "We need clear distinctions but certainly not closed borders or narrow confines. A boundary is not a wall" (232). (Those who think of Rhine as a conservative may be startled to read this, but his case is probably not one of conservatism but of perfectionism. He just does not care to waste time studying things that cannot be proven, as he explains in *New World of the Mind:*

> To try to believe unverified supernatural, occult or mystical hypotheses would be to desert our basic scientific standards. *This is not to say that there is nothing in any of these supernatural hypotheses,* the point is that in science it is not fruitful to explain one unknown by another...(231) [Italics mine]

It is just this, that the occulty beliefs cannot be proven, that makes the right-wingers want to avoid them. It is the possibility that they will yield fresh insights into the problems of parapsychology that tempts the left-wingers over the boundary.

It would seem that, as is usual, both groups are right and both are wrong. Occulty ideas are seldom provable themselves, yet, brought back into the laboratory, subjected to controlled conditions, may they not shed much-needed light on the psi process? The pharmaceutical laboratories are still seeking and finding uses for little-known plants from little-known regions of the world. The fact that the natives of these regions use the plants in their own rituals—which we may brand as superstitious—does not make the plant itself less efficacious when it is brought back to the lab and analyzed.

This chapter is devoted to unexplained phenomena and reports that call for further research. None of it stands by itself as a matter of science—though some may as a matter of faith. None of the material is original, but it is re-presented here with the hope that something in it may prompt further, properly controlled research.

One continuing phenomenon claimed by sensitives is the ability to see the human aura. The aura is claimed to be a surround of colored light around each person, with the colors varying according to his or her mood, personality, and health. Some sensitives claim to be able to diagnose illnesses from it, and in fact Dr. Shafica Karagulla has done considerable research with two such subjects, testing their diagnoses against those of the patients' doctors, with some success (138).

Harold Saxton Burr, for a long time professor of anatomy at Yale University School of Medicine, claimed that he had discovered a force, the Life-field or L-field, which surrounded every living thing. According to Burr the L-field not only changes with the health and well-being of the life form it belongs to, but it also seems to *guide* the physical development of that life form (38). With such two-way feedback between L-field and body, each responding to and having an effect on the other, not only should diagnosis by means of physical or clairvoyant measuring of the field be possible, but so should healing by PK. Presumably the healer could "PK" the field into a more beneficial form, and the field would then have its effect on the body. Interestingly, this is exactly how some healers have long claimed to work.

One red herring related to auras—one from which parapsychology took a while to withdraw—was Kirlian photography. Originally named after two Russian researchers, the Kirlian process consists of placing objects in contact with photographic film while in a high-frequency electrical field. The procedure uses no light and is carried out in a darkroom or a photographer's black bag. The resulting photographs show an electrical corona that appears as an aura of light surrounding almost any object, and, in the case of living tissue, frequently takes the form of rays radiating from the subject. Like the aura, the Kirlian corona is said to vary according to the health and mental state of the subject.

Greeted as "proof of the existence of the aura" and as a new diagnostic tool, Kirlian photography became an instant fad in the early 1970s despite warnings from more conservative researchers. The apparatus is comparatively simple (though potentially dangerous if it is not put together properly) and not too expensive. Apart from being quite beautiful, Kirlian photography can show, as I have discovered myself, very interesting and contrasting reflections of before and after situations. Medication, coffee, cigarettes, exercise, changes in mood, all appear to bring about changes in the Kirlian aura, but nobody was quite sure, to start with, what caused the changes and the beautiful colors.

Eventually it was realized that many of the color variations were brought about by ultraviolet sparks arcing between the equipment and the film or the object and the film (78). Further variations were due to dampness (an absolutely dry object provided little variation) and to chemical gases given off by the skin. The salt content of perspiration changes the picture as much as does the amount of moisture. The relaxed individual perspires little so there is little sodium in the atmosphere near his skin, and the corona is blue. If the tension level is raised, the hands perspire, making the skin a better conductor and changing the makeup of the gases around it, and red starts to appear in the corona. Whether these two discoveries explain *all* Kirlian variations is not yet clear, but it does appear that most Kirlian phenomena can be explained in normal physical terms. Few parapsychologists are now interested in working with the Kirlian technique for itself, but some do consider it a potentially useful tool. For example, the corona of metallic objects is comparatively stable and should be a good target for psychokinetic research. Even fingertip photos can be targets, although, being less stable, they are less satisfactory. Can a PK subject make the corona larger? Smaller? Change its shape? In a preliminary experiment of this type, Geller was asked to make the corona around his fingertip take specific shapes as it was photographed (123). Because the photography was done in the dark one cannot be sure that no sleight of hand occurred, but careful controls guarded against this eventuality. The photographs show results that are extremely hard to explain except by fraud or paranormal effects. This type of use seems very promising, so the Kirlian diversion may not have been a total waste of time.

The relevance to PK is that the aura, if eventually proven to exist, may be susceptible to control by people with certain abilities. We know that the body is surrounded by many "envelopes" of energy—electrical energy, heat energy, and so on. It is possible that the aura represents some kind of energy (unseen by most of us) that may be connected with psi.

Dr. Richard Dobrin of the Institute of Bio-Energetic Analysis in New York is reported to have experimented with a subject whose body emits light (as do most people, it seems from Dobrin's work) and who actually can control this light, increasing and decreasing it on command (193). Such phenomena may not in themselves be paranormal. For years the claims of Indian swamis to be able to control their heartbeats and other physiological functions were considered to be either fantasy, fraud, or paranormal, but eventually it was discovered that with proper feedback many people can learn similar control. The next question is whether such light energy and its control relate to psychic phenomena. Can it be converted into other forms of energy? Are there other hitherto undetected but controllable energies around the body? Could they be compressed, concentrated, to form something resembling Ochorowicz' "rigid rays" (Chapter 8)? Ochorowicz found evidence of these rays, he thought, in his work with Palladino and with Stanislawa Tomczyk. He believed that they emanated from a medium and, at times, from the sitters, and that they could support, repel, or attract objects. He took photographs that appeared to show them and believed that they could penetrate very small spaces, such as the gap between the lid and lip of a loosely stoppered jar, but not a complete seal (299).

Interestingly, many of the "mini-Gellers" tested by John Taylor (Chapter 5) have similar problems when the object on which they are to use their PK is in a hermetically sealed container, and it seems that Kulagina may have the same difficulty (211). This problem could be psychological, but a study in which the subjects did not know which containers were hermetically sealed and which were not might be extremely valuable, though it could not be conclusive because ESP might be used to break the blind condition.

The idea of fine threads that could join to make rigid bundles suggests the protuberances reported by many observers of the better mediums. Two witnesses claimed to have seen arms and hands, "prolongations" and "a kind of stump" growing from Palladino's body during one session. A female witness helped her undress after the seance (for many seances she wore specially designed clothes at the request of the investigators) but "there was no sign of any machinery" (101).

Home, too, was seen to have "extra hands" and protuberances that patted and prodded his sitters from time to time.

Such reports have usually been regarded as evidence of either faulty observation or mechanical fraud, and there may indeed be no more to them than that. At the same time, certain odd coincidences make one wonder.

Carlos Castaneda is a controversial figure, said to be either an adept or a hoaxer, depending upon who is writing. His books, however, based on a study of Indian beliefs, may be revealing even if we do not quite believe his tales of apprenticeship to an Indian *brujo*. In one incident, Castaneda reported seeing Indian *brujo* Don Genaro performing seemingly impossible feats as he climbed and crossed an extremely high waterfall. Later his teacher, Don Juan, is said to have rebuked him for not having been able to *see* (clairvoyantly in our understanding) how Don Genaro had done it.

> He said that...human beings were, for those who "saw," luminous beings composed of something like fibers of light, which rotated from the front to the back....The most astonishing part...was a set of long fibers that came out of the area around the navel....(47)

With these fibers, Don Juan said, Don Genaro had crossed the waterfall, extending them, wrapping them around boulders, and using them to maintain balance and to pull himself forward. Later Don Juan spoke of "the place of your luminous fibers," and pointed to his abdomen. Castaneda questioned him further and he explained, "It's an opening. It allows a space for the will to shoot out, like an arrow.... Will is what sends a sorcerer through a wall; through space; to the moon, if he wants" (48).

Elsewhere Castaneda writes of Don Juan's reference to the fact that similar though less durable lines could be produced from the hands and the eyes, and that such lines also are given off from the world itself (49). The lines from the body and from the earth could have a physical effect on others.

All very fanciful, for we do not even know for sure whether Don Juan exists. Yet the way in which explanations agree with one another, even though they come from opposite ends of the earth, should perhaps make us stop and think.

Psi is sometimes said to be space-time independent and therefore to function as well over great distances as over short ones. It is hard to imagine such "rods" covering immense distances in order to achieve their PK objective, even if Don Juan did say that they could take one to the moon. However, in actual fact most of the better evidence for long-distance psi comes from work with ESP, not PK, and, as we saw in Chapter 6, some of the superstars have definite limits to their PK reach (though, again, these may be more psychological than physical). Many anecdotal references to emanations from the bodies of sensitives make the point that they are strongest from the abdomen and the fingers. While pursuing this rather shaky line of thought perhaps we might wonder why Graham Watkins and Roger Wells, working with capacitors whose time constants seemed to vary from normal when they were being concentrated on by sensitives, found the effect greatest when the capacitor was held to the navel (334).

Occult lore is full of the idea that some kind of energy, *prana*, or vital force can be taken into and concentrated by the body. Breathing techniques are often suggested as a way of controlling this energy, and, interestingly, Dobrin's light-radiating subject is reported to control his emanations by doing breathing exercises.

Breathing control and meditation are also two main yogic techniques for attaining control over matter (Chapter 11). Unfortunately, though many parapsychologists are themselves interested in yoga, very little work has been done so far to discover whether breathing techniques may have any bearing on success in psi.

The idea that PK is achieved by manipulation of molecules or atomic particles rather than the gross object itself is intriguing. Paramahansa Yogananda (341) has suggested that it is by rearrangement of the vibratory nature of matter (an electron has the nature of a wave or vibration, as well as of a particle) that many materializations are performed. An object that appears is not made out of *nothing;* it is made out of *something.* Air is, after all, composed of atoms just as real as the atoms of a chair or a table, and those atoms, he says, can be rearranged, though not by any presently known force.

As far as the movement of objects is concerned, it should be remembered that an object remains in one place only because (1) gravity causes it to press against whatever is supporting it, increasing friction and stopping it from sliding around, and (2) the pressure of air molecules all around it is the same from every side. The movement of a solid object may be hard to accept. However, it is easier to imagine that, just as a spinning coin or random number generator may be affected to turn up slightly more of one side or target than another, it might be possible to cause slightly more air molecules to press on one side of an object than on the other. This would cause the object to move in the direction of the lower pressure, particularly if it were also slightly levitated so as to reduce friction between itself and whatever it is resting on, or if it were suspended and very light, like a feather (270).

Of course that so-called solid object is hardly solid anyway, but consists of a mass of constantly moving electrons circling atomic nuclei with relatively large amounts of space between them. However, since this fact—mind-blowing though it is in some ways—is plain old physics and not the least bit far out or speculative, we will not deal with it in this chapter.

In the previous chapter we considered briefly the possibility that one might affect the nature of an object by the type of thought one thinks about it, as in the case of the discarded bone that acquired the characteristics of a holy relic.

In writing of Tibetan Lamaism, Alexandra David-Kneel (69) refers to the belief that objects can be charged by mental energy waves so as to act as accumulators. This belief was for years dismissed as superstition, but may now deserve renewed attention in light of recent evidence for the linger effect.

Not only were objects charged beneficially, to bring about healing, protection, or whatever, as in the blessing of objects, but they could be used for harm, too. Sorcerers, David-Kneel was told, were believed to be able to "charge" a knife, for example, in such a way that when an intended victim picked it up, he would abruptly be impelled to stab himself. Even among the lamas, and even then, more than fifty years ago, however, the ESP/PK controversy was evident. Some lamas told David-Kneel that the rituals and mental concentration of the sorcerer on the knife made the knife itself cause the stabbing (the PK explanation), but others told her that during the weeks or months of preparation the sorcerer actually affected the *mind* of the proposed victim (the ESP explanation). The act of stabbing himself with that particular knife would be so impressed on the victim's unconscious mind by telepathy that, when he found himself holding the knife, he would automatically do it.

This idea of objects being used as accumulators of PK energy is not confined to Lamaism. The subject is commonly discussed at psychotronics conferences in Europe, though it has aroused little interest in the United States. If the linger effect exists, then such accumulators, or generators as they are sometimes called, are logically possible. Presumably the trick would be to find some design and material that do not allow the energy to dissipate too quickly.

Then there is the matter of apparitions, ghosts, and what have you. Since the earliest days of psychical research—and probably long before—people have argued about what ghosts are, assuming that such things *are*. Is a ghost the manifestation of a discarnate entity? Is it a hallucination that you think you see (but really don't) because you've picked up an image of it by clairvoyance from the surroundings, or by telepathy from someone else? In the case of collective viewing, where several people claim to see the same ghost at the same time, is the image picked up by only one person and rebroadcast telepathically to his companions, so that all "see" exactly the same picture? Or is it, perhaps, something more substantial than a hallucination? Is the image an energy pattern, perhaps, that actually exists—not quite physical, not quite mental—as a reflection of the impression of it created by that clairvoyance or telepathy? This suggestion was made in the 1930s by philosopher Professor H. H. Price and has been revived at intervals ever since (315). Again, the linger effect could give some support to this idea.

There has long been a debate within occultism as to whether the "demons" alleged to be conjured up by adepts are unreal, real with a separate existence, or real but created by the minds of the adepts. According to David-Kneel, they are created, but the student must subject himself to long years of apprenticeship before he truly becomes aware of this fact and is able to handle both the creation and dissolution of such a thought form. She says she herself created such a *tulpa*, in the shape of "a monk, short and fat, of an innocent and jolly type." After several months of solitude and concentration, and the appropriate rites, the phantom monk "grew gradually *fixed* and life-like looking." Madame David-Kneel set off on a journey, and the monk went along, behaving, as *tulpas* are expected to do, with considerable independence. He "walked, stopped, looked around him." He was seen by at least one other person who took him for a real lama. And he began to change. He "assumed a vaguely mocking, sly malignant look. He became more troublesome and bold. In brief, he escaped my control." It took six months of "hard struggle" for Madame David-Kneel to dissolve her creation.

A fairy story? The fantasy of a Western woman who had spent too long in the alien, masculine environment of rugged Tibet? Probably. No doubt the first knowing question of the psychiatrist would be, "In just what way did he become troublesome and bold?" And yet such a creation, be it called a familiar, daemon, *tulpa*, or control, occurs in so many disparate cultures that one cannot help but wonder why these diverse groups would have produced such similar ideas if they were not based on something. Could it be that the creative mind really can use and mold the energy around it so that a new energy pattern, neither physical nor mental, is formed?

Sensitive Rosalind Heywood, a great British lady who has approached her gift with healthy skepticism all her life, has reported some experiences that may be relevant. She has seemed to encounter Beings who impress her deeply as being far greater and more profound than anything she herself could have imagined (121). She suggests (122) that such Beings may have been formed by a gradual accretion of man's thoughts over the centuries, rather like the "group soul" of the occultists. A Being may be localized, as when it relates to the members of a group that meets in a certain place, such as a church or, as in one of Heywood's experiences, the British Houses of Parliament. At other times, perhaps, it relates to a concept, as in the case of what psychologists call *archetypes*. In other words, regardless of whether an archetype *originally* had independent existence, it is possible that an independent Being resembling an archetype now exists because it has been created by the thoughts of millions of people over the centuries. Thus there would be archetypes representing Light, the Great Mother, Nature, and so on, all created by man's mind. (And if you think about her long enough, perhaps there would be an archetype of your Aunt Millie—even if survival in the spiritualist sense is not a fact.)

If such Beings do exist, and were created by man's PK, then the question of *where* they exist may be relevant to the mysteries of psi. Beings are, in our theory, not exactly material, not exactly mental. It used to be fashionable to speculate about the existence of a fourth dimension, or even a fifth or sixth dimension. In recent years the word *dimension* has been nudged aside in favor of the concept of realities. LeShan writes of Sensory, Clairvoyant, and Transpsychic Realities (148), Castaneda of ordinary and nonordinary realities. Both maintain that events that would be impossible in what is generally accepted as being our everyday reality are not only possible but normal in other realities. Such events may include both psi and transcendent Beings.

Studies of altered states of consciousness are beginning to hint that in specific states we become aware of specific nonordinary realities. Perhaps in those states we do indeed "turn on" to things of which we cannot become aware in our normal state of awareness. Gardner Murphy has referred to ordinary, sensory reality as being like the outside surface of a cube (176). If it is possible to break through that surface to the interior of the cube, one can short-cut from one place to another; this, he suggests, is what happens when psi takes place. Perhaps the inside of that symbolic cube is the nonordinary reality in which psi is normal.

However, Murphy considers that by short-cutting through the cube one can only reach information (in ESP) or achieve ends (in PK) that one could eventually reach or achieve by normal sensorimotor means. In other words, the *end* is still in our ordinary reality; it is only the means of attaining that end that may be paranormal. Whether this would jibe with the sensing of nonordinary Beings and planes reported by those who claim to have been there is questionable. Perhaps that is only one cube of many. Perhaps there are cubes within cubes and realities within realities, and perhaps we are not yet willing to admit the consequences of such thoughts.

Such reluctance is hardly logical.

Parapsychologists are used to being considered "fringy" by many of their colleagues from other disciplines. Perhaps, rather than fighting the designation with ever more rigid adherence to scientific attitudes, they should recognize that the scientific attitude is to see things as they *are* and accept them that way. Parapsychology *does* border on the occult, the fringy, and the fantastic. Even though the field itself may remain strictly scientific, the border cannot be denied. A foreigner, observing a country with fresh and unjaded eyes, can sometimes make observations that one born and raised there cannot. So perhaps those parapsychologists born to science may do well to remain open to the observations of those from across the border. If we are reluctant to do so, perhaps we should ask ourselves whether it is not our own world view that we are protecting. Perhaps we are not ready to risk opening that ancient "see it, touch it, or it isn't there" door, long locked against childhood fears and chaos. Yet if there *is* such a door, to deny it would hardly be scientific.

A cautious study of some of these rather fringy subjects may well bring us closer to what parapsychology is presently lacking—a theory that can account for all the phenomena of psi, including psychokinesis.

Part 3

Where Now?

Chapter 13

"Let George Do It" (But Who and Why Is George?)

...We can try to define PK generally as a principle that makes the outcome of a random event depend on the effects produced by this outcome.

Helmut Schmidt (269)

So far we might be said only to have made short excursions along the shores of psiland. It may prove to be a bigger and more surprising place than we have generally dared to imagine.

Rex G. Stanford (286)

One of the earliest conclusions of researchers was that psi is basically unconscious. Early researchers came to this conclusion because subjects knew neither *how* they did whatever they did to achieve good psi results nor *when* they were achieving them. Later came experiments in which subjects apparently achieved good PK results when they were not even aware what die face, for example, was the target. A still later development was the series of experiments to discover whether subjects could achieve good results when they were not even aware that any psi test was taking place (mentioned briefly in Chapter 6). Though most of the preliminary work involved ESP, and so is not examined in detail in this book, some of the later, more elaborate tests did involve PK. Taken together, the results seem to establish fairly clearly that in experimental conditions subjects *do* use psi when they are not consciously aware that they are involved in a psi situation.

Interlinked with this work was Rex Stanford's major theory of psi-mediated instrumental response (PMIR) (283, 284).* The reader may remember Stanford's suggestion that, if people use psi unknowingly to get themselves into a more comfortable situation or to achieve other desired ends in the laboratory, it is logical to assume that they use it in the same way in real-life situations. Such use of psi may involve affecting the environment, but apparently it more commonly involves use of ESP to attain required information.

Many people have had the experience of noticing a word or subject that is new to them, only to have a clarification of that same thing turn up "by coincidence" within a few days. This may be an example of PMIR, particularly since there seems to be a tendency for the follow-up findings to occur in situations where random choices have been made. It is often the casually selected magazine that provides an example of just the word that interested us a few days previously; yet we could as easily have chosen any one of half a dozen others. What guides our choice? Is it PMIR?

Examples of PMIR through ESP are more common than those for PK, and are often quite dramatic. Stanford tells of a vegetarian couple traveling to Washington, D.C., with no knowledge of vegetarian restaurants at their destination. They stopped to eat at a service area restaurant, sat down, then, for no reason that they could pinpoint, decided to move to another booth. Moments later another group of people entered, sat down at the booth next to them, and *proceeded to discuss vegetarian restaurants in Washington.* They spoke loudly enough for the couple to acquire all the information they needed. As the couple left, they noticed that the people were eating meat, so were not themselves vegetarian (285). What had prompted the numerous decisions of timing and placement that had brought the couple to just that one place where they could get the information they sought? Coincidence? PMIR?

Why, when seeking a name for a new cat, did I pick up a magazine manifestly of no interest to me, only to find, buried near

* Much of what follows in this chapter and in Chapter 15 concerns Stanford's PMIR and conformance models. However, he is responsible for only those aspects of these models that are directly attributed to him. All other ideas and speculations are the responsibility of the author and should not in any way be blamed on Stanford!

the end, an anecdote about Confucius that gave me a name precisely suited to the circumstances?

Why, on the day they discovered that their beloved dog had epilepsy, did a friend and her husband stay up late for a talk show they hardly ever watched? They were deeply distressed by the dog's convulsions and disturbed because they had not previously known that dogs could have epilepsy. Was the fact that they watched this particular show an unconscious psi-mediated response to the fact that a guest on the show would be talking about *his* dog, which also had epilepsy, and of how his family was coping with the problem? Certainly what he had to say was of great comfort to them.

After knowing for several months that I needed to consult Panati's *The Geller Papers* before writing Chapter 5 of this book, I had begun to give up hope of getting a copy without buying one (and I was very short of funds). My local library did not have a copy, and none of my friends owned a copy. I had been told not to bother looking for books on parapsychology in the library of a nearby town because it had very few, so I never bothered to go in there even though I drove past it at least once a week. Why, then, did I one day change directions in mid-shopping trip, go straight to that library, check the index, tell a helpful librarian that I was looking for *The Geller Papers,* and watch her pick it up from where it was lying out on the counter, apparently waiting for me? Why was it out on the counter? Had I unconsciously tuned in to the fact that someone that morning was returning the book? If so, then PMIR was operating.

How often has an impulsive change of plan, or even an apparently absent-minded mistake, resulted in a desirable end? Many people, on examining the idea, find that these occurrences, usually dismissed as rare coincidences, are quite frequent.

Few such examples of spontaneous PK-PMIR are reported in the literature, apart from the oft-repeated tale of Jung and Freud's argument over the validity of parapsychology, during which loud noises are said to have come from Jung's bookcase. We cannot tell how often PK-PMIR is used in the form of MOBIA (mental or behavioral influence of an agent; see Chapter 4), for this would simply result in our influencing people to do something helpful to us. When such an event occurs unexpectedly we tend to attribute it to their kindness or say "You must have read my mind; that's just what I needed," without considering whether we might actually have played an active role in obtaining their help.

Another odd incident that may have involved PK-PMIR is known to the writer. A young woman who lived away from home was paying a brief visit to her parents. Her boyfriend had arranged to drive over later in the week, stay a day or two to get to know her family, and then drive her back to where she was living. Since her parents frequently disapproved of her boyfriends, and she was extremely serious about this one, she was somewhat tense about the proposed first meeting. During the few days before the boyfriend arrived, three electrical appliances that she had used many times before without mishap "died" as she was operating them quite normally. (Some people seem to "zap" electrical gadgets quite often, but this young lady did not.) Just as her parents were on the point of forbidding her to touch anything electrical, enter white knight in shining armor. Her boyfriend, who had considerable electrical skill, arrived and proceeded to fix all three appliances. Result—he was an immediate hero in the eyes of her hitherto suspicious parents.

Is it possible that my friend had unconsciously settled on one thing that her future husband could do that would win her parents' approval? That she had then given him the opportunity to do it by using PK, quite unconsciously, to affect the appliances? According to the PMIR theory, it is. Stanford believes that the stronger a person's need, the more efficiently PMIR is likely to work, and the need for parental approval in this case was, I believe, quite strong.

To discover whether PK could be used in such a way, a group of researchers headed by Stanford set up a laboratory experiment (293). Forty subjects were given a PK test using a random event generator with one chance in six of getting a hit. Then they were told that they were to take part in a motor skills test, which involved following the very slow movement of a light on a rotor. This task was extremely boring and could last up to forty-five minutes. Meanwhile, unknown to the subjects, the PK machine in another room was started up again. If, during the course of the forty-five minutes, the machine showed seven hits in any block of ten trials the experimenter immediately allowed the subject to stop the rotor tracking task and set him to work rating a series of pictures of attractive females in various stages of undress. Since all subjects were college-age males, it was assumed that this would be a more desirable condition than rotor tracking for most of them. Subjects might, therefore, unconsciously "discover" this way of escaping the rotor task and use their PK to bring about the desired score.

Although by chance alone fewer than three of the forty subjects should have attained the desirable condition, in fact eight did ($P = .0069$), indicating that PMIR did seem to be working.

Then came another question. Could it be proven that PMIR works more effectively in response to strong needs than to weak ones?

Once again Stanford and his colleagues turned to the rotor tracking task and sexually arousing pictures as undesirable and desirable conditions for seventy-two college-age male subjects in a PMIR-ESP experiment (292). Each subject was assigned to one condition or the other on the basis of a word association test. Among the words was a key word, randomly chosen in each case, to which the subject was to make either his fastest or his slowest response in the entire list. (Whether slowest or fastest was also decided randomly.) If the subject performed as required he entered the pleasant condition when the word association test was over. If he did not, he entered the boring condition. The test was unconscious because subjects had no knowledge that it involved anything other than word association, which they believed was part of a study of thought processes. The experimenter giving the test was blind to which was the key word and whether the desired response was fast or slow.

The "strength of need" part of the test was manipulated by having half the experimenters be males and the other half attractive females. It was hypothesized that subjects who had been talking with and tested by an attractive coed would be "at least somewhat sexually aroused" and therefore would have a greater need for the pleasant condition in which they studied pictures of females. As it turned out, quite a difference occurred in the scores of those tested by females and by males, with the former getting into the favorable condition significantly more often than did the latter.

Another preliminary test tackled the question of helping behavior, which might have been unconsciously brought about by MOBIA.

Again, Stanford used the word association test, with one randomly chosen key word as the target requiring the fastest response. In this case, however, it was not the person being given the test (the "potential helper") who would perform the rotor tracking or picture rating task. Unknown to him or her, a "helpable person" in a nearby room was waiting to be told whether he had been assigned to a "vigilance task" (the rotor) or a "person-perception task" (the pictures). If the potential helper scored a hit, the helpable person was assigned to the pictures; if not, he had the boring rotor task. While three people would be expected by chance to receive the more pleasant task, given the number of subjects involved, in fact 7 of them did. Apparently, although neither the helpable people nor the potential helpers knew that the former needed help (nor did either even know of the existence of the other), help was provided. We cannot say for sure that MOBIA was involved, that the helpable subjects used PMIR to discover their need (a need not to be assigned the boring task) and then used PK, in the form of MOBIA, to affect the potential helper's reactions, but it is a possibility (290).

Stanford's complete ESP-PMIR theory, which in many respects applies also to PK, was summarized in nine points (284), paraphrased as follows:

1. People (and probably animals) use psi as well as their five "normal" senses to scan the environment for whatever will help fill their needs.

2. If need-related information is obtained through psi, then a response to that information is likely.

3. One may unconsciously make changes in thinking, emotions, and so on, as preparation for PMIR.

4. Whether or not a PMIR will result is partly influenced by the strength and importance of the need involved, how fully the event, object, or information would fill that need, and how soon the event or information would be encountered.

5. PMIR may be totally unconscious to the extent that a person may not know that he is using psi, that he is attempting to fulfill a need (or even that he *has* a need), or that he is doing anything other than what he would normally do.

6. PMIR may use already existing behavior and thought patterns, memories and so on, to achieve its ends.

7. PMIR, like all psi, seems to be goal-oriented and to work in the most direct and economical way possible.

8. PMIR cannot work in all situations. Sometimes it is impossible for a person to respond to his psi-mediated impulses.

(Obviously if psi is prevented from operating, then PMIR cannot work. Equally, if a person is insufficiently flexible in his behavior, because of either outside circumstances or his own personality traits, then the impulse will be ignored. The personality factors mentioned by Stanford as hindering PMIR in this way are "behavioral rigidity, inhibitions, stereotypy, response chaining and strong preoccupations" [284], or, to put it colloquially, the inability to "stay loose.")

9. Just as people can psi-miss in the lab, so can they psi-miss in PMIR. Psychological factors such as (to quote Stanford again) "neuroticism, a negative self-concept, and direct motivational conflicts such as guilt or an approach-avoidance conflict" make it likely that one will psi-miss, failing to create the desirable situation or even actually using PMIR *against* one's own best interests.

In the same paper and elsewhere (288) Stanford suggests that PK may operate best when the subject believes that *not he but someone or something else is responsible for it:*

> The most dramatic of possible-PK events seem almost invariably associated with beliefs that some efficacious agency outside oneself is responsible for their occurrence, albeit usually with one's consent, request, supplication, etc., as in the case of appeal for such events to God, supernatural beings or forces, spirits, etc.

This suggestion is backed by several experiments indicating that people do better at PK tasks when they are told *not* to concentrate on them (Chapter 6).

We have seen that contemporary table-tipping work (assuming its validity for now) works best when the sitters are involved in joking and singing, rather than concentrating on the task at hand. In addition, the reader may remember that a "cheat," a psychological primer, was permitted to get things going by faking phenomena at the start of each sitting. As I have mentioned, many parapsychologists disapprove of this technique, and certainly it sets a questionable precedent. However, one effect could be that the other sitters would tend to relax more, thinking something like:

"Okay, it's happening even though I'm not doing anything, so I don't have to worry."

In other words, to use a popular old British expression, "Let George do it"—George being anyone other than the speaker.

Considerable evidence indicates that the "George" concept is helpful in PK. If we know *we* are doing it we *try,* we exert *effort,* we examine ourselves and our sensations to discover whether we are doing it right—even though no one knows what is right and what is wrong in this case. A belief that the outcome, though we would like it to be thus-and-such, is up to someone or something else seems to produce a more psi-conducive state of mind. This factor has been noticed many times and was well summarized in 1976 by Suzanne Padfield, herself a sensitive, who had originally used such a "George-type" figure, but later taught herself to take responsibility for her own PK with as much success as before (192).

It may be argued that this "let George do it" theory cannot be valid because many PK specialists seem to need to be under stress for PK to operate. However, the mind moves so fast that we cannot be sure of anyone's feelings at a particular moment. A major feature of most people's thinking under stress is that they reach a point characterized by one of the following:

"Oh, what's the use; I give up."

"I can't do anything more."

"If it's going to happen then it's going to happen; there's nothing I can do about it."

Or, in the more religiously inclined, "Please God, I can't do it. If you want it to happen then you'll have to help."

Such a moment seems to have occurred when Parise exclaimed, "abracadabra" and turned the compass needle (Chapter 6). From her flippant use of the word, it was clear that she had suddenly given up being serious about the whole thing.

Such moments may not be noticed at all by the experimenter in the normal course of events. Our culture frowns on giving up, so most subjects would immediately get back to work, almost ashamed of such a lapse and determined to show that they could do whatever the task might require. Nonetheless, it is quite possible that PK success is achieved in these fleeting moments of near desperation.

This idea has been suggested by experimental results (26) and studied directly by Stanford and Charles Fox (289). In their experiment, thirty-six subjects attempted to affect the electrical resistance of a photocell. After each trial they were instructed to read aloud from a magazine in an attempt to take their minds off the PK task. In three different testing conditions, the changes in electrical resistance were significantly greater during the twenty seconds *after* the subject had finished the trial than during the ten-second trials themselves. If this finding is supported by replication it seems to suggest that the actual effort of trying to do PK gets in the way of success, but the moment of release of effort may also be the moment when success is achieved. It may not be that *any* effort interferes with PK, but that *wrong* effort interferes—and the majority of people, it seems, use the wrong type of effort.

Some researchers believe that qualitative ESP tests, in which the subject tries to guess a picture or scene that could be absolutely *anything,* are more successful than quantitative tests for just this reason. In the qualitative test no information about the target is available and the subject has to start from scratch. Obviously this is an apparently impossible and therefore very stressful task. It has been suggested that in such a situation the intellect metaphorically throws up its hands in horror and quits—leaving exactly the attitude in which success is possible: "I can't do anything about it; if it's going to come to me it will."

Remember the tendency for the RSPK (poltergeist) agent to be someone who is frustrated and under stress, but who feels unable to make changes in his world. He feels helpless, so it would not occur to him—at least at first—that he could alter his environment normally, let alone throw plates or shift furniture paranormally. Yet, in a PMIR-like way, he achieves just what he wants to achieve. While believing that he is helpless to affect his environment, he manages to shake up his family, attract attention, and often bring in psychologists/parapsychologists who are interested in his feelings, who study the family relationship that often caused the stress in the first place, and who give advice that may help the family deal with its problems.

Parapsychologists have often noted that when they arrive on the scene RSPK events tend to weaken and become less frequent than previously reported. This apparent decrease may be due to exaggeration and credulity on the part of untrained earlier witnesses. However, it is common for a family afflicted with poltergeist phenomena to blame the events on a "spirit" once they have ruled out normal trickery to their own satisfaction. Comfortably provided with a spirit George to shoulder responsibility, a poltergeist agent would be free to vent subconscious angers and frustrations unchecked. Only when psychical researchers arrive and explain their theory that the agent's own PK is responsible would belief in George begin to fade, and the phenomena with them.

Perhaps we can account for the disappearance of the great physical mediums in the same way. It has often been suggested that physical mediums disappeared because today's researcher is too sophisticated to be hoodwinked by fraudulent tricks. This may be the case, but it should also be noticed that they started to disappear at about the time scientists announced that it was the mediums themselves, not spirits, who were responsible for the physical phenomena. Perhaps this, again, sowed the seeds of self-doubt so that mediums were no longer confident that they could slide comfortably into trance and let George do it. Once responsibility for the phenomena was placed firmly on their own shoulders, they were unable to produce the phenomena.

We know that many people have claimed to develop PK ability after seeing Geller. One wonders how many more actually develop and demonstrate it, happily thinking that it is good old Uri on the TV who is bending their spoons and starting the watches that they place before the set (if these things ever happen as they are alleged to).

Geller, in turn, used to think that not he but extraterrestrial beings were responsible for his PK (104), though he has now moved away from this belief.

In the help/hinder experiments (132) it is possible that the real subject, the person actually *doing* the PK, was the helper. He might have been able to perform quite spectacularly simply because he believed the official subject was doing the experiment—in other words, was "George"—and the helper considered his own task comparatively minor so was able to relax more. In the hinder part of the experiment he would have expected the subject to do less well, and so would have done less well himself. Another possibility is that the official subject regarded the helper/hinderer as a "George," was able to tell by ESP which condition was in force at which time, and performed accordingly.

An occult fad much despised by most parapsychologists involves the alleged ability of pyramids of certain proportions to keep razor blades sharp, preserve organic substances from decomposition, and encourage the growth of plants placed within them. Some sincere people believe that they have had success with these apparently outlandish experiments, although well-controlled attempts to verify the effect scientifically have not been successful. One is tempted to speculate that the pyramid is in fact just another George, and that those involved produce the success of their experiments with their own PK, released and able to work unconsciously because they are confident that the pyramid is doing it. Skeptics, of course, would bring about the results they expected—nothing whatsoever— because they have no faith in George-the-pyramid.

The implications of PMIR, of "let George do it" (not Stanford's choice of words), and of the apparently goal-oriented nature of psi led Stanford to suspect that the psychobiological theory of psi, in which the individual makes psychic events happen, might not be the real explanation for psi.

Eventually he came up with a new model, that all psi can perhaps be explained by what he calls *conformance behavior* (286, 288). Conformance behavior seems to be almost a law of nature: Given a number of alternative outcomes and a "disposed system" (an organism that needs or wants something) and given that one of the possible outcomes can fulfill the need, then *that* outcome is more likely than the other possible outcomes. So if a person has a need or a wish to do well in a PK test, the random number generator is the source of randomness and will tend to provide him with high scores. (Note that the word *behavior* does not necessarily apply to the behavior of the person with the need, but to the universe in general. It is not how we behave that causes the PK, but the fact that circumstances are "balanced" in such a way that our needs can affect that balance, bringing about a need-favorable event.)

This theory also relates well to ESP, in which the brain, with its multitude of neurons that may or may not fire, is the random event generator that will tend to bring to consciousness the desired target. This suggestion has been made elsewhere and has been formulated mathematically by physicist Evan Harris Walker (327). In ESP the random event generator is apparently usually inside us; in PK it is a part of the outside world.

This theory neatly does away with all the complex questions regarding the kind of energy link that exists between man and PK target. The force that moves or bends or breaks is a universal energy not necessarily related to the PK subject at all except that it does respond to his needs. In some way, presumably, this response relates to the subject's attitude or state of mind, so some kind of causal link still exists—the vital difference between synchronicity (see Chapter 14) and the PMIR and conformance models. However, the conformance model does not, as yet, deal with just *how* this is achieved. As Stanford himself has said of the whole concept, it "is in need of much conceptual and empirical refinement. It is simply one possible starting point."

As a starting point the conformance model opens up a whole new set of questions about psi and indeed about mankind. Does the universe conform more for some people than others? What of needs that work against other people's needs? Does this conformance relate to one's progress through life? To leadership? Power? Charisma? Luck?

While himself remaining on scientific ground, Stanford has thrown into the air a ball that may well land in some very non-scientific areas, as we shall see in Chapter 15. But before venturing into them, let us examine some of the more traditional theories of PK.

Chapter 14
How and Why?

I submit that we will not know any more about psi unless we begin to think in more positive terms about what psi is and subject our thoughts to experimental verification.

K. Ramakrishna Rao (223)

Comparatively few people can truthfully call themselves full-time parapsychologists. Most must have another, bring-home-the-bacon, career from which they earn their living. If they are lucky the two, vocation and avocation, will complement each other. If not, their interest in parapsychology may be a constant threat to their ability to support themselves and their families.

Shortly before writing this book I met two men, a geologist and a clinical psychologist, who had recently been denied tenure at the university at which they worked, almost certainly because of their work in parapsychology. Many other parapsychologists admit that much of their mental energy has to be used in seeking diplomatic ways of easing the tension between their two fields. Some publish little so that their academic colleagues will remain unaware of their interest. Others gamble, speak frankly about their work with psi, and keep going, knowing that an unlucky speculation or conclusion, or a slight change of political climate at work, may cost them their ability to earn a living.

Perhaps because of this feeling of insecurity, some parapsychologists are so anxious to conform to the concepts of the hard "scientific" sciences that many have put aside field observations such as poltergeist studies and observations made about the PK superstars.

Since these events did not occur under totally controlled conditions we are sometimes told that we have to ignore them. ("This cannot be true, therefore exclude it from the books.")

Obviously caution within science is not only desirable but essential. Without it, science is not science. Yet caution should not be confused with tunnel vision. In recent years, parapsychologists have been accused, often rightly, of being overly concerned with minutiae, with decimal point statistics, with the scientific status quo. Sometimes it is suspected that they are so determined to prove their scientific dependability that they have lost sight of the enormity of their field. They are so busy counting and measuring trees that they have forgotten that the forest even exists.

Laymen who have this feeling might be startled to know that their fears are shared by many people within parapsychology, too, particularly in very recent years.

Parapsychologists increasingly feel that none of the present theories of psi are enough. All are too timid, or untestable, or in some other way do not provide what is needed. There is a cry for a quantum jump, for someone to step out and produce a theory that will be global enough to explain the bewildering array of events known as psi, yet precise enough to be tested. It must either measure up to the known facts of other, harder sciences, or give us—not suggest or hint at but *give us*—a new view of life that can include both psi *and* the rest of reality—or the rest of the realities, if that be the case. Stanford's PMIR and conformance theories and their extensions begin to do this but still leave a large How? There may be a law of nature that helps fulfill our needs, but that does not tell us how such a law is carried out. Man is not usually content to leave laws of nature in such unsatisfactory, unexplained states. To find out how things work we have to send the kite up into the thunderstorm, and before we can know *what* to send up into *where*, and *why*, we have to have a theory.

A number of theories of psi were excellently discussed by Rao in 1966 (221), but unfortunately that was before the PK revival and almost all the ideas mentioned were focused on ESP. (It is in the realm of theory that ESP and PK most have to be separated, since a postulated system for ESP reception by the brain, for example, cannot easily be extended to cover a die or a random number generator.)

Existing theories range from the utilization of quantum mechanics to an unspecified universal energy and include such terms as *bioplasma* and *Shin* along the way, but none is complete. Each leaves a gap somewhere; some part of the psi process between man and object remains unexplored, and there are no near prospects of a breakthrough. In 1969 R. H. Thouless considered that although psi was unlikely to be generally accepted until it could be properly explained, we could not expect such an explanation to be swift in coming. "That is likely," he remarked, "to be a long time ahead, since the difficulties of the research are much greater than any in the physical sciences" (312).

An even more discouraging note was sounded in 1971 when David Rogers, pointing out that the unconscious is not rational, and that psi is an unconscious, and therefore nonrational function, said "The question remains if it is logically possible for the conscious and rational researchers to explain an unconscious and irrational phenomenon" (250).

A similar view is expressed by those who doubt that psi is physical and question whether a nonphysical function can be explained, let alone detected or measured by way of proof. Some go so far as to maintain that if a physical explanation for PK and ESP were found, "both phenomena would obviously be taken over by physics; and they would just as obviously no longer be of interest to parapsychology" (164).

Rhine has long been the foremost proponent of the nonphysical view. In his opinion physicists who believe that "paraphysics" is a more accurate term than parapsychology should first try to find some physical condition that does affect psi, in order to show that psi is subject to physical laws. Rhine does not feel that this has yet been done (236).

Against this view are theorists who maintain that if PK can physically move objects then it must be physical, and therefore subject to the laws of physics, even if we do not yet understand those laws. Haakon Forwald held that his work showed a clear relationship between the distance his various cubes moved and the atomic weight of the metal foil by which they were covered, and that his work showed gravity to be the force involved (94). However, as we have seen, Forwald's results may also be explained by the experimenter effect.

The poltergeist studies made by William G. Roll (Chapter 9) show a decrease in movements of objects as one gets farther away from the poltergeist agent. This fact is interpreted as evidence that poltergeist phenomena follow physical laws. An objection may be made on grounds that the poltergeist agent is more likely to be aware of objects near him, and therefore unconsciously focus his energy on them, making the attenuation a psychological phenomenon. However, we must remember that Dr. John Artley and Roll showed the attenuation rate very closely fitted a curve known as the exponential decay function (4). This function (discussed in Chapter 9) is, after all, a strictly physical, not psychological, function. The fact that attenuation resembles a physical function is a strong point in favor of its having a physical, rather than psychological, basis.

William Joines has also presented an analysis showing that wave theory seems to fit a number of psi manifestations. He refrains from judging what kind of wave might be involved, commenting only that "all forms of energy now known to us manifest themselves as wave motions," and that therefore we might expect psi energy to fit wave theory even if it is a new form of energy (134).

Still other researchers hold that the physical/nonphysical argument is pointless, that so much information will have to be gathered before the issue can be decided that both parapsychology and physics will by then have become completely different sciences from what they are now. Even J. G. Pratt, who in general tends toward the nonphysical line, does so with the *caveat* that future discoveries in physics may show a relationship to psi that is not presently apparent (210).

The various theories of psi may be broken down in many ways, but for our purposes and to avoid too much psychological and philosophical jargon the format shown in the accompanying table has been chosen. The theories are divided into Nonexistent ("PK does not exist"), Physical, Nonphysical, and External, the latter proposing the involvement of some force, entity, or law of nature totally external to man. Some of the divisions are arbitrary and some overlap, but this short survey does not allow a more complete analysis.

The nonphysical designation is included because it is a long-accepted term. In this writer's opinion, when discussing energies or forces in general it is semantically impossible to describe them as "nonphysical." Any energy is physical. What may be meant is that PK involves a form of energy presently unimaginable and unmeasurable by man, much as radio waves, electricity, and ultraviolet light once were. We arbitrarily divide the electromagnetic spectrum into cosmic, gamma, and X-rays, ultraviolet, visible, and infrared light, and Hertzian and radio waves and think of them according to how they affect, or can be manipulated to affect, our senses. Often we forget that these various terms simply describe different wavelengths of the same basic energy (as different octaves in music). In the same way, some currently unmeasurable forms of energy, perhaps (or perhaps not) related to currently unproven dimensions or planes of existence, may be named "nonphysical" or "spiritual," but as a semantic convenience, not a true division from the physical. Such "energy" may equally well be truly nonphysical or spiritual, but then it is not an energy in the generally accepted sense of the word.

Theoretical Explanations for Psychokinesis
A. Nonexistent.
B. Physical
   1. Presently known forces
      a. Quantum physics
      b. Electromagnetic energy
      c. Electrostatic energy
      d. Gravity
   2. Unknown ways of organizing known energies
   3. Unknown physical energy or field yet to be discovered
      a. As part of man
      b. Ubiquitous energy
C. Nonphysical
   1. *Shin*
   2. Etheric
   3. Alternative dimension/reality/state of consciousness

D. External
   1. Superordinate energy
      a. Personal
      b. Teleological
   2. Spirits, discarnate entities
   3. Synchronicity
   4. Conformance behavior

A. NONEXISTENT

The first theory holds that PK does not exist. If this is the case then the research discussed in this book, and more, can be explained only by allegations of fraud and/or inadequately controlled experiment (coincidence comes under the heading of Synchronicity). It seems unlikely that the scientific community of parapsychologists could have allowed either possibility to escape their notice for so long. Indeed, whether motivated by professional jealousy or an honest desire to keep the field operating at the highest level of control and integrity, many scientists will pounce on the slightest error or lack of experimental control by another without a moment's hesitation. Not even the most revered or best-loved researchers are immune from criticism. Certainly the personalities involved are far too disparate to allow for any possibility of the "global intrigue" theory that has occasionally been hinted at by those frustrated in their efforts to find fault with some of the more successful experiments.

Researchers are not infallible. Throughout this book, *caveats* have accompanied descriptions of experiments that were not as well controlled as one would hope, or for which differing interpretations of the results are possible. Some experiments cited may have alternative explanations of which the writer is unaware. Nevertheless, given the bulk of work that has been done, particularly in recent years, it does not seem possible that all can be dismissed so casually.

B. PHYSICAL

1. Presently Known Forces

a. Quantum physics: For many years there were those who maintained that psi was impossible, and believers who accepted psi and maintained that it related to nonphysical energies. The two were incompatible, and those who believed that psi could be explained physically were few and far between. However, as theoretical physics has progressed since the development of quantum physics, the physicist's world has become less and less physical in the classic sense of the word. The more physicists describe subatomic particles and quantum physics, the more what they say resembles what the mystics and great religious leaders have said about reality. Parapsychologist LeShan went so far as to write a paper (147) in which he presented an assortment of statements on man, matter, reality, existence, causation, time, and space. The trick was that half the statements were made by mystics and half by physicists, and he challenged anyone to distinguish them without using the key. For those unfamiliar with either field, it was almost impossible. LeShan perhaps oversimplifies the similarities between the fields somewhat, and his work has been criticized. However, it is an interesting concept.

A few physicists have had similar ideas and have started a search for ways in which quantum physics might correlate with psi and so make parapsychology a more scientifically acceptable field. They little knew the battle they were getting into. Some feel that the job is done, the model already demonstrated (327). They point to the fact that almost every psychic phenomenon has its parallel at the subatomic level. To those who say that psi energy must decrease over distance if it is physical, they point out that certain forces involved in the study of elementary particles appear to increase, not decrease, with distance (89).

They add that the tachyon, a postulated subatomic particle, is never slower than the speed of light (but its existence is questioned by many researchers). They write of positrons moving backward in time. They remind us that in quantum physics the state of everything is uncertain *until the moment it is measured,* and that prior to the time of measurement calculations can only show the combination of states in which whatever is being measured may be found. Which state will be the final one is uncertain until the moment of measurement. (Yet what exactly constitutes a measurement is unknown.) Some hypothesize that the *consciousness of the person making the measurement* may affect which state is the the final one, in which case PK would be demonstrated, but others dispute this.

While looking at the matter of causality, physicists point to the Einstein-Podolsky-Rosen (EPR) paradox (273). The EPR paradox is usually illustrated somewhat like this. Assume a certain kind of atom that decays into two photons, which take off in opposite directions. If one photon is observed meeting a polarizing filter it will become polarized, either vertically or horizontally. It has an equal chance of going either way and yet, whichever way it becomes polarized, the photon going in the opposite direction must always become polarized in the opposite direction. How does the other photon "know" which way to become polarized, or even that the first photon has become polarized? Where is the causation? None is apparent.

Perhaps, say some, this indicates that whenever things have been connected, they always remain linked in some mysterious way. Or perhaps they are demonstrating instantaneous information transmittal over a distance. Is this subatomic telepathy? Or does one *affect* the other? Subatomic PK? A paradox indeed, and one from which we might suspect that we had discovered a scientific basis for sympathetic magic. However, since we are being physicists at the moment, we can safely back away from that troubling thought.

There are, however, other disquieting concepts, such as that of quantum tunneling. Quantum tunneling is an established phenomenon in which a particle passes through a barrier—somewhat as though a tennis ball were to pass through a brick wall. And anything that can happen on the quantum level *could* happen on a larger scale. The molecular components of an object are constantly in motion; it is only the fact that their motion is random and incoherent that causes the object as a whole to remain apparently motionless. If a conglomerate of the components "decided" to do the same thing at the same time, the object would move too. As a general rule this does not happen, fortunately. The question is, does it perhaps happen in psi?

Does an object in a box suddenly appear out of the box because of something resembling quantum tunneling? Do all the atoms at one end of an iron bar "decide" to move in relation to those at the other end, so making the bar bend? The ideas strike a receptive chord in the minds of some who have long pondered the "hows" of PK. Yet, in spite of the popularization of the idea of parapsychology as quantum physics, most physicists and parapsychologists still believe that the two are not yet compatible. Philosopher C. T. K. Chari, who has long been involved in parapsychology, says flatly that "all attempts to crack the riddles of psychical research by relying on quantum mechanics are, for the moment, premature and hazardous" (51).

J. H. M. Whiteman, who is both a philosopher and a professor of mathematics at the University of Cape Town, also holds to the view that quantum physics does not *explain* psi (337). He believes, however, that quantum physics may exhibit a way in which things can contradict the common-sense view of the world yet still be scientific, paving the way for a similar approach to psi. If this aspect of quantum physics is accepted, then parapsychology can no longer be denied on the grounds that "things like that can't happen." At the quantum level they *can* happen—but whether parapsychological phenomena in the "upper world" have any direct connection with quantum physics has yet to be discovered.

Many of the physicists who care about parapsychology (few as they may be) agree with Edwin May in acknowledging an apparent parallel between physics and psi (159) while remaining content to wait a while for future developments that may or may not demonstrate a closer link. Parallel lines, after all, do not ever join. Quantum physics is still in a state of development and controversy. Sundry interpretations, theorems, and paradoxes continue to be disputed with as much heat as are school taxes and detente. Many postulated subatomic particles are postulated only because their existence makes sense, not because any trace of them has yet been found. Some believe that the field can hardly be expected to provide the answers to parapsychology's questions when it does not yet have answers to its own, while others think that the paradoxes of quantum physics can *only* be resolved by acceptance of the existence of psi phenomena.

b. Electromagnetic energy: When one thinks of ESP as "mental radio," the idea that electromagnetic (EM) energies may be involved in psi is extremely attractive. Some researchers believe that such energies also may be somehow harnessed to bring about

PK. Most EM wavelengths were eliminated as possibilities early in the psychical research game by the simple expedient of putting the subject into a Faraday cage, which excludes most of the EM spectrum. We have seen that Ted Serios continued to produce apparent PK effects while in a Faraday cage, and in fact so many Faraday cage experiments have been done that EM waves are conclusively ruled out, with the possible exception of extremely low frequency (ELF) waves, which are not excluded by a Faraday cage.

ELF waves can travel completely around the earth, guided by the ionosphere, which keeps them from dissipating into space. Michael Persinger is a psychophysiologist at Laurentian University, Canada. He has pointed out that (1) the frequency of ELF waves is such that under some conditions they may resonate with the human brain; (2) ELFs are more easily transmitted from west to east than vice versa; (3) more ELFs occur between midnight and 4 A.M. than at other times; (4) ELFs tend to follow the magnetic lines of the earth; and (5) ELFs are disturbed by geomagnetic disturbances (198).

According to Persinger, a study of reported spontaneous telepathy cases fits this profile: more occur when the agent is to the west of the percipient; numerically they peak in the early hours; and fewer occur during geomagnetic disturbances. He suggests that good psi subjects are those whose alpha waves peak at a frequency coinciding with ELF frequencies. To make the transfer to PK, he feels that if ELF waves "carry" telepathy, the reverse may also be true, and the energy of ELF waves can in some way be harnessed by man's body to be used in PK. (The phrase "in some way" perhaps puts this theory into a later category, "unknown ways of organizing known energies.")

A major difficulty with the ELF theory lies in the question of the body's ability to function as an antenna for waves this long. It has been hazarded that, although man's body is not long enough, perhaps the neural system as a whole is, but the mechanism of reception has yet to be shown clearly. The nerves are surrounded by liquid, which is a better conductor than they are, so it seems unlikely that the waves could get through to them.

To confirm the ELF theory it would be necessary to use a Faraday cage with concrete walls five feet thick, which would screen out about 99 percent of the ELF waves (151), or extremely thick steel walls, and even they would not be 100 percent efficient.

c. Electrostatic energy: Researchers have produced some evidence that electrostatic energy is used for some PK phenomena. It has been noted that Vinogradova appears to use electrostatic forces; yet she can work just as well when grounded. Because many successful PK experiments could not have been due to electrostatic forces, however, modern parapsychology cannot give the subject serious consideration except possibly as a source of energy that can be converted to some other form of energy.

d. Gravity: Forwald suggested that gravity helps explain his results and that the atomic weight of the metals is relevant, but he admitted an unanswered question: "Through which mechanism might nuclear energy within matter be converted into gravitational potential differences?" (94).

Forwald's work, however, took place prior to the development of the Schmidt machines and work with Geiger counters, magnetometers, and other definitely nongravitational experimental techniques. If gravity is involved it would seem to come into a later category, either as a known energy organized in an unknown way or as what some researchers call biogravity, which is perhaps arbitrarily assigned to (3) below.

2. Unknown Ways of Organizing Known Energies

In a way this heading covers all of the above, for we do not understand any way in which man may be able to convert known energies to paranormal use. However, this section primarily includes ways in which man might gain access to enough energy to enable him to move a die, or affect a magnetometer, even though science assures us that man does not give off enough energy himself to do this.

For example, it has long been noticed that many anecdotal accounts of psi phenomena include mention of a drop in temperature. A typical case is one mentioned by Myers, quoting a Mr. C. who had carried out some mediumistic experiments: "On *all* occasions, both at seances and privately, immediately before and during any manifestation, we all felt a sudden chill, like either a wave of

intensely cold air passing, or a rapid decrease of temperature"
(179).

In October 1971 a letter appeared in the *Journal of the American
Society for Psychical Research* (163) suggesting that such drops in
temperature might be the source of the energy used to move objects
in poltergeist cases (and, by extension, in other forms of PK
phenomena). J. T. McMullan of the School of Physical Sciences,
New University of Ulster, calculated that the air in an average size
room, if cooled through 1°C., would make available sufficient
energy to raise a 25-kilogram (55-pound) table about 200 meters
(656 feet)—far more than the height of the average room! The only
energy the PK subject would need to provide, therefore, would be
that needed to make the conversion and control the energy so
produced.

In discussing this suggestion, J. H. Rush later pointed out that,
using known methods, as much energy would be needed to extract
the heat energy as was actually extracted, leaving little or none for
poltergeist activity (260). However, he did not think that the theory
should be dismissed entirely, recalling a statement by Dr. Hans
Bender that the voices apparently heard on Raudive tapes are
always near the background noise level, as though perhaps that
noise level were itself the source of energy for the voices, a theory
noted briefly in Chapter 10.

Sometime after this exchange, Richard Mattuck of the University
of Copenhagen examined a fairly similar model of thermal noise as
PK energy source in some detail and concluded that it could account
for "a variety of PK phenomena" (157).

To explain the various concepts involved in organization of
known available energies, an analogy borrowed from Harold Puthoff
(217) may be helpful. Perhaps the effect is similar to that of a
laser, in which unfocused and incoherently bouncing energy is put
into phase to become a very powerful and controlled energy source.
Perhaps what we are looking for is not the energy involved, which
may already be available in one form or another, but simply
whatever puts it into phase.

"Noise energy" is always available in the atmosphere to some
degree. Furthermore, in Chapter 8 we saw that in the pseudo-
seance sessions of Batcheldor and Brookes-Smith, and of the

Toronto Society for Psychical Research, raps would not come when the group meditated or sat silently, but required songs, jokes, and conversation. In other words, perhaps an increased noise level served as an increased source of energy to fuel the raps, quite apart from helping the participants get into the right frame of mind for PK.

Perhaps the reason different experiments suggest different forms of energy in PK is that this organizing force of psi can actually make use of any available form of energy. Support for this concept of energy conversion also comes from the fact that the exponential decay function, which fitted analyses of object movements in poltergeist cases, is usually associated with changes from one form of physical energy to another.

An objection to this theory arises when we consider the phenomenon of teleportation. Hans Bender has pointed out that if an object dematerializes when it transfers from one closed space to another, "transformations of energy would be necessary which far surpass those of a hydrogen bomb" (14).

(Bender suggests that an alternative explanation for such transfers might be a fourth dimension, adding, "There is no *a priori* argument against higher space but there seems to be no evidence from other fields of science in its favor.")

We cannot lightly dismiss teleportation, since a certain amount of evidence for it exists, particularly from some poltergeist cases. However, it is one of the least proven forms of PK and is certainly so rare that it may be a special case apart from PK in general. Perhaps quantum tunneling does have some strange equivalent in the "upper world." Perhaps there is some other explanation.

In spite of objections regarding apparent teleportation, the possibility that PK is due to an organizing energy is so promising and so susceptible to experimentation that one hopes it will be studied closely in the future.

3. Unknown Physical Energy or Field Yet to Be Discovered

a. As part of man: Is it possible that man gives off energies not yet noticed by science? Is a mysterious psi field responsible for ESP and PK? As discussed in Chapter 12, many measurable fields surround the body, and Harold Saxton Burr proposed an L-field as a kind of force that not only surrounds us but perhaps guides the development of the physical body. This seems to relate very closely to Roll's belief, stated in 1969, "that each of us exists at the center of a psychokinetic force field which is a factor in directing our lives" (252).

The questions that arise are whether any of these fields can be controlled and used, and whether there may be others as yet undetected that can be controlled and used. If the answer to either question is yes, we may have grasped the *how* of PK—once we know how to control and use these fields. Much of the theorizing in this area has been done by the Russians and has arrived in the Western Hemisphere via the one or two specialists who devote much time and energy to following and translating Eastern European work in parapsychology. One of the foremost Soviet theoreticians is Aleksandr P. Dubrov, whose theory of "biogravitation" has been published in English in *The Parasciences,* one of a series of books published by UNESCO. Dubrov suggests that the molecular structure of living cells may give rise to a form of gravitational energy that could be directional and may interact with other such energy fields. Just how this directional effect could be controllable is not made clear (152), but the theory could be investigated without too much difficulty. As Dubrov himself has said, if the effect is gravitational and if a laser beam were between a PK subject's hand and the object being affected, then the beam would bend slightly (144). (Work is in fact being done on PK and laser beams in this country, but no information on results is yet available to me.)

To be subject to fluctuation or control, biogravity, if it exists, would have to be so different from gravity as we know it that it would probably be better classified under a different heading. But whether or not gravitational energy is involved, the force fields surrounding the human body certainly demand closer investigation in view of the hints from so many areas of paranormal endeavor.

Another human energy that may be involved in PK is muscle energy. Objects have been reported to move just as or just after a medium has made a spasmodic jerk. To the suspicious this observation confirmed that manipulatory fraud using threads or rods was involved, and that the medium's writhings were just a cover.

Perhaps not, however. Perhaps a kind of "leakage" occurs. As Hereward Carrington put it:

> It is quite *conceivable,* at least, that the nervous force which actuates the body might, under certain exceptional circumstances, extend beyond the periphery of the bodily frame, and exert an influence over the external, material world. (43)

We will come back to this idea in discussion of the *Shin* theory below, but for the moment let us look at some reports of muscle movements that seemed to have a paranormal effect.

In 1956, Mrs. Tubby, longtime secretary to the late Dr. James H. Hyslop, one of the founders of psychical research in this country, was quoted in the *Journal of Parapsychology* (37) as writing of the "musical telepaths," a husband and wife team who had been investigated by Hyslop. The wife would sit at the piano in one room, the husband in another. When given the title of the target tune the husband would make "rhythmical muscular movements," upon which the wife would start to play the tune. Probably a magician's parlor trick, for we are given little information as to the controls imposed, and yet Hyslop was no fool and does not seem to have discovered any form of fraud.

More recently L. L. Vasiliev of the Soviet Union wrote of experiments conducted by both Rudolph Reutler, then of Rosh Pina, Palestine, and a student under Vasiliev's direction, who conducted some rather distasteful experiments with cockroaches and cockchafers. The insects were decapitated and their abdomens opened up and placed in saline solution under a glass cover. Normally under these conditions the intestines will contract rhythmically for several hours. It was found that the rhythm of the contractions would often respond sharply to the experimenters' breathing patterns and to contractions of their legs, though the experiment was not successful under cold conditions (323).

Unfortunately no mention is made of any attempt to determine the maximum distance over which this effect took place. Muscle movements are known to give off electrical energy over short distances, and such energy might stimulate the intestines when the insects were close to the experimenter. In most cases the experimenter sat quite near what was left of the insect, so that he could observe the contractions through a magnifying glass. However, of the original Palestine experiments, Vasiliev says that "as soon as the experimenter entered the room, and increasingly so when he sat down to observe the preparation . . . the movements grew stronger and more rapid." This seems to indicate an effect over a fair distance—apparently across the room—but whether the vibrations of footsteps and an opening and closing door might have caused the first reaction we cannot tell, nor do we know who made the observation that "the intestines contracted in a slow rhythm" while the experimenter was gone and speeded up as soon as he entered the room, since we are also told that the room was empty while he was gone.

However, anecdotally and from observations made of mediums and superstars (many of whom move quite convulsively when attempting PK) we may wonder whether the theory that muscle activity in some way contributes energy to PK should be investigated further. As the reader will remember, Honorton found that subjects under the "muscle tension" condition scored better than those in the "muscle relaxation" condition (Chapter 6).

We may also wonder about the cause/source of this muscle activity. A recurring question since the early days of mediumship has been the possible connection between psi and sexual energies. It has been noted that the majority of poltergeist agents are approaching or just past puberty. The disturbances around at least one poltergeist agent, Eleonore, ceased as soon as she started to have her menstrual periods. In mentioning this incident writer Paul Tabori commented that powers of mediumship often either stop or start with the onset of puberty (301). Since many adult mediums have told of being mediumistic in childhood this cannot always be the case, but it is an interesting observation. We noticed that Eusapia Palladino writhed "orgasmically" during seances. E. R. Dodds, a past president of the SPR, has been quoted as writing that physical medium Rudi Schneider "was found to have had an emission of semen" during every successful sitting for the SPR. Schneider also explained a series of unsuccessful sittings as due to the fact that he was at that time having an affair (75).

More recently Professor Jean C. Dierkens, reporting on his work with Jean-Pierre Girard (Chapter 5), commented, "Girard is well conscious that creating PK is similar to experiencing an orgasm," and drew an analogy between Girard's movements when stroking a bar to bend it and the movements involved in masturbation—though Girard's EEGs were not identical under the two conditions (76).

Again, even if sexual energy is involved, just how it may be converted for use in PK we do not know. Subjects' performances in Faraday cages make it clear that any electrical energy from body movement is not what we are looking for, since this could not get through the Faraday barrier. Might it, however, be the smaller controlling energy that brings some other, unknown energy into phase so that, laserlike, the unknown energy can leap a Faraday cage in a single bound?

b. Ubiquitous energy, with acknowledgement of Robert Morris, who first used the terms "message ubiquity" and "superordinate source" in relation to ESP (174). The term *ubiquitous energy* implies that an unknown energy may exist everywhere around us, just waiting to be tapped. Most occult traditions claim this to be a fact, as do many religions. Regardless of whether it is called *prana, ki, od,* or the Holy Spirit, it is said that we all have access to it and can use it in apparently miraculous ways. Author John White has listed forty-seven different names for and "discoverers" of what he considers to be more or less the same type of energy (335). It is usually recommended that one practice meditation and breathing exercises, as well as mental and/or spiritual disciplines, in order to be able to control such an energy.

No doubt if it should be "discovered" at last and accepted by science it will not be until many more names and discoverers have been added to the list, and as yet no serious scientific work has been done in this area.

C. NONPHYSICAL

Bear in mind the point mentioned earlier, that if a "nonphysical" energy exists, it cannot be measured with physical equipment, for if it could be measured, it would be classified as physical. Therefore, if any of the hypothetical energies mentioned in this section are ever confirmed as fact, they will undoubtedly have to be reclassified as physical. If they are not physical it seems unlikely that they will be discovered by science as we know it. They may still exist, however, within some other dimension or plane of being, and may be perceivable at some other level of perception than our usual here-and-now level of awareness.

1. Shin

Exactly what is it that decides to move your little finger? Where is that decision made, and, once made, how is it communicated and how and why does the finger eventually move? Ask a biologist, and the odds are that, after more or less floundering around, depending on the nature of your chosen biologist, he or she will admit that although we know a lot, we cannot trace the entire transaction. Somewhere in or around our bodies something happens that we do not understand and yet that undeniably happens. Since we cannot discover a way in which the process conforms to known physical or psychological laws, the process of moving your finger could legitimately be called paranormal, if we wanted to stretch semantics to an extreme point of logic.

In 1948 Thouless and Dr. B. P. Wiesner (310) elaborated on a concept originally suggested by Myers and endorsed by Rhine. They used the word *Shin*, a Hebrew letter, to mean "that which perceives and wills"—a meaning very close to that of the word *soul* but without its religious connotations. They suggested that under normal conditions the *Shin* of each person directs the sensorimotor system, though by exactly what means we and our biologist do not know. Normally *Shin* confines its attentions to one person's body (though it is not necessarily attached thereto) but at times leakage may occur. *Shin* may bypass the sensorimotor processes and establish "direct relations" with the object it is perceiving (ESP) or affecting (PK).

This theory could have a bearing on the possible connection between RSPK and epilepsy or other CNS eruptions mentioned in Chapter 9. Some forms of epilepsy manifest as uncontrollable muscular spasms, and an extension of these beyond the body could be the cause of some types of poltergeist phenomena.

The *Shin* theory also accounts for *two* types of telepathy, one in which the sensory part of *B*'s *Shin* contacts *A*'s sensory system and discovers what is there (active percipient telepathy) and one in which the motor part of *A*'s *Shin* affects the motor part of *B*'s, so causing *B* to do physically what he is willed to do (active agent telepathy or MOBIA). This division would explain some questions about telepathy that have been bothering parapsychologists for some time.

Psychiatrist Jan Ehrenwald has suggested that this extension of *Shin* is an exact mirror image of conversion hysteria or hysterical paralysis, in which it seems to the patient that parts of his body are no longer in contact with the ego (or *Shin,* to use our terminology). He cannot feel or move them, although organically nothing is wrong. In the *Shin* theory it is not *less* than the body that is in contact with *Shin,* but *more* than the body (79).

Since the *Shin* theory does not explain what energies are involved, one assumes that this is a nonphysical process, for *Shin* itself is apparently nonphysical. However, the possible correlation with the muscle movement theory is obvious, as is the possible connection between poltergeist phenomena and epilepsy. Perhaps *Shin* does not totally bypass its sensorimotor system, as Thouless and Wiesner suggest, but goes through and beyond it.

2. *Etheric*

Murphy described what he called the "'etheric' theory (Myers-Newbold)" by way of acknowledging its similarity to both Myers' metetherial theory and the ideas of W. R. Newbold of the University of Pennsylvania (178). As Murphy put it, "There is a sphere of psychic events which is intermediate between the bodily sphere and a transcendent sphere." In other words, the etheric sphere is neither physical nor spiritual, but something in between, with something in common with both—a possibility we considered in Chapter 12. Murphy refers to it particularly in connection with apparitions, but one is reminded also of the aura, of the *something* "slightly visible to the clairvoyant" that is alleged to leave the body during out-of-body experiences, and of what the Soviets call bioplasma. Just how this etheric energy would interact with a solidly material die is not entirely clear. What is clear is that such an etheric energy might seem far from etheric if one were on/in another plane or state of consciousness.

3. *Alternate Dimension / Reality / State of Consciousness*

The anecdotes of Castaneda (46, 49), Robert A. Monroe (170), and many others who believe they have been out of body (66) make it clear that when one is in a nonordinary reality many material things seem etheric, whereas one perceives ethereal energies that seem as solid as a rock. The idea of a hyperspace—a fourth, fifth, or sixth dimension giving such impressions—has been the plaything of science fiction writers and a starting point for philosophical speculation for many years. Carrington has pointed out that if fourth dimension exists, no other explanation is needed for materializations and teleportations (41).

Mediums have long reported the existence of other planes impinging upon ours. Most of theirs are occupied by the departed, but persons having OBEs also report beings of other types (170), as have some who have had "back from death" experiences (66, 171). For the most part these planes seem to have no physical contact with our "normal" here-and-now reality, but perhaps an occasional slippage may occur, the beloved "lost door" of the fantasy writers may open, and for a moment there is interaction.

Gardner Murphy has suggested (178) that it may be the transition from one mental state or level to another that releases the apparent psychical energies, just as a change of state in matter involves a release of energy. Perhaps this is indeed a matter of slippage. How many altered states does the mind have access to? Some we know well; we are accustomed to sliding back and forth between alertness and sleep, meditation, or reverie. Some people are actually aware of a sensation almost like a click just before they fall asleep. We know from many reports (302) that people experience far more states than most of us are familiar with. Perhaps, then, at the moment of "sliding down" (for want of a better term) into one of our usual states we may actually cross a different threshold from the usual and enter a state of consciousness in which the ethereal is the solid. This theory does not of course deal with the problem of how an apparently nonphysical energy may interact with a physical die. Perhaps it is at the quantum level of consciousness.

When researching this concept of awareness of quantum levels one gets very tired of running across mention of Maxwell's ubiquitous demon, a fantasy figure proposed by physicist James Maxwell as an illustration of how matter might be operated on at the molecular level. The demon, he said, would be able to sort one type of molecule from another. It has long been shown that such an operation is not possible—but that decision was of course made by someone operating in the here-and-now reality.

Myers, pointing to the immense amount of space within every atom and molecule (if the nucleus of an atom were the size of a basketball, the electrons, proportionately, would be over a mile away), remarked, "To pass through matter may be a problem like that of the puzzles which consist of rings to be threaded together: there is plenty of space if you know where the chinks are."

We know that the forces of the atom are not easily manipulated, but at the molecular level things are a little less tricky. The "glue" holding together the atoms that make up each molecule is less strong and less explosive. Some people reporting altered state experiences have seemed to be describing the entering of matter (214). Could an ethereal energy somehow be capable of manipulating molecules? Such manipulation is usually the province of the chemist, but it is not impossible *per se* to do mechanically. It is only impossible because we and our tools are too large. Something more delicate might be more effective.

If we accept the fact that by PK some people can affect some—not all, just some—of an extremely high number of electronically generated random events, is it not possible that they can somehow "mess with" the molecules of matter? This possibility was mentioned in connection with materialization and yoga in Chapter 12 and would result in a macro effect brought about by a micro procedure.

It should be remembered, as V. A. Firsoff of the Royal Astronomical Society has pointed out (90), that the laws of nature are at best statistical laws, laws that "describe the most probable behavior of large numbers of elements." Just as human nature permits of maverick behavior by individuals without materially altering the average, so does the nature of physics permit individual atoms to behave atypically. Is it possible that in PK one is simply creating a larger number of atypical atoms or molecules—a sort of micro-mass-hysteria?

D. External

The external category includes those explanations that remove responsibility for PK from man.

1. Superordinate Energy

a. Personal: Personal superordinate energy is some entity outside of man that takes responsibility for "miracles" performed by PK and perhaps for many other unexplained facts of life. Whether regarded as a God, a devil, a saint, or a meddling extraterrestrial, it is presumed to have some kind of intelligence, to work with, for, or against man, and to be capable of doing things far beyond the capabilities of man. The existence of such a being, or beings, is more a matter of faith than of proof, but such a faith may, in a "let George do it" way, improve one's chances of PK regardless of the being's actual existence or nonexistence.

b. Teleological: Is there a teleological system guiding man to some future end? Are we, unknowingly, drawn forward in some way toward man's ultimate destiny? And if so, how? And how would this relate to PK?

Though both the Personal and Teleological theories would be almost impossible to investigate scientifically, increasing numbers of researchers are wondering whether such a study should nevertheless be attempted (281). It would seem more theological or philosophical than scientific, but that might be all to the good. Many others besides myself have long maintained that parapsychology is the area in which science will be proven to religion and religion will be proven to science.

2. Spirits, Discarnate Entities

As we have seen, this is where psychical research came in. Whether or not survival research eventually manages to demonstrate that something of man survives bodily death, it is unlikely, according to present trends of thought, to show that dear departed

Aunt Liza was responsible for Felicia Parise's moving a compass needle or for the Watkins' rapidly reviving mice. It is a possibility that cannot be ruled out, but it is not considered probable by most parapsychologists.

3. Synchronicity

Psychologist Carl Jung articulated the theory of synchronicity (137). It is simply that some principle of nature dictates that things happen which appear to be connected and yet which are acausal: neither one is the cause of the other. In other words, the long arm of coincidence is a whole lot longer than we think it is.

While synchronicity is superficially similar to PMIR (psi-mediated instrumental response) and conformance, they are actually quite different. In PMIR we seem unconsciously to cause events to happen through active ESP or PK. Conformance theory makes the causation less direct, since we do not *make* anything happen ourselves, but yet it happens because we have needs to which the universe may conform. In synchronicity we and our needs have no effect—the events just "happen to happen" at the same time.

The theory of synchronicity is almost impossible to prove, if one regards psi as a reasonable alternative. For example, the patient's dream of some object or animal which actually and "coincidentally" appeared as she was telling Jung about it can be regarded as precognitive, a PMIR way of catching the psychologist's attention by making something unusual happen, or one can deny psi and hold synchronicity responsible. One can say that it is because of PK that Psifi produces a run of more tails than heads at the same time that tails are the target, or we can look to synchronicity. However, while synchronicity may be the skeptic's answer to the parapsychologist, the theory actually presents no final answers. We know no more about *how* or *why* it happen, and perhaps less, than we know about how or why PK happens.

4. Conformance Behavior

As discussed in Chapter 13, the conformance theory may be a useful explanation for the *why* of what we call PK, but it does nothing to help us in our search for the *how*.

It may seem at first glance that the various theories discussed here must be mutually exclusive, that only one, or perhaps two overlapping, can explain PK. This need not necessarily be so.

It may be that there is indeed an energy, presently unknown to us and therefore classified as nonphysical, that will eventually be found and discovered to conform to physical laws as they are by then understood. It may be that our knowledge of those laws will by then be more refined, that a quantum jump upward from quantum physics will have been made, or that at least the present bickering over quantum interpretations will be finished and the whole subject clarified.

Perhaps such an energy is indeed universal. If so, it may be a function of living cells to convert it to more usable form. Perhaps every living cell is a "disposed system." Perhaps the energy can be gathered and concentrated into those cells even more efficiently by proper breathing, can be given off willy-nilly and incoherently by muscular action, and yet be capable of being brought into phase and under control by some mental technique that may one day be understood. Perhaps that technique may involve our becoming more in tune with the universe so that its conformance behavior becomes even more responsive to our needs. Perhaps the breathing and relaxation help do just that.

The search for the key, the converter that can change or channel such an energy and carry out such a law, is ongoing. Perhaps life itself is the answer. Perhaps if we knew the answer we would know *all* the answers.

But this last is far less than a theory and is undisputably unscientific. It is just a thought, a far distant *maybe,* for in science there must be room for these, too.

Chapter 15

What Does It All Mean?

Psi itself is not important except in the context of our understanding of the nature of man.

Robert Van de Castle (322)

If PK does not exist, then obviously it has no meaning. In this final chapter, a chapter in search of the implications of PK research, I am assuming, therefore, that PK is a fact, that it does exist. If it exists, then its implications are far-reaching, to put it mildly. (Vasiliev is reported to have considered the discovery of psi energy to be more important than the discovery of nuclear energy. Perhaps parapsychologists cannot yet lay claim to the actual discovery of psi energy, as he believed, but it does appear that in dealing with psi, regardless of how it works, we are dealing with something far more fundamental than the ability to influence dice.)

The idea of PK is mind boggling, but perhaps during the course of this book we have become somewhat desensitized, so that our minds are now more or less boggle free. Thus, rather than gasping at the mere concept of "mind over matter," we can consider its implications from various viewpoints.

For science, probably the first and most important implication is that *the word* objective *becomes meaningless.*

Consider the experimenter effect, the preferential effect, the subconsciousness and the need/goal orientation of PK. If all these factors are combined, there can be no such thing as a truly objective experiment. The subject/object split that has long been a part of any well-controlled experiment is simply not relevant in psi situations *(which, we have to realize, may be* all *situations)*. This was tacitly recognized by William Braud when, in reporting his second series of experiments with aggressive fish (Chapter 3), he made the experimenters a part of the experiment by referring to "person-fish teams" rather than to the fish as subjects and the people as experimenters (28).

This finding applies not only to parapsychology, but to experiments of any kind. The chemist awaiting an unknown reaction, the psychologist testing a new theory, the physicist studying the behavior of an alloy or a subatomic particle, each has his hopes, needs, and beliefs regarding the research. None, therefore, is an objective observer of the process, but is at the subjective center of the whole thing. (Nor can any experiment be truly blind, because of the possibility of ESP.) This fact alone, presenting as it does the impossibility of a perfectly controlled experiment, is enough to make any scientist wish to deny the existence of psi.

The biological implications of PK cannot be ignored either. If PK can heal, can it also harm? If PK is simply a form of "leakage" of something that normally controls the body, then could not a form of internal psi-missing be responsible for some diseases? Do psi-missers have a higher incidence of illness than psi-hitters?

What about external harm—harm to someone else—via PK? Kulagina once seemed to affect the heartbeat of an experimenter. (Lest we suspect that this could have been caused by a normal male-female situation *a la* Palladino, it should be remembered that Kulagina also caused a frog's heart to stop beating under laboratory conditions.) Can we extend this idea to so-called hex deaths, which, though often explained psychologically, do not *always* fit into the psychological mold? E. Brockhaus of the University of Freiburg reported in 1968 on some studies that he had made in West Africa. After observing various rituals, he noted not only "extremely rapid healing of self-inflicted knife wounds" but also that "hens were killed apparently without physical agency." The latter was observed repeatedly, and eventually Brockhaus learned to do it himself, using a fetish. Yet he remarked that "a normal cause for the hen's death is not apparent to me" (32). Was the fetish the "George" that enabled him to kill, either by stopping the heart or in some other way, by PK?

If PK can affect living things, can it affect heredity, the combinations of chromosomes? And even evolution?

Jule Eisenbud (85) has cited a number of nonparapsychologist biologists who feel that pure chance and natural selection are not sufficient to explain some evolutionary developments. He points out that many functions and organs, although useful for survival in their developed form, would have had to develop over the course of generations, or even eons, *before* they would have become efficient enough to have survival value. The theory of natural selection does not, therefore, entirely explain their development, and the possibility of some form of influence, perhaps via psi, is suggested. We may remember Burr's "L-field," which seems to affect and guide physical development, in support of this idea, although it is not clear where the psi would come from. Could it be that, unknowingly, the species did have a need for that kind of function, and the universe conformed by gradually affecting the developing cells until the organ was complete?

Eisenbud also suggested that the behavior of animals with one another, particularly in the predator-prey relationship in which animals sometimes almost seem to cooperate in being caught, may also be affected by psi. Such behavior could be prompted because of individual needs, species needs (according to population sizes and pressures), or overall environmental needs.

The "let George do it" theory itself has powerful implications for parapsychologists. If the majority of the population needs to believe that someone else is "doing PK" in order to be able to do it themselves, then a new design for PK experiments may be required. For example, belief that a PK applied specialist, "a real expert," is working on the same experiment in another room (even if he is actually nonexistent) might enable the average subject to score far better than when he or she is simply asked to affect a random number generator alone.

This brings up the difficult subject of sophistication. It seems that once people have started to score well, some can train themselves to fade out thoughts of George and take responsibility for their own PK. However, for some of them it may be important to show good results *before* George is removed. If they become aware of the theory before finding out that they can cause PK, then PK may be more difficult for them because they will no longer believe in their particular George. (From this point of view, books such as this one may actually be harmful to the production of high PK scores.) Such effects are only a matter of individual attitude, and should not occur if one can overcome the old, buried taboos. A number of para-psychologists who are well acquainted with the theory are able to produce high scores, so apparently it is partly a matter of motiva-tion. If you really want or need to score well, you should be able to do so—provided you don't try too hard. However, some researchers may feel even more inclined to use subjects who know compara-tively little about psi to ensure that this problem does not arise. Another good source of subjects would be those who are deeply involved in the oft-scorned (by parapsychologists) spiritualist and occult groups, who provide their own Georges and whose belief in them is unlikely to be shaken.

In field situations one wonders to what extent the para-psychologist should immediately try to "educate" a poltergeist family, for example. Should he try to observe the events for a few days without saying that it may not be the spirit of Great-Uncle George who is causing all the pandemonium? Or should he explain immediately that the disturbances are probably due to PK from someone in the family, even though he knows that this explanation could cause the events to fade away before he can even find out what, if anything, is happening? The decision will have to be reached by each investigator individually and will presumably depend partly on whether the people involved are in a state of real terror or are merely inconvenienced by what is happening, as well as on other circumstances varying with each case.

Another aspect of "George" that may make poltergeist investiga-tion more difficult is the fact that events are apparently more likely to occur when people expect someone or something else to make them occur. It follows that disturbances are more likely to occur if the people involved *think* that haunting or contact by discarnates is likely. A death, or the anniversary of a death, or stories that an old house is haunted may promote expectations of events, lowering the blocks and freeing the unconscious PK of the people who have the expectations. (Perhaps we should say that they have a need to have their expectations met.) Since their expectation is of events caused by a George, disturbances may well occur. The investigator is then faced with some facts that appear to support the discarnate entity hypothesis, even though the events may be caused by PK.

One case that was reported to me (though not thoroughly investigated) started when a young man was speaking rather strongly against religion, making some other people in the group present feel quite uncomfortable. I do not know whether any of them were actually thinking, in the cliche of TV's Maude, "God'll get you for that," but it seems likely from what I was told. A box promptly fell off a refrigerator and hit him. Other events are said to have followed.

While we wonder whether sophistication is really desirable where psi is concerned, it is interesting to note that many myths and fairy tales about "supernatural powers" indicate that it is not desirable to seek knowledge and explanations for them.

The idea that the universe may tend to fulfill our needs is somewhat frightening. Any casual student of psychology is aware that we all harbor emotions that can be destructive, either to ourselves or to others. If our PK could help us act out our emotional needs, just what might happen?

A classic science fiction movie, *The Forbidden Planet,* illustrates the problem well. It concerns an expedition to a distant planet for the purpose of finding out what had happened to a previous expedition. Upon arrival the hero, the expedition leader, finds three things: (1) Only two people, a scientist and his beautiful (of course) daughter, survived the earlier expedition; (2) they have discovered that the previous civilization of the planet, now extinct, had almost conquered mind over matter by mechanical means at the time it mysteriously disappeared; and (3) his group is being destroyed, as were the personnel of the previous expedition, by fearsome monsters that cannot be seen, but can be kept away by some form of force field.

It turns out that members of the previous civilization had been destroyed by "monsters from the Id" because they had in fact completed their mind-over-matter equipment, not realizing that it would respond not only to conscious commands but also to unconscious wishes. Normal rivalries and subconscious angers and resentments then caused the destruction of the entire civilization through the mind-over-matter apparatus (which continued to function). The scientist's resentment at the intrusion of his would-be rescuers, and at the hero's interest in his beautiful daughter, were now responsible, through the equipment, for the attacks on the new expedition.

Normal PK is hardly likely to produce forces that can melt metal doors (as in the film), but if it could be used to fulfill destructive emotional needs it would hardly be a boon to mankind, and the elimination of our more unpleasant urges would become imperative if man were to survive. It may be fortunate that PK's power seems to be limited.

Perhaps Stanley Krippner was thinking of something like this when he told an interviewer for *Psychic Magazine:*

> I . . . think that there are forces for good and forces for evil in the universe, and that many of these forces rest within ourselves. Each of us must ally ourselves on the side of the positive, creative, and life-fostering forces, because it's far easier to destroy something than to build something. (144)

Lack of success and lack of self-confidence often seem to be combined, psychologically, with hostility and destructiveness. It seems possible that they may also be tied to psi-missing. Could this be a fail-safe mechanism in some way built into us to prevent the destruction of the species? If the hostile individual is a psi-misser he cannot aim his PK well, and society avoids the consequences of his hostility. However, the PMIR theory holds that psi-missers not only may use PMIR in ways that avoid fulfilling their needs, but may actually use it against their own best interests.

In other words, if you psi-miss, it is possible that the decisions you base to a certain extent on hunches will tend to be incorrect, so you will find it harder to achieve success and will become less self-confident than someone who, consciously or unconsciously, psi-hits during the decision-making process.

An experiment by Graham Watkins showed that male lizards who were subordinate in the pecking order of their group tended to psi-miss while dominant males psi-hit strongly and those with undetermined social position psi-hit slightly (330). This finding is somewhat supported by very preliminary findings regarding male mice in an ESP experiment being conducted by the writer.

Lest you question that people use psi as an aid to success in decision-making, at least one lengthy experiment conducted by Douglas Dean, a former president of the Parapsychological Association, showed that of a large group of business leaders and executives, those who had recently been successful in their companies were psi-hitters, whereas those who had not tended to be psi-missers (73).

(On the subject of leadership, if mental or behavioral influence of an agent [MOBIA] is a reality, it may be that the charisma that seems necessary for most forms of successful leadership relates to an ability to influence and/or attract others by using PK on those neurons which, when fired, result in the individual being attracted to or trusting you.)

A survey of material on sports and psi by Rhea A. White of the American Society for Psychical Research (336) has also examined the possible use of both ESP and PK by the successful, this time relating to athletes and rooting sections. (The latter might partially explain the home game advantage, since home teams usually have more spectators cheering for them.) Some of White's material suggests that many athletes have a feeling akin to the mystical during high points in their games, and that there may indeed be a place for psi in sports.

If, then, it is the psi-hitters with whom nature "conforms" and who tend toward success, how can one become a psi-hitter? Strangely, the answers are so obvious—so corny, in fact—that one wonders how on earth something so trite can come from a voyage of discovery across something as exotic as PK. The answers are those that have been given by most psychologists, psychiatrists, and religious leaders since the first confused failure asked his witch doctor for advice.

What is it that Rex Stanford suspected might lead to blocking of the PMIR impulse? "Behavioral rigidity, inhibitions, stereotypy, response chaining, and strong preoccupations" (Chapter 13). These attributes do not prevent psi; they are behavioral patterns that prevent one from following the psi impulse by limiting the way in which one reacts. Presumably if we seek the healthy alternatives to these descriptions we have a picture of the psi-hitter. The opposites are flexibility, spontaneity, and openness, which enable one to make the appropriate response to the psi impulse even if that impulse is not one's usual kind of behavior.

The characteristics suggested as possibly causing psi-missing or self-destructive use of psi were "neuroticism, a negative self-concept, and direct motivational conflicts" (Chapter 13). In neurosis one's world view is distorted because of some earlier experience(s). A negative self-concept leads one to downgrade oneself, to see oneself as not worthy of success, so that PMIR would tend to work to withhold it. Again, one sees life in a distorted way. Motivational conflicts can be summarized as causing an approach/avoidance dilemma, an "I want to but I don't want to" approach to everything, from which no clear needs can become apparent for the universe to conform to since one does not know oneself whether success or failure is the real inner goal.

(Perhaps I should reemphasize that nobody believes that all psi-missers are necessarily rigid or neurotic or exhibit any of the foregoing traits. As we saw in earlier sections on psi-missing, we often do not know what causes it and when we do, the causes seem to vary widely. In an experimental situation, it is often the subject's feelings toward the experimenter or his co-workers, toward the general experimental situation, or even toward the guy who beat him to the last empty parking spot this morning that may bring about temporary psi-missing. Another cause may be an unconscious fear of psi itself. Outside the laboratory there are obviously many, many more known variables that can affect one's attitude and emotions, quite apart from all the unknowns that we have yet to discover. In other words, if you find that you psi-miss, you do not have to head for the nearest psychiatrist. The point here is that people with certain personality traits may unconsciously misuse psi, *not* that people who psi-miss have certain personality traits.)

The forms of "wrong-thinking" mentioned above as possibly leading to misuse of psi are, interestingly enough, tackled in the majority of the pop psychology, self-help, and New Thought books that regularly make the paperback best-seller lists. Rigidity and compulsive behavior are also dealt with, and advised against, in this type of literature. Understanding oneself and one's motivations, being open to the moment rather than rigid or preoccupied, are advocated by most of the philosophies and religions of the world, if one takes a look at their deeper meanings.

I quoted Rhine in Chapter 11 as saying that the founders of religion seem to have been giving advice on how to use psi. I would say that, more specifically, they have been giving advice on how to use psi properly by becoming a psi-hitter. And why not? It begins to appear that being a psi-hitter is the same thing as being attuned to the universe, resulting in more effective PMIR, which apparently brings a fulfillment of one's needs—the ultimate and truest form of success.

Might not the "let George do it" principle lie at the root of the many religious exhortations to have faith, because only those who have faith can perform miracles? When we believe that prayer can be answered by our chosen religious figure (whether it be God by whatever name or one of His proclaimed intermediaries), may we not simply be freeing ourselves from the blocks that normally stand between us and the conformance that will fulfill our needs?

The story of mankind, repeated over and over again by many religious leaders, is of a leadership that is in many ways relaxed, that speaks of obedience to the inner voice of God rather than to external laws,* of trust in Him for the needs of tomorrow, of having faith. Then, after the leader is gone, his followers start to codify his instructions, so that they will not be forgotten. As generations pass, these instructions are applied more and more rigidly, until later followers have little freedom to respond to their inner impulses. Eventually, yet another leader arises to free them, but, since he must tell them to be less concerned with the codifications of the existing religion than with the inner voice, he is considered to be a heretic. Eventually he will be either forgotten or accepted. If the latter, then the cycle, and the search for openness and self-understanding, start again.

It is somewhat frustrating, after starting a book intended to be a strictly scientific survey with only an occasional minor foray beyond

---

*Except perhaps in the case of Moses, the codifier *par excellence*. He had discovered that he could not preach his new religion in Egypt, and, in order to find a place of freedom, had first to discipline his followers, unused as they were to initiative and self-guidance, so that they could survive the journey ahead.

the walls of the laboratory, to find that the implications of much of the work surveyed are less scientific than philosophical and religious. Yet I believe that is the way it is.

However, on reflection, perhaps it is appropriate that the major implications of the study of PK should range far beyond the laboratory. The laboratory findings of science are only relevant if they can be transferred to the world at large so that, in some way or other, they can have meaning for life in general.

The implications I have drawn may not be correct. I hold no credentials as a philosopher, and parapsychology is, after all, a very young science. I have taken Stanford's admittedly speculative "starting point" of conformance behavior (which he suggests I take too seriously) and galloped madly away with it, ignoring the pleas of common sense, science, and Stanford. At the end of the journey I have found myself on the shores of an almost religiously oriented philosophy with which I have long been somewhat familiar, but which I had believed had no connection whatsoever with science. Now I am not so sure. I do think that the view from those shores may give us the glimmering of an answer to the question that the great F. W. H. Myers is said to have considered the most important of all: *"Is the universe friendly?"*

It may be that the real business of PK has no relation to its conscious use. Perhaps this is why some religions speak against deliberate use of psi, not because it is evil, but because its basic function is to work unconsciously. Perhaps this is why results achieved by conscious PK in experiments are usually so infinitesimally small. PK may be truly relevant only in the kind of PMIR situations that bring about those "lucky coincidences" that make the universe seem friendly indeed—*for those who approach it as friends.*

Perhaps this is the real significance of the statement "He stretched a plank" (though in any Sufi tale there are many layers of significance).

In its way perhaps the stretching of the plank *was* a miracle, but that was not what was significant, for, "Miracles as such do not matter. The only thing that matters is their Source..."(54).

Nor was stretching a plank significant as an attempt to prove to the skeptics that such a thing could happen.

Least of all would it have been significant for those who would have excluded the incident from the book—though for them it *could* have been the most significant. Their fear may indicate an awareness, conscious or otherwise, that such an event might mean the restructuring of their world view.

Perhaps the real significance lay in the simple fact that *the need of the carpenter and his Son was met* (always bearing in mind the difference between *need* and *want*).

It is a long step from deciding whether dice can be influenced by the mind to deciding that perhaps, if you get your head straight, the universe will automatically tend to fulfill your needs. It is a long step, but, if it is true, it is probably the most important step that anyone can take. All else follows.

Bibliography

1. Andre, E. "Confirmation of PK Action on Electronic Equipment," *J. Parapsychol.* 36:4, December 1972, pp. 283-93.
2. Andrew, K. "Psychokinetic Influences on an Electromechanical Random Number Generator during Evocation of 'Left-Hemispheric vs. Right-Hemispheric' Function," in *Research in Parapsychology 1974,* J. D. Morris, W. G. Roll, and R. L. Morris, eds. (Metuchen, N.J.: The Scarecrow Press, 1975), pp. 58-61.
3. Angoff, A., and Barth, D., eds. *Parapsychology and Anthropology* (New York: Parapsychology Foundation, 1974).
4. Artley, R. L., and Roll, W. G. "Mathematical Models and the Attenuation Effect in Two RSPK (Poltergeist) Cases," *Proc. P.A.* 5, 1968, pp. 29-31.
5. Averill, R. L., and Rhine, J. B. "The Effect of Alcohol upon Performance in PK Tests," *J. Parapsychol.* 9:1, March 1945, pp. 32-41.
6. Barrett, W. F. "Poltergeists, Old and New," *Proc. Soc. Psych. Res.* Part 64, August 1911.
7. Ibid. Primary source: *Atlantic Monthly.*
8. Barry, J. "General and Comparative Study of the Psychokinetic Effect on a Fungus Culture," *Proc. P.A.* 5, 1968, pp. 13-14.
9. Batcheldor, K. J. "Report on a Case of Table Levitation and Associated Phenomena," *J. Soc. Psych. Res.* 43:729, September 1966, pp. 339-56.
10. Bayless, R. Correspondence, *J. Am. Soc. Psych. Res.* 53:1, January 1959, pp. 35-38.
11. Beloff, J. Book review, *Superminds, an Enquiry into the Paranormal* by J. Taylor, *J. Parapsychol.* 39:3, September 1975, pp. 242-50.
12. Beloff, J., and Evans, L. "A Radioactive Test of Psychokinesis," *J. Soc. Psych. Res.* 41, March 1961, pp. 41-46. Cited in 241, p. 156.
13. Bender, H. "An Investigation of 'Poltergeist' Occurrences," *Proc. P.A. 5,* 1968, pp. 31-33.
14. Bender, H. "New Developments in Poltergeist Research," *Proc. P.A.,* 6, 1969, presidential address, pp. 81-102.
15. Bender, H. "Zur Analyse aussergewohnlicher Slimmphänomene auf Tonband, *Zeitschrift fur Parapsychologie,* 12:4, January 1971, pp.

226-38. Translation, "The Phenomena of Friedrich Jurgenson," *J. Paraphysics* 6:2, March/April 1972. Cited in 87.

16. Bender, H. "Parapsychology in Germany," *Para. Rev.* 3:5, September/October 1972, pp. 9-13. Originally presented at "Parapsychology Today: A Geographic View," Parapsychology Foundation Conference, August 1971.

17. Berendt, H. C. "Uri Geller—Pro and Con," *J. Soc. Psych. Res.* 47:762, December 1974, pp. 475-84.

18. The Bible, *Matthew* 8.

19. The Bible, *Luke* 8:22-25.

20. The Bible, *Luke* 9:12-17, *John* 6:5-14.

21. The Bible, *John* 14:12.

22. The Bible, *Acts* 3:2-8, 5:16, 9:33-34, 14:8-11, 28:8.

23. Bierman, D. J.; De Diana, I. P. F.; and Houtkooper, J. M. "Preliminary Report on the Amsterdam Experiments with Matthew Manning," *Eur. J. Parapsychol.* 1:2, May 1976, pp. 6-16.

24. Braud, W. G. "Psychokinesis in Aggressive and Nonaggressive Fish with Mirror Presentation Feedback for Hits, Some Preliminary Experiments," *J. Parapsychol.* 40:4, December 1976, pp. 296-307. (.02 statistic calculated by D.R. from data provided in article.)

25. Braud, W. G. "Allobiofeedback: Immediate Feedback for a Psychokinetic Influence upon Another Person's Physiology," paper presented at the P.A. Convention, Washington, D.C., August 1977, in *Research in Parapsychology* 1977, W. G. Roll, ed. (Metuchen, N.J.: The Scarecrow Press 1974), pp. 123-34.

26. Braud, W. G. "Recent Investigation of Microdynamic Psychokinesis, with Special Emphasis on the Roles of Feedback, Effort, and Awareness," paper presented at the 1977 Parascience Conference, London, England. In *Parascience Proc.* Vol. 2, in press.

26A. Braud, W. G. "Conformance Behavior Involving Living Systems," in *Research in Parapsychology* 1978, W. G. Roll, ed. (Metuchen, N.J.: The Scarecrow Press, 1979), pp. 111-15.

27. Braud, W. G., and Hartgrove, J. "Clairvoyance and Psychokinesis in Transcendental Meditators: A Preliminary Study," *Eur. J. Parapsychol.* 1:3, November 1976, pp. 6-16.

28. Braud, W. G., and Kirk, J. "Attempt to Observe Psychokinetic Influences upon a Random Event Generator by Person-Fish Teams," *Eur. J. Parapsychol.* 2:3, November 1978, pp. 228-36.

29. Braud, W. G., et al. "Psychokinetic Influences on Random Number Generators During Evocation of 'Analytic vs. Nonanalytic': Modes of Information Processing," in *Research in Parapsychology 1975*, J. D. Morris, W. G. Roll, and R. L. Morris, eds. (Metuchen, N.J.: The Scarecrow Press, 1976), pp. 85-88.

30. Breederveld, H. "Psychokinesis Experiments with a Subject under the Influence of a Stimulating Drug and a Tranquilizer," *Proc. P.A.* 4, 1967, p. 21.
31. Brier, R. "Parapsychological Principles from Anthropological Studies," *Para. Review* 5:1, January/February 1974, pp. 3-8, paper presented at "Parapsychology and Anthropology," Parapsychology Foundation Conference, August 1973, London, England.
32. Brockhaus, E. "Possibilities and Limits of Parapsychological Field Research in West Africa," *Proc. P.A.* 5, 1968, pp. 9-10.
33. Brookes-Smith, C., and Hunt, D. W. "Some Experiments in Psychokinesis," *J. Soc. Psych. Res.* 45:744, June 1970, pp. 265-81.
34. Brookes-Smith, C., and Hunt, D. W. "Data-tape Recorded Experimental P.K. Phenomena," *J. Soc. Psych. Res.* 47:756, June 1973, pp. 69-89.
35. Brookes-Smith, C., and Hunt, D. W. "Paranormal Electrical Conductance Phenomena," *J. Soc. Psych. Res.* 48:764, June 1975, pp. 73-86.
36. Broughton, R., et al. "A PK Investigation of the Experimenter Effect and Its Psi-Based Component," paper presented at the P.A. Convention, Washington, D.C., August 1977, in *Research in Parapsychology 1977*, W. G. Roll, ed. (Metuchen, N. J.: The Scarecrow Press, 1978), pp. 41-48.
37. Bruce, H. A. "James Hervey Hyslop—Pioneer," *J. Parapsychol.* 20:1, March 1956, pp. 44-52. Quoting a letter from Miss Tubby, Hyslop's secretary.
38. Burr, H. S. *Blueprint for Immortality: The Electric Patterns of Life* (London, England: Neville Spearman, 1972).
39. Byrd, E. "Uri Geller's Influence on the Metal Alloy Nitinol," *The Geller Papers*, C. Panati, ed. (Boston: Houghton Mifflin, 1976).
40. Camstra, B. "PK Conditioning," in *Research in Parapsychology 1972*, W. G. Roll, R. L. Morris, and J. D. Morris, eds. (Metuchen, N.J.: The Scarecrow Press, 1973), pp. 25-26.
41. Carrington, H. *The Physical Phenomena of Spiritualism* (Boston: Herbert B. Turner & Co., 1907).
42. Ibid, p. 363. Primary source: *Proc. Soc. Psych. Res.*, vol. 14, p. 136.
43. Ibid., p. 367.
44. Ibid., pp. 373-77. Primary source: Crookes, Sir William, *Researchers in Spiritualism*, pp. 34-42.
45. Ibid., p. 394. Primary source: Sargeant, Epes, *Planchette*, pp. 100-101.
46. Castaneda, C. *A Separate Reality* (New York: Pocket Books, 1972).
47. Ibid., p. 106.
48. Ibid., p. 147.
49. Castaneda, C. *Journey to Ixtlan* (New York: Simon & Schuster, 1972), p. 232.

50. Chari, C. T. K. "Some Disputable Phenomena Allied to Thought-ography," *J. Am. Soc. Psych. Res.* 63:3, July 1969, pp. 273-86.
51. Chari, C. T. K. "Precognition, Probability and Quantum Mechanics," *J. Am. Soc. Psych. Res.* 66:2, April 1972, pp. 193-207.
52. Coohill, T. P. "Filmed and Nonfilmed Events: On Uri Geller's Visit to Western Kentucky University," *The Geller Papers,* C. Panati, ed. (Boston: Houghton Mifflin, 1976), pp. 133-38.
53. Cornell, A. D., and Gault, A. "The Geophysical Theory of Poltergeists," abstracted in *J. Parapsychol.* 26:2, June 1962, p. 138. Primary source: *J. Soc. Psych. Res.* 41, 1961, pp. 129-47.
54. *A Course in Miracles* (New York: Foundation for Inner Peace, 1975), vol. 1, text, p. 1.
55. Cox, W. E. "The Effect of PK on the Placement of Falling Objects," *J. Parapsychol.* 15:1, March 1951, pp. 40-48.
56. Cox, W. E. "A Comparison of Spheres and Cubes in Placement PK Tests," *J. Parapsychol.* 18:4, December 1954, pp. 234-39.
57. Cox, W. E. "Five-Tier Placement PK," *J. Parapsychol.* 26:1, March 1962, pp. 35-46.
58. Cox, W. E. "The PK Placement of Falling Water," *J. Parapsychol.* 26:4, December 1962, p. 266.
59. Cox, W. E. "A Cumulative Assessment of PK on Multiple Targets," *Proc. P.A.* 2, 1965, p. 14.
60. Cox, W. E. "Multiple PK Placement using 135 Balls per Throw," *Proc. P. A.* 3, 1966, p. 9.
61. Cox, W. E. "Clock-Timed Cube-Placement Psychokinesis," *Proc. P.A.* 5, 1968, pp. 16-17.
62. Cox, W. E. "The Use of Pendulums in PK Measurements," *Proc. P.A.* 6, 1969, pp. 45-46.
63. Cox, W. E. "Note on Some Experiments with Uri Geller," *J. Parapsychol.* 38:4, December 1974, pp. 408-11.
64. Cox, W. E. " 'Blind PK' with Automated Equipment," paper presented at the Southeastern Regional P.A. Convention, February 1977. Abstracted *J. Parapsychol.* 41:1, March 1977, pp. 37-38.
65. Cox, W. E. "Direct Observation of Metal Bending," paper presented at the Southeastern Regional P.A. Convention, February 1977. Abstracted *J. Parapsychol.* 41:1, March 1977, p. 50.
66. Crookall, R. *The Study and Practice of Astral Projection* (New Hyde Park, N.Y.: University Books, 1966).
67. Dale, L. A. "The Psychokinetic Effect: The First ASPR Experiment," *J. Am. Soc. Psych. Res.* 40, 1946, 123-51.
68. Dale, L. A., and Woodruff, J. L. "The Psychokinetic Effect: Further ASPR Experiments," *J. Am. Soc. Psych. Res.* 41, 1947, pp. 65-82.
69. David-Kneel, A. *Magic and Mystery in Tibet* (New York: Dover, 1971). First published as *Mystiques et magiciens du Thibet* (Paris: Plon, 1929).

70. Davis, J. Personal communications, February and August, 1977.
71. Dean, D. "Molecular Effects of 'Healers,'" Proc. First Canadian Conference on Psychokinesis and Related Phenomena, *New Horizons,* June 1974, pp. 215-19.
72. Dean, D. Personal communication, August 1977.
73. Dean, Douglas, et al. *Executive ESP* (New York: Prentice-Hall, 1974).
74. De Diana, I.P.F., and Houtkooper, J. M. "Physiological Variables and PK," in *Research in Parapsychology 1976,* J. D. Morris, W. G. Roll, and R. L. Morris, eds. (Metuchen N. J.: The Scarecrow Press, 1977), pp. 72-74.
75. Devereux, G. "Trance and Orgasm in Euripedes: Bakchai, " in *Parapsychology and Anthropology* (New York: Parapsychology Foundation, 1974). Quoted and reviewed by R. A. White, *J. Am. Soc. Psych. Res.* 69:3, July 1975, pp. 285-92.
76. Dierkens, J. C. "Psychophysiological Approach to PK States: Experiments with Jean-Pierre Girard," "Psi and States of Awareness," 26th International Conference, Parapsychology Foundation, Paris, August 1977. Proceedings, in press.
77. Dingwall, E. J. "The Early World of Psychical Research," *Para. Rev.* 6:5, September/October 1975, pp. 6-9.
78. Dobervich, C. "Kirlian Photography Revealed," *Psychic* 6:1, December 1974, pp. 34-39.
79. Ehrenwald, J. "Parapsychology and the Seven Dragons: A Neuropsychiatric Model for Psi Phenomena," in *Parapsychology,* G. R. Schmeidler, ed. (Metuchen, N.J.: The Scarecrow Press, 1976), pp. 246-63.
80. Eisenbud, J. *The World of Ted Serios* (New York: William Morrow, 1967).
81. Eisenbud, J. "Two Camera and Television Experiments with Ted Serios," *J. Am. Soc. Psych. Res.* 64:3, July 1970, pp. 261-76.
82. Eisenbud, J. "The Serios 'Blackies' and Related Phenomena," *J. Am. Soc. Psych. Res.* 66:2, April 1972, pp. 180-92.
83. Eisenbud, J. "Psychic Photography and Thoughtography," *Psychic Exploration,* E. Mitchell and J. White, eds. (New York: G. P. Putnam's Sons, 1974), pp. 314-31.
84. Eisenbud, J. "On Serios' Alleged 'Confession,'" *J. Soc. Psych. Res.* 48:765, September 1975, pp. 189-92.
85. Eisenbud, J. "Evolution and Psi," *J. Am. Soc. Psych. Res.* 70:1, January 1976, pp. 35-54.
86. Eisenbud, J., et al. "Two Experiments with Ted Serios," *J. Am. Soc. Psych. Res.* 62:3, July 1968, pp. 309-20.
87. Ellis, D. J. "Listening to the 'Raudive Voices,'" *J. Soc. Psych. Res.* 48:763, March 1975, pp. 31-42. Primary source: Locher, T., "Wie

fragwürdig ist unser Hörvorgang?" *Schweigerisches Bulletin für Parapsychologie,* November 1971, pp. 7-8 and 15.

88. Ellison, A. J. "Some Problems in Testing 'Mini-Gellers,'" in *Research in Parapsychology 1976,* J. D. Morris, W. G. Roll, and R. L. Morris, eds. (Metuchen, N.J.: The Scarecrow Press, 1977), pp. 203-6.

89. Feinberg, G. During discussion of T. Bastin, "Connections between Events in the Context of the Combinatorial Model for a Quantum Process," in *Quantum Physics and Parapsychology,* L. Oteri, ed. (New York: Parapsychology Foundation, 1975), pp. 229-51.

90. Firsoff, V. A. "Life and Quantum Physics," in *Quantum Physics and Parapsychology,* L. Oteri, ed. (New York: Parapsychology Foundation, 1975), pp. 109-28.

91. Flammarion, C. *Haunted Houses,* (n.p.: D. Appleton & Co., 1924), p. 347.

92. Ibid. p. 302ff. Primary source: *Proc. Soc. Psych. Res.* vol. 7, p. 183.

93. Forwald, H. "Extract from Records of Sittings Held during 1949." Unpublished report.

94. Forwald, H. *Mind, Matter and Gravitation* (New York: Parapsychology Foundation, 1969).

95. Franklin, W. "Metal Fracture Physics Using Scanning Electron Microscopy and the Theory of Teleneural Interactions," in *The Geller Papers,* C. Panati, ed., (Boston: Houghton Mifflin, 1976), pp. 83-106.

96. Franklin, W. "Prof. Franklin Retracts," Readers Forum, *The Humanist,* 37:5, September/October 1977, pp. 54-55.

97. Frey, H., et al. Letter, *J. Am. Soc. Psych. Res.* 62:3, July 1968, pp. 330-31.

98. Fukurai, T. *Clairvoyance and Thoughtography* (London: Rider, 1931). Discussed in 83.

99. Gardner, M. "Geller, Gulls and Nitinol," *The Humanist,* 37:3, May/June 1977, pp. 25-32.

100. Gauld, A. *The Founders of Psychical Research* (New York: Schocken Books, 1968), pp. 226-31. Primary source: *J. Soc. Psych. Res.* 6, 1894, pp. 350-51 and 355-57.

101. Ibid., p. 236. Primary source: unpublished notes from Soc. Psych. Res. archives.

102. Ibid., p. 213. Primary source: *J. Soc. Psych. Res.* 4, 1889, pp. 124-26.

103. Gauld, A. "A Series of 'Drop In' Communicators," *Proc. Soc. Psych. Res.* 55, Pt. 204, July 1971, pp. 273-340.

104. Geller, U. *My Story* (New York: Praeger, 1975).

105. Gibson, E. P.; Gibson, L. H.; and Rhine, J. B. "A Large Series of PK Tests," *J. Parapsychol.* 7:4, December 1943, pp. 228-37.

106. Gibson, E. P., and Rhine, J. B. "The PK Effect: III. Some Introductory Series," *J. Parapsychol.* 7:1, March 1943, pp. 118-34.
107. Gorer, G. *Africa Dances: A Book about West African Negroes* (New York: Knopf, 1935). Quoted in 128.
108. Grad, B. "Some Biological Effects of the 'Laying on of Hands,' a Review of Experiments with Animals and Plants," *J. Am. Soc. Psych. Res.* 59:2, April 1965, pp. 95-127.
109. Grad, B. "A Psychokinetic Study Using the Production of Carbon-Dioxide from Sugar by Yeast as the Target," paper presented at the 1965 P. A. Convention, discussed in *Proc. P.A.* 2, 1965, pp. 15-16.
109A. Grad, B. "The Biological Effects of the 'Laying on of Hands' on Animals and Plants: Implications for Biology," in *Parapsychology: Its Relation to Physics, Biology, Psychology, and Psychiatry,* G. R. Schmeidler, ed. (Metuchen, N.J.: The Scarecrow Press, 1976), pp. 76-89.
110. Gregory, A. "The Physical Mediumship of Rudi Schneider," *Proc. P.A.* 5, 1968, pp. 19-21.
111. *Guinness Book of Records,* N. McWhirter, ed. (New York: Sterling Publishing Co., 1977), pp. 19-20.
112. Hansel, C. E. M. *ESP: A Scientific Evaluation* (New York: Charles Scribner's Sons, 1966). Primary source: Michael Faraday, "Experimental Investigation of Tablemoving," *Athenaeum,* July 1853, pp. 801-3.
113. Haraldsson, E., and Osis, K. "The Appearance and Disappearance of Objects by Sri Sathya Sai Baba," in *Research in Parapsychology 1975,* J. D. Morris, W. G. Roll, and R. L. Morris, eds. (Metuchen, N.J.: The Scarecrow Press, 1976), pp. 144-47.
114. Haraldsson, E., and Thorsteinsson, T. "Psychokinetic Effects on Yeast: An Exploratory Experiment," in *Research in Parapsychology 1972,* W. G. Roll, R. L. Morris, and J. D. Morris, eds. (Metuchen, N.J.: The Scarecrow Press, 1973), pp. 20-21.
115. Hasted, J. B. "My Geller Notebooks," in *The Geller Papers,* C. Panati, ed. (Boston: Houghton Mifflin, 1976), pp. 197-212.
116. Hasted, J. B. "Experiments on Psychokinetic Phenomena," in *The Geller Papers,* C. Panati, ed. (Boston: Houghton Mifflin, 1976), pp.183-96.
117. Hasted, J. B. "An Experimental Study of the Validity of Metal Bending Phenomena," *J. Soc. Psych. Res.* 48:770, December 1976, pp. 365-83.
118. Herbert, B. "Report on Nina Kulagina," *Para. Review* 3:6, November/December 1972, pp. 8-10.
119. Herbert B. "Spring in Leningrad: Kulagina Revisited," *Para. Review* 4:4, July/August 1973, pp. 4-10.
120. Herbert, B. "Paris Parapsychology Conference," *Para. Review* 6:3, May/June 1975, pp. 11-12.

121. Heywood, R. *ESP: A Personal Memoir* (New York: E.P. Dutton, 1964). First published as *The Infinite Hive* (England: n.p., n.d.).
122. Heywood, R. "Illusion—or What?" *Theta* 4:1, Winter 1976, pp. 5-10. Excerpted from R. Heywood, *Man's Concern with the Nature of Life after Death* (London: Weidenfeld Publishers Ltd., n.d.).
123. Hickman, J. L. "A High-Voltage Photography Experiment with Uri Geller," in *Research in Parapsychology 1976,* J. D. Morris, W. G. Roll, and R. L. Morris, eds. (Metuchen, N.J.: The Scarecrow Press, 1977), pp. 15-18.
124. Hill, S. "PK Effects by a Single Subject on a Binary Random Number Generator Based on Electronic Noise," in *Research in Parapsychology 1976,* J. D. Morris, W. G. Roll, and R. L. Morris, eds. (Metuchen, N.J.: The Scarecrow Press, 1977), pp. 26-28.
125. Home, D. D. *Incidents in My Life* (Secaucus, N.J.: University Books, n.d.). First published by Longmans, 1871 (sources differ on original date; some say 1862 and 1863).
126. Honorton, C. "Apparent Psychokinesis on Static Objects by a 'Gifted' Subject," in *Research in Parapsychology 1973,* W. G. Roll, R. L. Morris, and J. D. Morris, eds. (Metuchen, N.J.: The Scarecrow Press, 1974), pp. 128-31.
127. Honorton, C. "Has Science Developed the Competence to Confront Claims of the Paranormal?" Presidential Address, P.A. Convention, August 1975, in *Research in Parapsychology 1975,* J. D. Morris, W. G. Roll, and R. L. Morris, eds. (Metuchen, N.J.: The Scarecrow Press, 1976), pp. 199-223.
128. Honorton, C. "Mind at Large," paper presented at "Current Perspectives in Parapsychology," a seminar at the University of Bridgeport, March 1976.
129. Honorton, C. Personal communication, September 1977.
130. Honorton, C., and Barksdale, W. "PK Performance with Waking Suggestions for Muscle Tension Versus Relaxation," *J. Am. Soc. Psych. Res.* 66:2, April 1972, pp. 208-14.
131. Humphrey, B. M. "Paranormal Occurrences among Preliterate Peoples," *J. Parapsychol.* 8:3, September 1944, pp. 214-29.
132. Humphrey, B. M. "Help-Hinder Comparison in PK Tests," *J. Parapsychol.* 9:1, March 1947, pp. 4-13.
133. Janin, P. "Psychism and Chance," in *The Philosophy of Parapsychology,* B. Shapin and L. Coly, eds. (New York: Parapsychology Foundation, 1977), pp. 237-59.
134. Joines, W. "A Wave Theory of Psi Energy," *Research in Parapsychology 1974,* J. D. Morris, W. G. Roll, and R. L. Morris, eds. (Metuchen, N.J.: The Scarecrow Press, 1975), pp. 147-49.

135. Joines, William, et al. "Energy Focusing and Lingering Effects in Poltergeist Cases and Experimental Studies," in *Research in Parapsychology 1974,* J. D. Morris, W. G. Roll, and R. L. Morris, eds. (Metuchen, N.J.: The Scarecrow Press, 1975), pp. 134-49.

136. Joire, P. "De la suggestion mentale," *Annales des sciences psychiques,* no. 4, p. 193, and no. 5, p. 263. As reported in 323, p. 34.

137. Jung, C. G. "Synchronicity: An Acausal Connecting Principle," in *The Interpretation of Nature and the Psyche* (New York: Pantheon, 1955).

138. Karagulla, S. *Breakthrough to Creativity* (Los Angeles, DeVorss & Co. 1967).

139. Karger F. "Physical Investigation of Psychokinetic Phenomena in Rosenheim, Germany, 1967," *Proc. P.A.* 5, 1968, pp. 33-35.

140. Keil, H. H. J., and Fahler, J. "Nina S. Kulagina: A Strong Case for PK Involving Directly Observable Movement of Objects," *Eur. J. Parapsychol.* 1:2, May 1976, pp. 36-44.

141. Keil, H. H. J., et al. "Directly Observable Voluntary PK Effects," *Proc. Soc. Psych. Res.* vol. 56, part 210, January 1976, pp. 204-35.

142. Knowles, F. W. "My Experience in Psychic Healing and Parapsychology," *New Zealand Medical Journal* 74:474, pp. 328-31.

143. Krieger, D. "Therapeutic Touch: The Imprimatur of Nursing," *Am. J. of Nursing* 75:5, May 1975, pp. 784-87.

144. Krippner, S. "Interview: Stanley Krippner, Ph.D." *Psychic* 6:6, February 1976, pp. 48-58.

145. Lambert G. W. "Poltergeists: A Physical Theory," *J. Soc. Psych. Res.* 38:684, June 1955, pp. 49-71.

146. Layard, J. "PSI Phenomena and Poltergeists," *Proc. Soc. Psych. Res.* vol. 47, 1942-45, pp. 237-47.

147. LeShan, L. "Physicists and Mystics: Similarities in World View," *J. Transpersonal Psych.* 1:2, 1969. Reprinted in 148.

148. LeShan, L. *The Medium, the Mystic and the Physicist* (New York: Viking Press, 1974).

149. LeShan, L. "What It Feels Like to Be a Parapsychologist," paper presented at "Parapsychology: Today's Implications, Tomorrow's Applications," a symposium conducted by the Am. Soc. Psych. Res., New York, May 1974.

150. Locher, T. "Wie fragwurdig ist unser Horvorgang?" *Schweigerisches Bulletin für Parapsychologie,* November 1971, pp. 7-8. Quoted in 87.

151. Lucas, D., and Maresca, N. "Some Current Soviet Theories of Psi," paper presented at the Southeastern Regional P.A. Convention, February 1976. Abstracted in *J. Parapsychol.* 40:1, March 1976, p. 60.

152. Maddock, P. Book review: *The Parasciences, Impact of Science on Society* (UNESCO 24:4, October/December 1974), in *Para. Review* 6:4, July/August 1975, pp. 15-19.
153. Manning, M. *The Link* (New York: Holt, Rinehart & Winston, 1975).
154. Maslow, A. H. *The Farther Reaches of Human Nature* (New York: Viking Press, 1971), chapter 3.
155. Matas, F., and Pantas, L. "A PK Experiment Comparing Meditating Versus Nonmeditating Subjects," *Proc. P.A.* 8, 1971, pp. 12-13.
156. Mathews, F. M., and Solfvin, G. F. "A Case of RSPK in Massachusetts: Part 1. . . Poltergeist," in *Research in Parapsychology 1976,* J. D. Morris, W. G. Roll, and R. L. Morris, eds. (Metuchen, N.J.: The Scarecrow Press, 1977), pp. 219-23.
157. Mattuck, R. D. "Random Fluctuation Theory of Psychokinesis: Thermal Noise Model," in *Research in Parapsychology 1976,* J. D. Morris, W. G. Roll, and R. L. Morris, eds. (Metuchen, N.J.: The Scarecrow Press, 1977), pp. 191-95.
158. Mattuck, R. D., and Hill, S. "Psychokinetic Stretching of an Aluminum Bar by Jean-Pierre Girard," in *Research in Parapsychology 1976,* J. D. Morris, W. G. Roll, and R. L. Morris, eds. (Metuchen, N.J.: The Scarecrow Press, 1977), pp. 209-13.
159. May, E. C. Personal communication, March 1976.
160. May, E. C., and Jahagirdar, K. T. "From Where Does the Kum-Kum Come? A Materialization Attempt," in *Research in Parapsychology 1975,* J. D. Morris, W. G. Roll, and R. L. Morris, eds. (Metuchen, N.J.: The Scarecrow Press, 1976), pp. 150-52.
161. McConnell, R. A. "Parapsychology in the U.S.S.R." *J. Parapsychol.* 39:2, June 1975, pp. 129-34.
162. McDougall, W. *J. Parapsychol.* Editorial introduction to first issue, March 1937, quoted by J. B. Rhine in "A Backward Look on Leaving the JP," *J. Parapsychol.* 41:2, June 1977, pp. 89-102.
163. McMullan, J. T. "A Possible Physical Source for the Energy Needed in Poltergeist Activity," *J. Am. Soc. Psych. Res.* 65:4, October 1971, pp. 493-94.
164. "Mid-Century Inventory of Parapsychology," editorial, *J. Parapsychol.* 14:4, December 1950, pp. 227-43.
165. Millar, B. "Thermistor PK," in *Research in Parapsychology 1975,* J. D. Morris, W. G. Roll, and R. L. Morris, eds. (Metuchen, N.J.: The Scarecrow Press, 1976), pp. 71-73.
166. Miller, R. N. "Paraelectricity, A Primary Energy," *Human Dimensions* 5:1, 2, 1976, pp. 22-26.
167. Mischo, J.; Timm, U.; and Vilhjalmsson, G. "A Psychokinetic Effect Personally Observed," *Proc. P.A.* 5, 1968, pp. 37-38.
168. Mischo, J., and Weis, R. "A Pilot Study on the Relations between PK Scores and Personality Variables," in *Research in Parapsychology*

1972, W. G. Roll, R. L. Morris, and J. D. Morris, eds. (Metuchen, N.J.: The Scarecrow Press, 1973), pp. 21-23.
169. Mishra, R. S. *The Textbook of Yoga Psychology* (New York: Julian Press, 1963), p. 279.
170. Monroe, R. *Journeys Out of the Body* (Garden City, N.Y.: Anchor Press/Doubleday, 1977).
171. Moody, R. A., Jr. *Life After Life* (Covington, Ga.: Mockingbird Books, 1975).
172. Morris, R. L. "Further PK Placement Work with the Cox Machine," *Proc. P.A.* 2, 1965, pp. 14-15.
173. Morris, R. L. "The Psychobiology of Psi," *Psychic Exploration,* E. Mitchell, and J. White, eds. (New York: G. P. Putnam's Sons, 1974), pp. 237-45.
174. Morris, R. L. "Tacit Communication and Experimental Theology," Presidential Address, P.A. convention, 1974, in *Research in Parapsychology 1974,* J. D. Morris, W. G. Roll, and R. L. Morris, eds. (Metuchen, N.J.: The Scarecrow Press, 1975), pp. 179-98.
175. Murphy, G. *Challenge of Psychical Research* (New York: Harper Colophon, 1970), pp. 56-62. Primary source: Brugmans, H. I. F. W. "A Communication Regarding the Telepathy Experiments in the Psychological Laboratory at Groningen," in *Proceedings,* First International Congress of Psychical Research, Copenhagen, 1922.
176. Murphy, G. "Lawfulness Versus Caprice: Is There a 'Law of Psychic Phenomena'?" *J. Am. Soc. Psych. Res.* 58:4, October 1964, pp. 238-49.
177. Murphy, G. "The Discovery of Gifted Sensitives," *J. Am. Soc. Psych. Res.* 63:1, January 1969, pp. 3-20.
178. Murphy, G. "Are There Any Solid Facts in Psychical Research?" *J. Am. Soc. Psych. Res.* 64:1, January 1970, pp. 3-17.
179. Myers, F. W. H. "On Alleged Movements of Objects, Without Contact, Occurring Not in the Presence of a Paid Medium," *Proc. Soc. Psych. Res.* vol. 7, 1891-92, pp. 146-98.
180. Myers, F. W. H. *Human Personality and Its Survival of Bodily Death,* S. Smith, ed. (New Hyde Park, N.Y.: University Books, 1961), p. 265. First published by Longmans Green, 1903.
180A. Nash, C. B. "PK Tests of a Large Population," *J. Parapsychol.* 8:4, December 1944, pp. 304-10.
181. Nash, C. B. "An Exploratory Analysis for Displacement in PK," *J. Am. Soc. Psych. Res.* 50:4, October 1956, pp. 151-56.
182. Onetto, B. "PK with a Radioactive Compound: Cesium 137," *Proc. P. A.* 5, 1968, pp. 18-19.
183. Osis, K. "A Test of the Relationship Between ESP and PK," *J. Parapsychol.* 17:4, December 1953, pp. 298-309.
184. Ostrander, S., and Schroeder, L. *Psychic Discoveries behind the Iron Curtain* (Englewood Cliffs, N.J.: Prentice-Hall, 1970).

185. Owen, A. R. G. *Can We Explain the Poltergeist?* (New York: Helix Press/Garrett Publications, 1964).
186. Owen, A. R. G. "The Future of the Poltergeist," symposium, *Proc. P. A.* 7, 1970, pp. 33-37.
187. Owen, A. R. G. "Fifteen Years of Psychokinesis," *New Horizons,* 2:1, April 1975, pp. 4-7.
188. Owen, I. M. " 'Philip's' Story Continued," *New Horizons,* 2:1, April 1975, pp. 14-20.
189. Owen, I. M. "Continuation of the Philip Experiment," *New Horizons* 2:2, June 1976, pp. 3-4.
190. Owen, I. M., and Sparrow, M. H. "Generation of Paranormal Physical Phenomena in Connection with an Imaginary Communicator," *New Horizons* 1:3, January 1974, pp. 6-13.
191. Owen, I. M., with Sparrow, M. H. *Conjuring up Philip: An Adventure in Psychokinesis* (New York: Harper & Row, 1976).
192. Padfield, S. "Psychic Support Figures and Their Relevance to the Production of Paranormal Phenomena," paper presented at the Institute of Parascience Conference, 1976. In *Parascience Proc. 1976,* in press.
193. Panati, C. *Supersenses* (New York: Quadrangle/New York Times Book Co., 1974), pp. 250-52.
194. "Parapsychology and Biology," editorial, *J. Parapsychol.* 14:2, June 1950, pp. 85-94.
195. Parise, F. "Personal Experiences with the Para-Normal," paper presented at "Current Perspectives in Parapsychology," seminar at the University of Bridgeport, March 1976.
196. Pauli, Enrique. "PK on Living Targets as Related to Sex, Distance and Time," in *Research in Parapsychology 1972,* W. G. Roll, R. L. Morris, and J. D. Morris, eds. (Metuchen, N.J.: The Scarecrow Press, 1973), pp. 68-70.
197. Perovsky-Petrovo-Solovovo, Count. "Nikolaefe: A Little Known Russian Physical Medium," *Proc. Soc. Psych. Res.* vol. 47, 1942-45, pp. 261-66.
198. Persinger, M. "ELF Waves and ESP," Proc. First Canadian Conference on Psychokinesis and Related Phenomena, *New Horizons,* June 1974, pp. 232-35.
199. Pierce, H. W. *Science Looks at ESP* (New York: Signet/Mystic/New American Library, 1970), pp. 86-87.
200. "PK Research at the Point for Decision," *J. Parapsychol.* 8:1, March 1944, pp. 1-2.
201. Podmore, F. *Mediums of the 19th Century* (New Hyde Park, N.Y.: University Books, 1963), vol. 1, pp. 39-40. First published as *Modern Spiritualism,* 1902.
202. Ibid., vol. 2, p. 8. Primary source: *Medical Times & Gazette,* June 11, 1853.

203. Ibid., p. 82. Primary Sources: *Echo,* England, June 8, 1871; *Medium,* June 15, 1871; *Spiritualist,* June 15, 1871; and *Spiritual Magazine,* July 1871.
204. Ibid., p. 123.
205. Ibid., pp. 244-69.
206. Ibid. p. 255. Primary sources: *Psychic Power—Spirit Power: Experimental Investigation,* London, 1871; and *Report to the Committee of the Dialectical Society* by Lord Lindsay, p. 214.
207. Popenoe, C. *Wellness* (New York: Random House/Yes! 1977).
208. Pratt, J. G. "Target Preference in PK Tests with Dice," *J. Parapsychol.* 11:1, March 1947, pp. 26-45.
209. Pratt, J. G. "The Cormack Placement PK Experiments," *J. Parapsychol.* 15:1, March 1951, pp. 57-73.
210. Pratt, J. G. "Some Notes for the Future Einstein of Parapsychology," *J. Am. Soc. Psych. Res.* 68:2, April 1974, pp. 133-55.
211. Pratt, J. G., and Keil, H. H. J. "Firsthand Observations of Nina S. Kulagina Suggestive of PK upon Static Objects," *J. Am. Soc. Psych. Res.* 67:4, October 1973, pp. 381-90.
212. Price, E. "The Uri Geller Effect," *The Geller Papers,* C. Panati, ed. (Boston: Houghton Mifflin, 1976), pp. 247-312.
213. Price, M., and Rhine, J. B. "The Subject-Experimenter Relation in the PK Tests," *J. Parapsychol.* 8:3, September 1944, pp. 177-86.
214. Progoff, I. *The Symbolic and the Real* (New York: Julian Press, 1963), p. 129.
215. Puthoff, H. E., and Targ, R. "PK Experiments with Uri Geller and Ingo Swann," in *Research in Parapsychology 1973,* W. G. Roll, R. L. Morris, and J. D. Morris, eds. (Metuchen, N. J.: The Scarecrow Press, 1974), pp. 125-28.
216. Puthoff, H. E., and Targ, R. "Information Transmission under Conditions of Sensory Shielding," *Nature* 252:5476, October 18, 1974, pp. 602-7.
217. Puthoff, H. E., and Targ, R. "Physics, Entropy and Psychokinesis," in *Quantum Physics and Parapsychology* (New York: Parapsychology Foundation, 1975), pp. 129-50.
218. Randall, J. L. "An Attempt to Detect Psi Effects with Protozoa," *J. Soc. Psych. Res.* 45:744, June 1970, pp. 294-96.
219. Randall, J. L. "Experiments to Detect a Psi Effect with Small Animals," *J. Soc. Psych. Res.* 46:747, March 1971, pp. 31-39.
220. Randi, J. "The Amazing," in *The Magic of Uri Geller* (New York: Ballantine Books, 1975).
221. Rao, K. R. *Experimental Parapsychology* (Springfield, Ill.: Charles C. Thomas, 1966).
222. Rao, K. R. "An Autobiographical Note," *Para. Review* 4:4, July/August 1973, pp. 13-15.

223. Rao, K. R. "Frustrations and Challenges in Parapsychology," invited address at the Southeastern Regional P.A. Convention, February 1977, in *J. Parapsychol.* 41:2, June 1977, pp. 119-35.
224. Raudive, K. *Breakthrough* (New York: Taplinger, 1971).
225. Rhine, J. B. *Extrasensory Perception* (Boston: Branden, 1964). First published by the Boston Society for Psychic Research, 1934.
226. Rhine J. B. "Dice Thrown by Cup and Machine in PK Tests," *J. Parapsychol.* 7:3, September 1943, pp. 207-17.
227. Rhine, J. B. "The PK Effect: Early Singles Tests," *J. Parapsychol.* 8, 1944, pp. 287-303.
228. Rhine, J. B. "Early PK Tests: Sevens and Low-Dice Series," *J. Parapsychol.* 9:2, June 1945, pp. 106-15.
229. Rhine, J. B. "The Psychokinetic Effect: A Review," *J. Parapsychol.* 10:1, March 1946, pp. 5-20.
230. Rhine, J. B. "The Forwald Experiments with Placement PK," *J. Parapsychol.* 15:1, March 1951, pp. 49-56.
231. Rhine, J. B. *New World of the Mind* (New York: Morrow, 1971), p. 299. First published by William Sloane Associates, 1953.
232. Rhine, J. B. Untitled article, *Parapsychology Bulletin* 19, 1971.
233. Rhine, J. B. "Can Parapsychology Help Religion?" paper presented at the Spiritual Frontiers Fellowship Convention, Chicago, 1973.
234. Rhine, J. B. "A New Case of Experimenter Unreliability," *J. Parapsychol.* 38:2, June 1974, pp. 215-25.
235. Rhine, J. B. "Second Report on a Case of Experimenter Fraud," *J. Parapsychol.* 39:4, December 1975, pp. 306-25.
236. Rhine, J. B. Personal communication, February 1977.
237. Rhine, J. B. "A Backward Look on Leaving the JP," *J. Parapsychol.* 41:2, June 1977, pp. 89-102.
238. Rhine, J. B., and Humphrey, B. M. "The PK Effect: Special Evidence from Hit Patterns. I. Quarter Distributions of the Page," *J. Parapsychol.* 8:1, March 1944, pp. 18-60.
239. Rhine, J. B., and Humphrey, B. M. "PK Tests with Six, Twelve, and Twenty-Four Dice per Throw," *J. Parapsychol.* 8:2, June 1944, pp. 139-57.
240. Rhine, J. B., Humphrey, B. M., and Averill, R. L. "An Exploratory Experiment on the Effect of Caffeine upon Performance in PK Tests," *J. Parapsychol.* 9:2, June 1945, pp. 80-91.
241. Rhine, L. E. "Placement PK Tests with Three Types of Objects," *J. Parapsychol.* 15:2, June 1951, pp. 132-38.
242. Rhine, L. E. "Toward Understanding Psi Missing," *Proc. P.A.* 2, 1965, pp. 61-78.
243. Rhine, L. E. *Mind Over Matter* (New York: Macmillan, 1970), p. 78.
244. Ibid. pp. 158-60. Primary source: Wadhams, P., and Farrelly, B.A. "The Investigation of Psychokinesis using Beta Particles," *J. Soc. Psych. Res.* 44:736, June 1968, p. 281-88.

245. Ibid. pp. 160-62. Primary source: Chauvin, R., and Genthon, Jean-Pierre, "Eine Untersuchung uber die Moglichkeit Psychokinetscher Experimente mit Uranium und Geigerzähler," *Zeitschrift für Parapsychologie und Grenzgebiete der der Psychologie* 8, 1965, pp. 140-47.

246. Ibid. pp. 242-46. Primary source: Cox, W. E., "The Effect of PK on Electromechanical Systems," *J. Parapsychol.* 29:3, September 1965, pp. 165-75.

247. Rhine, L. E., and Rhine, J. B. "The Psychokinetic Effect: I. The First Experiment," *J. Parapsychol.* 7:1, March 1943, pp. 20-43.

248. Richmond, N. "Two Series of PK Tests on Paramecia," *J. Soc. Psych. Res.* 36, 1952, pp. 577-88.

249. Riley, F. J. "Production of 'Electronic Voices' by a Group Practised in Psychokinesis," *New Horizons,* June 1977, pp. 16-21.

250. Rogers, D. "Of Powdered Eggs and Hens," *Proc. P. A.* 8, 1971, pp. 35-37.

251. Rogo, D. S. "Eusapia Palladino and the Structure of Scientific Controversy," *Para. Review* 6:2, May/April 1975, pp. 23-27. Primary source: Morselli, E., "Eusapia Palladino and the Genuineness of her Phenomena," *Annals of Psychical Research,* May 1907, pp. 391-460.

252. Roll, W. G. Book review: *Prophecy in Our Time* by M. Ebon, *J. Am. Soc. Psych. Res.* 63:1, January 1969, pp. 99-104.

253. Roll, W. G. "The Newark Disturbances," *J. Am. Soc. Psych. Res.* 63:2, April 1969, pp. 123-74.

254. Roll, W. G. "Poltergeist Phenomena and Interpersonal Relations," *J. Am. Soc. Psych. Res.* 64:1, January 1970, pp. 66-99.

255. Roll, W. G. *The Poltergeist* (Garden City, N.Y.: Doubleday, 1972).

256. Roll, W. G. "Understanding the Poltergeist," paper presented at the P.A. Convention, 1977, in *Research in Parapsychology 1977,* W. G. Roll, ed. (Metuchen, N.J.; The Scarecrow Press, 1978), pp. 183-95.

257. Roll, W. G.; Burdick, D. S.; and Joines, W. T. "Radial and Tangential Forces in the Miami Poltergeist," *J. Am. Soc. Psych. Res.* 67:3, July 1973, pp. 267-81.

258. Roll, W. G.; Burdick, D. S.; and Joines, W. T. "The Rotating Beam Theory and the Olive Hill Poltergeist," in *Research in Parapsychology 1973,* W. G. Roll, R. L. Morris, and J. D. Morris, eds. (Metuchen, N.J.: The Scarecrow Press, 1974), pp. 64-67.

259. Roll, W. G., and Pratt, J. G. "The Miami Disturbances," *J. Am. Soc. Psych. Res.* 65:4, October 1971, pp. 409-54.

260. Rush, J. H. "On 'A Possible Physical Source for the Energy Needed in Poltergeist Activity,' " *J. Am. Soc. Psych. Res.* 66:2, April 1972, pp. 229-30.

261. Ryzl, M. "Parapsychology in Eastern Europe," in *Parapsychology Today: A Geographic View (1971),* Procedures of an International Conference (New York: Parapsychology Foundation, 1971).
262. St. Augustine. *The City of God,* 21:8.
263. Schmeidler, G. Quoted in Roll, W. G., "Some Physical and Psychological Aspects of a Series of Poltergeist Phenomena," *J. Am. Soc. Psych. Res.* 62:3, July 1968, pp. 263-308.
264. Schmeidler, G. "PK Effects upon Continuously Recorded Temperature," *J. Am. Soc. Psych. Res.* 67:4, October 1973, pp. 325-40.
265. Schmidt, H. "PK Test with Electronic Equipment," *Proc. P.A.* 7, 1970, pp. 75-76.
266. Schmidt, H. "PK Experiments Involving Animals," *Proc. P.A.* 7, 1970, pp. 7-8.
267. Schmidt, H. "PK Effect on Random Time Intervals," in *Research in Parapsychology 1973,* W. G. Roll, R. L. Morris, and J. D. Morris, eds. (Metuchen, N.J.: The Scarecrow Press, 1974), pp. 46-48.
268. Schmidt, H. "Comparison of PK Action on Two Different Random Number Generators," *J. Parapsychol.* 38:1, March 1974, pp. 47-55.
269. Schmidt, H. "Psychokinesis," *Psychic Exploration,* E. Mitchell and J. White, eds. (New York: G. P. Putnam's Sons, 1974), pp. 179-93.
270. Schmidt, H. "PK Tests with a High-Speed Random Number Generator," *J. Parapsychol.* 37:2, June 1973, pp. 105-18.
271. Schmidt, H. "Observation of Subconscious PK Effects with and without Time Displacement," in *Research in Parapsychology 1974,* J. D. Morris, W. G. Roll, and R. L. Morris, eds. (Metuchen, N.J.: The Scarecrow Press, 1975), pp. 116-21.
272. Schmidt, H. "Instrumentation in the Parapsychology Laboratory," in *New Directions in Parapsychology,* J. Beloff, ed. (Metuchen, N.J.: The Scarecrow Press, 1975), pp. 13-37.
273. Ibid. pp. 30-31. The first statement of the EPR Paradox appeared in *Physics Review,* 47:777, 1935.
274. Schmidt, H. "PK Experiment with Repeated Time-Displaced Feedback," in *Research in Parapsychology 1975,* J. D. Morris, W. G. Roll, and R. L. Morris, eds. (Metuchen, N.J.: The Scarecrow Press, 1976), pp. 107-9.
275. Schmidt, H., and Pantas, L. "Psi Tests with Internally Different Machines," *J. Parapsychol.* 36:3, September 1972, pp. 222-32.
276. Shah, I. "Why the Clay Birds Flew Away," *Tales of the Dervishes* (New York: E. P. Dutton, 1970).
277. Smith, J. "Paranormal Effects on Enzyme Activity," *Proc. P.A.* 5, 1968, pp. 15-16.
278. Smith, S. *The Enigma of Out of Body Travel* (New York: Garrett/Helix, 1965; New American Library, 1968).
279. Solfvin, G. F., and Mathews, F. M. "A Case of RSPK in Massachusetts: Part 2, The Haunting," in *Research in Parapsychology 1976,*

J. D. Morris, W. G. Roll, and R. L. Morris, eds. (Metuchen, N.J.: The Scarecrow Press, 1977), pp. 223-27.
280. Solfvin, G. F., and Roll, W. G. "A Case of RSPK with an Epileptic Agent," in *Research in Parapsychology 1975,* J. D. Morris, W. G. Roll, and R. L. Morris, eds. (Metuchen, N.J.: The Scarecrow Press, 1976), pp. 115-20.
281. Spedding, F. Book review: *Psi Und Psyche,* E. Bauer, ed. (Stuttgart: Deutsche Verlags Anstalt), referring to paper by H. Schmidt, *J. Soc. Psych. Res.* 48:764, June 1975, pp. 112-14.
282. Stanford, R. G. " 'Associative Activation of the Unconscious' and 'Visualization' as Methods for Influencing the PK Target," *J. Am. Soc. Psych. Res.* 63:4, October 1969, pp. 338-51.
283. Stanford, R. G. "An Experimentally Testable Model for Spontaneous Psi Events: I. Extrasensory Events," *J. Am. Soc. Psych. Res.* 68:1, January 1974, pp. 34-57.
284. Stanford, R. G. "An Experimentally Testable Model for Spontaneous Psi Events: II. Psychokinetic Events," *J. Am. Soc. Psych. Res.* 68:4, October 1974, pp. 321-56.
285. Stanford, R. G. "Extrasensory Factors in Everyday Life Experience," paper presented at Current Perspectives in Parapsychology, seminar at the University of Bridgeport, Connecticut, March 1976.
286. Stanford, R. G. "Are Parapsychologists Paradigmless in Psiland?" in *The Philosophy of Parapsychology,* B. Shapin and L. Coly, eds. (New York: Parapsychology Foundation, 1977), pp. 1-18.
287. Stanford, R. G. Comments after 133.
288. Stanford, R. G. "Experimental Psychokinesis: A Review from Diverse Perspectives," in *Handbook of Parapsychology,* B. E. Wolman, ed. (New York: Van Nostrand Reinhold, 1977), pp. 324-81.
289. Stanford, R. G., and Fox, C. "An Effect of Release of Effort in a Psychokinetic Task," in *Research in Parapsychology 1974,* J. D. Morris, W. G. Roll, and R. L. Morris, eds. (Metuchen, N.J.: The Scarecrow Press, 1975), pp. 61-63.
290. Stanford, R. G., and Rust, P. "Psi-Mediated Helping Behavior: Experimental Paradigm and Initial Results," in *Research in Parapsychology 1976,* J. D. Morris, W. G. Roll, and R. L. Morris, eds. (Metuchen, N.J.: The Scarecrow Press, 1977), pp. 109-10.
291. Stanford, R. G., and Stio, A. "A Study of Associative Meditation in Psi-Mediated Instrumental Response," *J. Am. Soc. Psych. Res.* 70:1, January 1976, pp. 55-64.
292. Stanford, R. G., et al. "Motivational Arousal and Self-Concept in Psi Mediated Instrumental Response," *J. Am. Soc. Psych. Res.* 70:2, April 1976, pp. 167-78.
293. Stanford, Rex G., et al. "Psychokinesis as Psi-Mediated Instrumental Response," *J. Am. Soc. Psych. Res.* 69:2, April 1975, pp. 127-34.

294. Steilberg, B. J. " 'Conscious Concentration' Versus 'Visualization' in PK Tests," *J. Parapsychol.* 39:1, March 1975, pp. 12-20.

295. Stevenson, I. "Are Poltergeists Living or Are They Dead?" *J. Am. Soc. Psych. Res.* 66:3, July 1972, pp. 233-52.

296. Stevenson, I., and Pratt, J. G. "Exploratory Investigations of the Psychic Photography of Ted Serios," *J. Am. Soc. Psych. Res.* 62:2, April 1968, pp. 103-29.

297. Stevenson, I., and Pratt, J. G. "Further Investigations of the Psychic Photography of Ted Serios," *J. Am. Soc. Psych. Res.* 63:4, October 1969, pp. 352-64.

298. Sudre, R. *Treatise on Parapsychology* (New York: The Citadel Press, 1960), p. 8. Primary sources: Ochorowicz, "Un nouveau phenomene mediumique," *Ann. de sc. psych.,* 1-5, 1909; and R. C. Le Clair, ed., *The Letters of William James and Theodore Flournoy* (Madison: University of Wisconsin Press, 1966).

299. Ibid., pp. 248-50. Primary source: Ochorowicz, "Les Rayons Rigides et les Rayons X," *Ann. des Sc. Psych.* April/December 1910.

300. Ibid., p. 260.

301. Tabori, P. *Companions of the Unseen* (New Hyde Park, N.Y.: University Books, 1968), p. 184.

302. Tart, C., ed. *Altered States of Consciousness* (Garden City, N.Y.: Doubleday/Anchor, 1972).

303. Tart, C. "A Psychophysical Study of Out-of-the-Body Experiences in a Selected Subject," *J. Am. Soc. Psych. Res.* 62:1, January 1968, pp. 3-27.

304. Tart, C. "A Second Psychophysical Study of Out-of-the-Body Experiences in a Selected Subject," *Parapsychology,* December 1967, pp. 251-58.

305. Tart, C. "Card Guessing Tests: Learning Paradigm or Extinction Paradigm?" *J. Am. Soc. Psych. Res.* 60, 1966, pp. 45-55.

306. Tart, C., letter, *J. Soc. Psych. Res.* 47:762, December 1974, pp. 531-32.

307. Tart, C., personal communication, March 1976.

308. Taylor, J. *Superminds* (New York; Viking Press, 1975).

309. *Theta,* Psychical Research Foundation, Durham, N.C., all issues.

310. Thouless, R. H., and Wiesner, B. P. "The Psi Processes in Normal and 'Paranormal' Psychology," *J. Parapsychol.* 12:3, September 1948, pp. 192-212.

311. Thouless, R. H. "A Report on an Experiment in Psychokinesis with Dice, and a Discussion on Psychological Factors Favoring Success," *J. Parapsychol.* 15:2, June 1951, pp. 89-102. Also, *Proc. Soc. Psych. Res.* 49, February 1951.

312. Thouless, R. H. "Parapsychology during the Last Quarter of a Century," *J. Parapsychol.* 33:4, December 1969, pp. 283-99.

313. Thurston, H. *The Physical Phenomena of Mysticism,* J. H. Creham, ed. (Chicago: Henry Regnery Co., 1952).

314. Tizane, E. "Sur La Piste de L'Homme Inconnu," (On the Search for the Unknown Man), in *Les Phenomenes de Hantise et Possession* (Paris: n.p., 1951). Cited in 14.

315. Tyrrell, G. N. M. *Apparitions* (New York: Macmillan/Collier Books, 1963).

316. Ullman, M. "An Informal Session with Nina Kulagina," *Proc. P.A.* 8, 1971, pp. 21-22.

317. Ullman, M. "PK in the Soviet Union," in *Research in Parapsychology 1973,* W. G. Roll, R. L. Morris, and J. D. Morris, eds. (Metuchen, N.J.: The Scarecrow Press, 1974), pp. 121-25.

318. Van de Castle, R. L. "An Exploratory Study of Some Personality Correlates Associated with PK Performance," *J. Am. Soc. Psych. Res.* 52:4, October 1958, pp. 134-50.

319. Van de Castle, R. L. "Psi Abilities in Primitive Groups," Presidential Address, *Proc. P.A.* 7, 1970, pp. 97-122.

320. Ibid. Primary sources: Rose, L., and Rose, R., "Psi Experiments with Australian Aborigines," *J. Parapsychol.* 15, 1951, pp. 122-31; Rose, R., "Experiments in ESP and PK with Aboriginal Subjects," *J. Parapsychol.* 16, 1952, pp. 219-20; Rose, R., "A Second Report on Psi Experiments with Australian Aborigines," *J. Parapsychol.* 19, 1955, pp. 92-98; and Rose, R., *Living Magic: The Realities Underlying the Psychical Practices and Beliefs of Australian Aborigines* (New York: Rand McNally, 1956).

321. Van de Castle, R. L. "Is There a Madness to Our Methods in Psi Research? *Proc. P.A.* 8, 1971, pp. 40-46.

322. Van de Castle, R. L. "Some Possible Anthropological Contributions to the Study of Parapsychology," paper presented at "Parapsychology: Today's Implications, Tomorrow's Applications," symposium conducted by the Am. Soc. Psych. Res., New York, May 1974.

323. Vasiliev, L. L. *Experiments in Mental Suggestion* (Church Crookham, Hants., England: Institute for the Study of Mental Images, 1963), pp. 55-57. First published in Russia, 1962.

324. Vasse, P., and Vasse, C. "A Comparison of Two Subjects in PK," *J. Parapsychol.* 15:4, December 1951, pp. 263-70.

325. Vaughan, A. "The Phenomena of Uri Geller," *Psychic* 4:5, June 1973, pp. 12-18.

326. Vaughan, A. *Patterns of Prophecy* (New York: Hawthorn Books, 1973), p. 154.

327. Walker, E. H. "Foundations of Paraphysical and Parapsychological Phenomena," in *Quantum Physics and Parapsychology,* L. Oteri, ed. (New York: Parapsychology Foundation, 1975), pp. 1-53.

328. Walther, G. "Willy Schneider: 1903-1971," *Para. Review* 3:2, March/April 1972, pp. 4-5. Primary source: A. von Schrenz-Notzing, *Experiments der Ferbewgung* (Stuttgart: Union Deutsche Verlagsgesellschaft, 1924).

329. Wärndorfer, A. "Report of a 'Poltergeist' Case," *J. Soc. Psych. Res.* 13:239, May 1907, pp. 66-79.

330. Watkins, G. K. "Possible PK in the Lizard *Antis sagrei,*" *Proc. P.A.* 8, 1971, pp. 24-25.

331. Watkins, G. K., and Watkins, A. M. "Possible PK Influence on the Resuscitation of Anesthetized Mice," *Proc. P.A.* 8, 1971, pp. 27-28.

332. Watkins, G. K., and Watkins, A. M. "Apparent Psychokinesis on Static Objects by a 'Gifted' Subject," in *Research in Parapsychology 1973,* W. G. Roll, R. L. Morris, and J. D. Morris, eds. (Metuchen, N.J.: The Scarecrow Press, 1974), pp. 132-34.

333. Watkins, G. K.; Watkins, A. M.; and Wells, R. A. "Further Studies on the Resuscitation of Anesthetized Mice," in *Research in Parapsychology 1972,* W. G. Roll, R. L. Morris, and J. D. Morris, eds. (Metuchen, N.J.: The Scarecrow Press, 1973), pp. 157-59.

334. Watkins, G. K., and Wells, R. A. "Possible PK Effects on an Electrical System," paper presented at the Southeastern Regional P.A. Conference, January 1975; abstracted, *J. Parapsychol.* 39:1, March 1975, pp. 29-30.

335. White, J. "X Energy and Consciousness," *Psychic* 6:6, February 1976, pp. 37-41.

336. White, R. A. "Sports and ESP," *Psychic* 6:1, November/December 1974, pp. 44-49.

337. Whiteman, J. H. M. "Quantum Theory and Parapsychology," *J. Am. Soc. Psych. Res.* 67:4, October 1973, pp. 341-60.

338. Whitton, J. "The Psychodynamics of Poltergeist Activity and Group P.K." Proc. First Canadian Conference on Psychokinesis and Related Phenomena, *New Horizons,* 1:5, January 1975 pp. 202-11.

339. Whitton, J. "Qualitative Time-Domain Analysis of Acoustic Envelopes of Psychokinetic Table Rappings," *New Horizons* 2:1, April 1975, pp. 21-24.

340. Whitton, J. "Paramorphic Table Rappings: Acoustic Analysis," *New Horizons* 2:2, June 1976, pp. 7-9.

341. Yogananda, P. *Autobiography of a Yogi* (Los Angeles: Self-Realization Fellowship, 1946).

342. Zeibell, I. "Through the Looking Glass with Uri Geller," *Psychic* 6:6, February 1976, pp. 16-19.

343. Zorab, G. "The Sitoebondo Poltergeist (Java, 1893): A Firsthand Account Written Soon After the Events," *J. Am. Soc. Psych. Res.* 67:4, October 1973, pp. 391-406.

Name Index

Subject Index